GABRIEL OROZCO

OCTOBER FILES

George Baker, Yve-Alain Bois, Benjamin H. D. Buchloh, Hal Foster, Denis Hollier, David Joselit, Rosalind Krauss, Carrie Lambert-Beatty, Annette Michelson, Mignon Nixon, and Malcolm Turvey, editors

Richard Serra, edited by Hal Foster with Gordon Hughes
Andy Warhol, edited by Annette Michelson
Eva Hesse, edited by Mignon Nixon
Robert Rauschenberg, edited by Branden W. Joseph
James Coleman, edited by George Baker
Cindy Sherman, edited by Johanna Burton
Roy Lichtenstein, edited by Graham Bader
Gerhard Richter, edited by Benjamin H. D. Buchloh
Gabriel Orozco, edited by Yve-Alain Bois

GABRIEL OROZCO

edited by Yve-Alain Bois

essays and interviews by Benjamin H. D. Buchloh, Jean Fisher, Guy Brett, Molly Nesbit, Gabriel Orozco, Briony Fer, and Yve-Alain Bois

OCTOBER FILES 9

The MIT Press
Cambridge, Massachusetts
London, England

MIT Press books may be purchased at special quantity discounts for business or sales promotional use. For information, please email special_sales@mitpress.mit.edu or write to Special Sales Department, The MIT Press, 55 Hayward Street, Cambridge, MA 02142.

This book was set in Bembo and Stone Sans by Graphic Composition, Inc. Printed and bound in the United States of America.

Unless otherwise noted, all images are courtesy of Marian Goodman Gallery, New York.

Library of Congress Cataloging-in-Publication Data

Gabriel Orozco / edited by Yve-Alain Bois.
p. cm.—(October files)
Includes bibliographical references and index.
ISBN 978-0-262-01318-5 (hardcover : alk. paper)—ISBN 978-0-262-51301-2 (pbk. : alk. paper)
1. Orozco, Gabriel, 1962—Criticism and interpretation.
I. Orozco, Gabriel, 1962–. II. Bois, Yve-Alain.
N6559.O76G33 2009
709.2—dc22

2009003625

10 9 8 7 6 5 4 3 2 1

Contents

Series Preface

OCTOBER Files addresses individual bodies of work of the postwar period that meet two criteria: they have altered our understanding of art in significant ways, and they have prompted a critical literature that is serious, sophisticated, and sustained. Each book thus traces not only the development of an important oeuvre but also the construction of the critical discourse inspired by it. This discourse is theoretical by its very nature, which is not to say that it imposes theory abstractly or arbitrarily. Rather, it draws out the specific ways in which significant art is theoretical in its own right, on its own terms and with its own implications. To this end we feature essays, many first published in *OCTOBER* magazine, that elaborate different methods of criticism in order to elucidate different aspects of the art in question. The essays are often in dialogue with one another as they do so, but they are also as sensitive as the art to political context and historical change. These "files," then, are intended as primers in signal practices of art and criticism alike, and they are offered in resistance to the amnesiac and antitheoretical tendencies of our time.

The Editors of *OCTOBER*

Acknowledgments

"Refuse and Refuge" by Benjamin H. D. Buchloh and "The Sleep of Wakefulness" by Jean Fisher were originally published in *Gabriel Orozco*, the catalog of an exhibition curated by Catherine de Zegher at the Kanaal Art Foundation, Kortijk (Belgium), in 1993. "Gabriel Orozco: The Sculpture of Everyday Life" by Benjamin H. D. Buchloh first appeared in the exhibition catalog *Gabriel Orozco*, edited by Bernard Bürgi and Bettina Marbach (Zurich: Kunsthalle, 1996). "Between Work and World: Gabriel Orozco" by Guy Brett was first published as "The Light Touch" in *Empty Club: Gabriel Orozco* (London: Artangel Afterlives, 1998). "The Tempest" by Molly Nesbit was first published in the exhibition catalog *Gabriel Orozco*, edited by Alma Ruiz (Museum of Contemporary Art, Los Angeles, 2000). Gabriel Orozco's "Lecture," delivered on January 30, 2001, at the Rufino Tamayo in Mexico City, was originally published in Spanish in *Textos sobre la obra de Gabriel Orozco* (Mexico: Turner Publicationes, 2005). It is published in English for the first time here. The conversation with Benjamin H. D. Buchloh took place on July 1, 2004, at the Goethe Institute in London, in conjunction with the artist's exhibition at the Serpentine Gallery. It is published here for the first time. "Spirograph: The Circular Ruins of Drawing" by Briony Fer and "Cosmic Reification: Gabriel Orozco's Photographs" by Benjamin H. D. Buchloh were first published in the exhibition catalog *Gabriel Orozco* (London: Serpentine Gallery, 2004). "Crazy about Saturn," an interview with the artist by Briony Fer, as well as "The Tree and the Knight" by Yve-Alain Bois, were first published in the exhibition catalog *Gabriel Orozco*, edited by Alexandra

Garcia Ponce (Mexico City: Museo del Palacio de Bellas Artes, and Turner Publicationes, 2006).

I would like first to thank the authors for their willingness to participate in this project, as well as Gabriel Orozco and the staff of the Marian Goodman Gallery for their help in gathering the included material. I would also like to thank the Galerie Chantal Crousel, Paris, and Kurimanzutto, Mexico City. A special debt of gratitude is due to Adam Lehner and Rachel Churner for their editorial assistance; to Kavior Moon for proofreading and indexing help; and to Ryan Reineck for his electronic expertise and last-minute aid.

Refuse and Refuge (1993)

Benjamin H. D. Buchloh

> Thus the art of Mexico has reached a turbulent maturity attained after a struggle against the bonds that held it fast to failed traditions. The liberation of Mexican art runs closely parallel to the social and political liberation of the nation itself, and if the participation of the artists in this struggle had been less ardent, perhaps modern Mexican art would have never shown its present vigor and new vision.[1]

The heroic moment that the painter Miguel Covarrubias evokes in his catalog introduction to the first (and thus far the only) survey exhibition of Mexican art at the Museum of Modern Art, in 1940, seems to have been lost on most of the common twentieth-century art histories: a moment when it appeared possible in Mexico (as it had shortly before in Weimar Germany and in the Soviet Union) that artistic practices and political change could be actively and intricately correlated, that new forms of artistic distribution and simultaneous collective reception (the mural and the printed broadsheet) would engage and activate the rural and urban masses in a continuous process of political information, consciousness raising, and growing self-determination.

The loss of this historical moment—or rather, the prohibition of this communicative model of aesthetic production and reception, and its subsequent replacement by the esoteric models of modernity—has affected the cultural contexts of post–World War II history with equal violence and has generated the peculiar hegemony of an aesthetic of willfully muted or voluntarily silenced objects.

In nuce, the loss of this utopian union of the political and artistic avant-garde in Mexico was already initiated in the very exhibition project at the Museum of Modern Art (and this is peculiarly evident in the translation of Covarrubias's text into the specific institutional language of the catalog, which shifted and falsified the terms of discussion to problems of cultural rather than sociopolitical history, emphasizing *artistic* struggles over *political* ones).[2]

When seen against this historical background it becomes easier to recognize the degree to which a sublimation of the political impulses must have been difficult but necessary before Mexican postwar culture could achieve the level of abstraction that would make it structurally and formally comparable to the most advanced forms of esoteric silence within European or American postwar modernism. Paradoxically, our historical and theoretical distance to this aesthetic of silence has gradually increased—partially as the result of a long and complicated archaeology of those moments exempted from the silence of modernism (e.g., John Heartfield or Leopoldo Mendez), and partially as the result of the recognition that this aesthetic of silence is not only a heroic achievement but also a fatal refuge from the difficult but necessary steps that can lead to radically redefined artistic and activist practices. This archaeology enables us at this point to reverse the perspective on criteria of aesthetic quality defined as they were in compliance with the principle of enforced hermeticism. Rather than asking how successful a work has been in suppressing its communicative aspirations, we can now question the degree to which works of the recent past have voluntarily embraced the conformity of silence; or to what extent they have at least attempted to initiate a critique of this structure of repression, operative within the very constituting principles of their aesthetic conventions, by challenging and refusing the quietist conditions of modernism from within.

Evidently, then, the relationships between the hegemonic institutions and discourses of postwar modernism and marginal cultures are fraught from the outset with numerous and complex questions. Any curatorial or critical gesture proclaiming to have overcome the contradictions and the oppression exerted in the unevenly developed field of cultural practices deserves our profound skepticism, if not suspicion. Every claim to remedy cultural exclusion, abandonment, and neglect is now immediately matched by a quest for the mining of previously undiscovered resources, and every argument for the inclusion of the obsolete and the marginal into the visibility of the fashion moment deserves our scrutiny.

As Homi Bhabha has argued convincingly, the concept of "cultural belatedness" and its counterpart "aesthetic quality" are structures of hegemonic thought establishing a typical double-bind of domination. Both are equally efficient as strategies of control and exclusion, since they position any form of articulation, contestation, and critique voiced by the marginalized and the previously silenced as a deviation from an established model of hegemonic cultural production. On the one hand, they acknowledge the inevitable entry of these communities into a status of linguistic competence (within or outside the terms of hegemonic discourse); on the other hand, they endlessly defer the recognition of these practices temporally along the paradoxical axis of the argument "you come too late but we will admit you later" and structurally along the axis of the argument "you have entered a symbolic system but it is inferior to the one by which we rule."

With these responses, the hegemonic voice not only reaffirms its own canon and established categories but also refutes from the outset (and ignores completely) that any *contestation of dominance* would obviously operate according to terms radically different from those of the dominant cultural model. Most importantly, hegemonic positions refuse to accept a definition of cultural practice that insists that the political effect of initiating language competence and cultural, institutional, and political representation is at any moment infinitely more important both culturally and politically than the rigorous enforcement of the supposed quality standards of classical modernism, or any other tradition, for that matter.

It is crucial to recognize that this exercise of power operates *intra*culturally, that is, in between the various phases and moments of the development within different cultural communities or groups of "speakers" differentiated by history, geography, class, gender, and, more importantly, by needs and investments in that language competence. It does so with the same violent prescriptions and exclusions with which it imposes its legislature *infra*culturally, that is, in its attempts to prescribe and prohibit the norms and paradigms of cultural production that are admissible within a particular history. This is evident, for example, in the interminable debates about the hierarchies of painting versus documentary photography, of abstraction versus figuration, of the seemingly autonomous and so-called poetic practices versus the seemingly instrumentalized, that is, activist and productivist models of cultural communication and intervention.

Within these debates (in fact, for the most part they are silently executed judgments), it is never a problem to enforce quietly the tautology of self-affirmation and perpetuation of hegemonic concepts (e.g.,"whatever you might have to say about John Heartfield, Matisse remains Matisse"). Yet it is more difficult to analyze how the specific reduction of the aesthetic to a tautological definition succeeds at all times to establish its inevitable link with power. Or, perhaps in reverse, how it is that power consistently searches out those artistic practices that seem to have forfeited any contestatory element, how it searches out work that—reappearing in the guise of aesthetic self-sufficiency—renews its ancient alliances with mythical forms of experience.

> [W]hile silence is defeat, it serves . . . both as a sanctuary and as a place of bondage. Silence is . . . a fated exile, yet also a home, a destination and a binding oath. To not return from this silence is rule rather than exception.[3]

Once again, current hopes expect artists of marginalized cultures (both of the urban ghettoes and the non-Western world) to redeem the crisis of the artistic object and reimbue it with a credible auratic dimension, defying as it were the now generally governing principles of simulation and political instrumentalization of artistic practices in the centers. Current cultural aspirations long for a renewed aesthetic opacity and simplicity that less trained or non-Western artists supposedly offer (a conception that had been inherent in Western constructions of primitivism from the very beginning). How can an artist escape these projections operative in the process of "othering," especially if, as is currently the case, that construction of a cultural other is an opportune institutional strategy that will disappear from the center of art-world attention as rapidly as it was moved there in the time of economic recession?

In a peculiar phenomenology of the postcolonial object, Gabriel Orozco's work traces these complicated relationships between the projections of the hegemonic world and the refusal to be subjected to these expectations, answering in each instance with a precise analysis of the mechanism of othering itself. Inasmuch as Orozco's sculptural objects seem to lure us even deeper into our primitivist projections and aspirations, they immediately respond by reminding us of the destruction that the Western world has historically brought about in the cultures from which it again and again claims aesthetic redemption. Orozco's sculptures articulate themselves within the most complex modes of reflection and within the idioms of Western European and American modernism. His emphasis on procedure and gesture and the morphology of his sculptures seem to reiterate the synthesis of industrial materials and gestural articulation that determined *arte povera* and postminimal sculpture of the late 1960s. Yet every work by Orozco immediately responds to the attempts to assimilate it within a European or American perspective ("you have acquired competence but you come too late") with an explicit articulation: asserting both its historic and geopolitical independence in terms of Orozco's cultural history, as much as its specific difference in terms of Western modernism.

Orozco seems to have understood very well that our expectation for a reconstitution of a separate category of the "sculptural" would be tantamount to immediate claims for a privileged mode of experience, intricately linked at this point to any of the traditional artistic categories asserting itself in unperturbed validity. How could the modes of experience inherent in these categories and the publics who claim to have access to them not inevitably end up in the confinement of the aesthetic fetish? And yet at this point sculpture promises the bodily experience of the "opacity of the signifier" more than any other form of aesthetic communication, seemingly a bastion against the finality of instrumentalized imagery, against the order of communicative action.

Typical of the desire to establish an opaque, irreducible, and indivisible material experience with artistic means is the recurrence of the indexical procedure, an operation that claims the material trace as strictly nontranscendable, as a pure material causality. Its supposed link with the performing body seems to guarantee that body's resistance against metaphysics (both that of origins as much as that of interpretation). Orozco's *My Hands Are My Heart* (1990) seems to respond directly to this desire for a reconstituted fiction of sculptural elementarism (figs. 1 and 2). Pressing and imprinting his hands into a lump of brick clay, Orozco produced a strange hybrid between late '60s purely indexical sculptural procedures (such as the casts of body parts in Bruce Nauman's work) and the specific Latin and Hispanic iconography of the heart. The apparent simplicity of the gesture and the commonality of the archaic industrial material, however, seem to engage precisely in a project of demythification of both the fetishization of the sculptural object and the loaded image of the heart in favor of a secular emphasis on the project of self-definition in the process of production. Orozco's materialist focus on the link between the production of identity and the physical and material transformation through

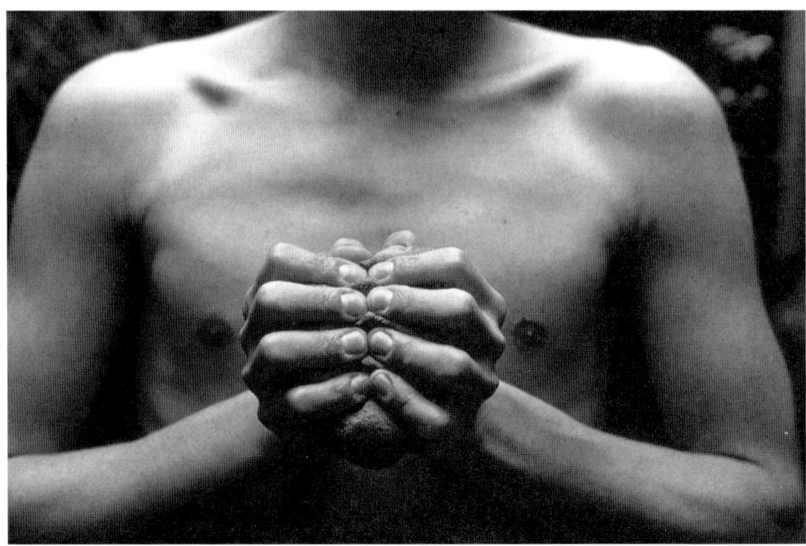

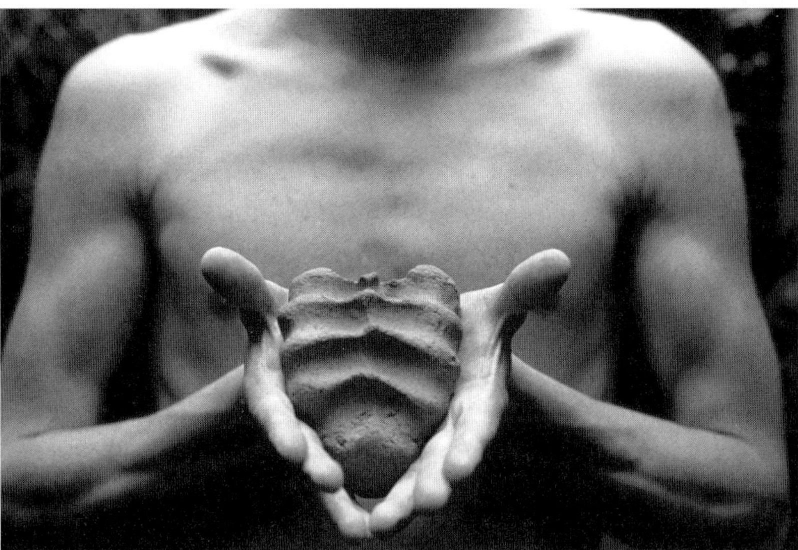

1, 2 *My Hands Are My Heart*, 1991.
Silver dye bleach print, two parts.
9 1/8 x 12 1/2 inches.

productive labor is reminiscent of an early and relatively unknown instance of that procedure of indexical inscription which the architect Antonio Gaudí produced for the interior ornamentation of the apartments of La Pedreira in Barcelona. Asking the artisans to imprint their knuckles, arms, and elbows in continuous and consecutive movements into the wet plaster as they proceeded to construct the doorjambs of the building's interior, Gaudí seems to have recognized that the traces of collective production could be made the sole and singularly credible origin of ornament in contemporary architecture.

Undoubtedly a work such as *My Hand Is the Memory of Space* (1991) seems unthinkable without a certain knowledge of the sculptural transformations that English sculptors such as Tony Cragg brought about in the mid- to late-1970s. And in fact Orozco has acknowledged that his encounter with British sculpture of that period during the year that he spent in Spain in 1986–87 was a crucial influence. Sculptors like Cragg were responding to both the romanticizing practices of British artists like Richard Long and Hamish Fulton as much as to the fact that Italian *arte povera* and American postminimal sculpture had avoided the mass cultural everyday object.

Yet the particular structure of these radiating elements that emanate from the negative shape of a hand and form a circular segment of peculiarly benign objects (wooden ice-cream spoons) resituate Orozco's work immediately within rather different parameters. At first the work's splendor seems to suggest a faint and latent reference to the hieratic ornamentation on elaborately carved stones in pre-Columbian architectural sculpture, while the manifest association of these wooden spoons shifts the reading inevitably into the present and the pleasures of the child: a present where tactile, oral, and scopic gratification are synthesized all in one as in the promises of fables and fairy tales told to console the deprived. The concreteness of this utopian promise (with its additional play on the thermal dynamics of the objects' context) seems to generate the radiating energy of this circular segment.

Orozco's *Recaptured Nature* (1990) inscribes itself into a doubly difficult sculptural tradition: the pneumatic sculpture and the spherical sculpture (fig. 3). Both have predecessors that are either such eminent exceptions or such conclusive statements that even the attempt to produce yet another inflated spherical object and to submit it for sculptural considerations could surprise. From Marcel Duchamp's *Air de Paris* (1917) to Piero Manzoni's *Artist's Breath* (1960) to Hans Haacke's untitled *Air*

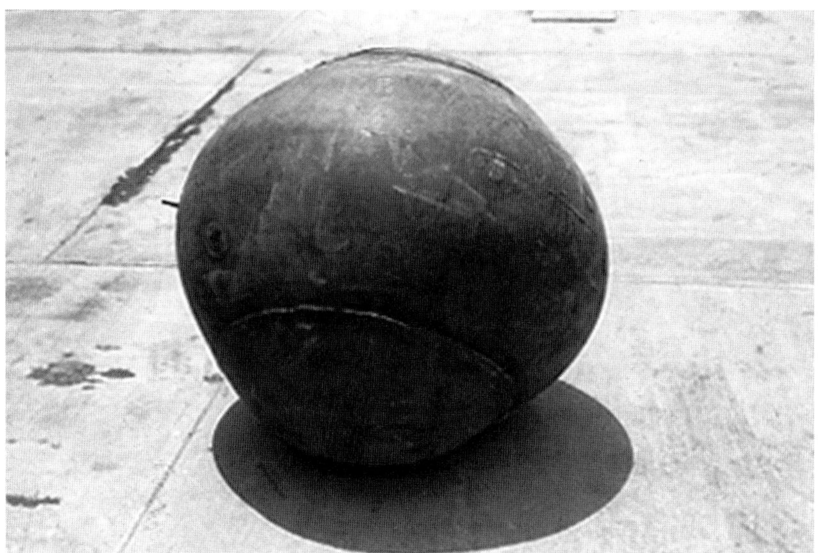

3 *Recaptured Nature,* 1990.
Vulcanized rubber.
37 3/8 x 37 3/8 x 37 3/8 inches.

Sculptures (ca. 1962–64), which detached Manzoni's pneumatic objects from their maker, the spherical and the pneumatic have operated in a secret fusion to render sculptural volume both formally and structurally anonymous. At the same time they have eliminated the question of the perfect sculptural form (Brancusi's quest) by directly choosing the purely stereometric object (in this instance the spherical) as the obvious answer articulated from the historical perspective of the readymade: pure pneumatics and pure stereometry displace the sculptor once and for all (or so it seemed).

But Orozco's rubber ball neither contains *air de Paris* nor the artist's breath; its hull is the inner tube of a truck tire inflated at the gas station. Sliced open laterally on one side and folded into a broad open cylinder, patched on the top and bottom with two rubber caps and revulcanized, the inner tube's original structure and the internal dynamic (resulting from the way the rubber was originally cast) have been reversed into a vertical position.

It is from this inversion that *Recaptured Nature* gains its spell: playing off the internal tension of this inverted object, the bulging rubber sphere gains an unexpected organic intensity. Like an organ from the past or a fruit of the future this giant's toy always reminds us of its origins in the mountains of industrial debris at the outskirts of every industrial metropolis, and it fuses the promise of pure corporeal bliss (that of plenitude or that of play) with the memory of imminent ecological suffocation and collapse.

A similar structure defines Orozco's peculiar installation entitled *Crazy Tourist* (1991). Here, once again, the typical projection with which we invest the images of exotic markets in rural economics (how many posters of markets with overburgeoning fruits have advertised our desire for natural plenitude in the phantasmagoria of primitive economic relations) is literally inverted to appear as the image of allegorical scarcity and of actually existing rural poverty.

The object-type that appears to us only in large accumulations (produce in markets), and as the naturalized serial object of industrial agriculture, appears in Orozco's object performance (where he placed single oranges on the tables of a Brazilian market after closing time) suddenly and precariously isolated.

Orozco's most recent sculpture *Yielding Stone* (1992) seems to reverse the principles of *Recaptured Nature* (fig. 4). Rather than departing from industrial residue this work defines itself by means of an admittedly minor

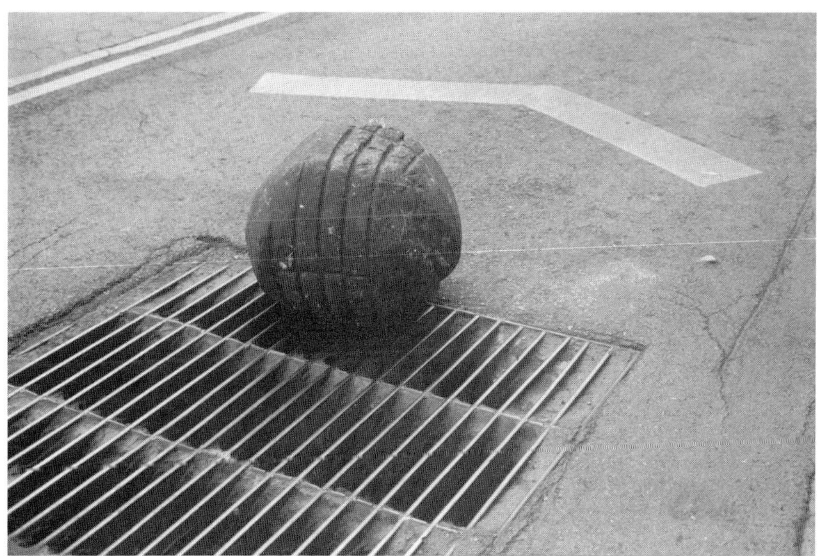

4 *Yielding Stone,* 1992.
Plasticine.
132.2 pounds.

studio material (plasticine) that is used for elementary sculptural sketching, in architectural model making, and for children's modeling games. As already indicated in the paradoxical title about the malleable stone, Orozco seems to search out the unified ire and contempt of all traditional sculptors for whom the resistance of the natural material is still an essential part of their code of honor. The vulgarity of highly malleable plastic paste in the shape of an amorphous lump and the artificiality of its material origins stand in stark contrast to the quest for the natural nobility of wood, stone, and steel with which sculptors up to Andre and Serra still limited their material horizon.

Worse yet, after having more or less formed this black lump in the weight of his own body, Orozco expels it into the street where it is supposed to absorb residue and particles, whatever accidental debris and dust its surface can collect and whatever texture and structure might imprint itself on its skin in the accidental constellations it encounters when being rotated.[4]

The hundreds of anonymous finger imprints—traces of spectators' secret touches during a recent exhibition, by which they clandestinely tried their hands and the plasticine ball's surface and materiality—make it probably a more accurate definition of the current conditions and possibilities of public sculpture than the hundreds of back-lit billboards, slide projections, and one-liner statements that have been paraded through the well-established channels of predetermined conceptions and institutions of public art. Orozco's atavistic object, with its relapse into a primary concept of mere tactility as a participatory mode, appears to prefer muteness over the myth of public speech. But this muteness would be in and of itself deeply reprehensible if it was presented emphatically and with reactionary conviction and minimalist spite, in the manner of Donald Judd, for example. Orozco's objects exude a silence that is always aware of its inflicted and transitory status, neither ostentatiously displayed as an aesthetic privilege nor internalized as an inescapable condition. It is the muteness of elementary materials before they achieve the status of an instrumentalized object (such as clay for the production of bricks, or plasticine, the juvenile and trivial material for elementary sculptural exercises), or it is the silence of discarded and dysfunctionalized materials (such as rubber tires) after a return to the margins. As such the silence of these objects as much as the atavistic definition of their participatory dimension circumnavigate the question of how sculptural objects at this point could enable or enact public speech under the circumstances of its immediate abrogation for and destruction within a symbolic system that has destroyed the dimension of public experience.

It is practically impossible not to think of Jose Guadalupe Posada in the discovery of *Horse* (1992), Orozco's strangely statuary photograph of a dorsal image of a malnourished horse (fig. 5). Perhaps Posada, the first Mexican modernist, was also the first truly allegorical artist in his consistent effort to make all bodies transparent and reduce them literally to the support structure of the skeleton. Allegorical perhaps also in his leveling of all classes along the axis of death: here radical hopelessness, the negative model of revolutionary thought, privileges the proletariat only in a realistic evaluation of its actual historical condition of having nothing to lose. Unlike in utopian vision where the proletariat functioned as the agent of revolutionary transformation, in the political moments of a radical denial of utopian thought, in the face of Fascist oppression as Posada confronted it in the massacres initiated by General Victoriano Huerta, the image of the people becomes that of an avant-garde of total annihilation.

Yet here in Orozco's photograph of the horse, with all the necessary refrain from the reference to class and social injustice that the aesthetic of the silenced object prescribes, the allegory is naturalized and transferred onto the level of the color photograph (if the allegorical model should be at all conceivable within photographs). But whereas in Posada the universal presence of death is politicized rather than mythified, Orozco's image of what appears to be the last horse on Earth is brought to us explicitly from the realm of a supposedly privileged experience of nature (the nonindustrialized worlds of the developing countries). Yet this horse's death devotion is inflicted precisely by those who expect from his world the redemption of the natural in the oppressed.

Orozco's work continuously alters its terms of identification between a Western European and American sculptural discursivity and its very specific and independent deviation from those principles. But these deviations do not invite an easy counteridentification at all; nothing could be less acceptable to him than the variety of *neomexicanismos* or *latinismos* currently entering the Western European and American art market. Whatever references we might discover in Orozco's work that remind us of the specific historic conditions of Mexican modernism and contemporary existence in Central America, those terms are never articulated in a manner that would allow us to relegate and confine him in a condescending and sentimental concept of the higher authenticity of the exotic.

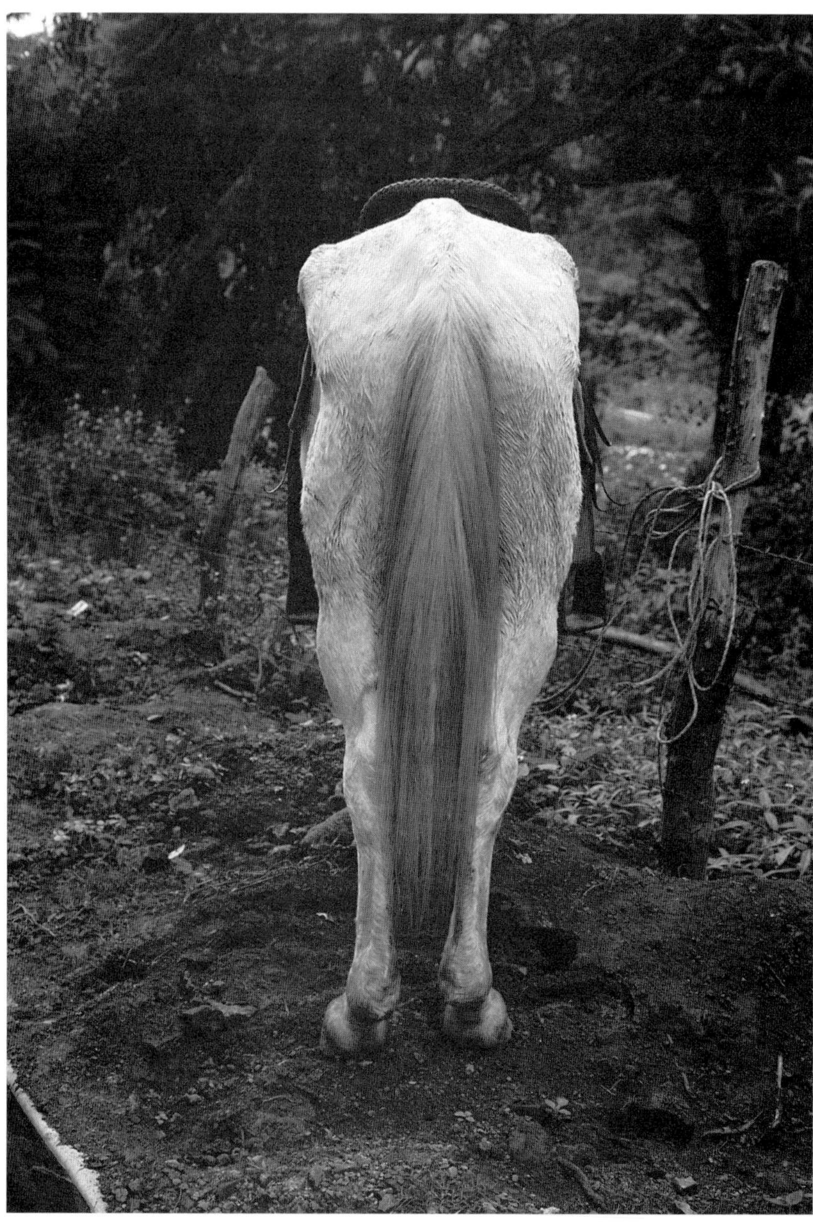

5 *Horse*, 1992.
Chromogenic color print.
20 x 16 inches.

Precisely the opposite takes place: Orozco's sense of identity seems to be intricately linked to a comprehension of the universal conditions of ecological destruction and global economic doom, those conditions that the advanced forms of capitalist production have wreaked on his own culture in the ever increasing invasions of tourism and the continuous expansion of commodity production and enforced consumption. What is "authentic" and guarantees the specifically "Mexican" identity of Orozco's work is the universal presence of debris and scarcity, the industrial waste through which he passes in search of sculptural refuse and the dialectical juxtaposition of these conditions with the historic neutrality of the romantic language of *arte povera* and the scientific optimism of postminimal sculpture. What is equally specific is the degree with which Orozco maneuvers his way through the fallacies (and opportunities) of being "othered" without ever pronouncing either a total disavowal of the specific cultures from which he emerges or a declamatory embrace of its legacies, which would inevitably relegate him to the most alienated forms of a "primitivized" identity.

Of course, each of Orozco's sculptural objects seems to resonate deeply with references to the ancient cultures of Mexico: the rubber ball to the games of the Maya courts, the red clay heart to the rituals and the symbolism in which Native American and Hispanic mythologies were fused, the black plasticine ball in its hermetic weight inevitably acquiring the features of the haunting sculptures of stone skulls we know mostly from dark black-and-white photographs, and the distribution sculpture constructed out of ice-cream spoons, which invokes the hieratic ornamentation of the elaborate stone carvings of temple architecture.

But the work consistently denies these references as explicitly as it seems to suggest them, continuously recalling them as mere chimera. The viewer's projections are engaged in a conscious reiteration of the very process of othering, returning our primitivizing projections onto these objects, whereas these objects return our exoticizing gaze back onto us. Orozco's objects achieve this continuous effect of distantiation by an unusual set of strategies. On the one hand they seem to insist on their sculptural competence as works that emerge from a complex dialogue with the sculpture of the recent past, from Penone to Serra; on the other hand these objects deny the validity of those traditions for themselves as much as the revelation of the archaic references are negated in the first instant even of their articulation.

And it is here that our argument introducing this essay should be reconsidered and perhaps modified at least in part. For if we said that each instance of the acquisition of language competence and of actual cultural representation is politically infinitely more important than the compliance with abstract criteria of quality and the obedience to standards set by Eurocentric and patriarchal traditions that have been hegemonic and exclusionary, then we should also say that an aesthetic definition restricted to the particularities of the projects of historic empowerment betrays all definitions of the aesthetic as a promise of an inherently universal experience. This question really would not be of more than philosophical concern if it were not for the fact that the increasing variety of highly specific and instrumentalized practices of artistic articulation already indicate the political ramifications of that definition. Outside the horizon of a universal conception of the political and a universal conception of the aesthetic, a new realm of idiomatic operations emerges (something like a model of artistic coalition politics), each one more specific and restrictive in its terms of operation and its modes of address and audiences.

The ensuing effect of a radical dedifferentiation of subjective experience, and of the dismantling of historical reflection as an integral element of the constitutive complexity of both authors and readers as traditionally subsumed in aesthetic constructs of a particular historical moment, is already an accomplished fact within most practices of current concern. And it is within this dialectic, between an increasingly instrumentalized definition of the aesthetic function as a tool of identity formation and the simultaneous restriction of the concepts of subjectivity to those of sexuality, gender, and ethnicity, that critical *aesthetic* and *political* questions emerge. The first one addresses the contradiction of an aesthetic definition that excludes the mnemonic dimension from its projects, and the second one addresses the contradiction of a subject definition that restricts itself from its initiating moment to the logic of culture as identity formation, political representation, and empowerment—an empowerment that is entirely defined with regard to the existing institutions of a hegemonic culture and, paradoxically, defines itself in the contestation of its canons in order to gain the institutional acceptance of that hegemonic culture. Worst of all, the current definitions of cultural production as a substitute for actual political empowerment and representation fail to recognize the paradox of the depoliticizing effect of the politicization of contemporary culture as much as the dismantling of subjectivity inherent in the strategies of cultural representation. Shoring up cultural memory in the way that the conservative reaction suggests cannot be but a profoundly reactionary and hopeless mechanism of defending privileges inevitably always already lost. But to accept a concept of subject formation that excludes the differentiation of historical experience from its radical demands for political and cultural representation in the present institutional system (if we limit our discussion to the questions of cultural representation in existing institutions and discourses) betrays emerging identities all the more: once again it cheats them of their historical rights as much as of their understanding of the legacies of oppression and destruction from which they originally emerged and to which they remain indebted.

Notes

1. Miguel Covarrubias, "Modern Art," in *20 Centuries of Mexican Art*, exh. cat. (New York: Museum of Modern Art, 1940), p. 145 (translation modified).

2. For example, the translator generously adds the word "European" to the concept of "failed traditions," when in fact it is fairly evident in the Spanish original that the "failed traditions" are the cultural traditions of the bourgeois class. In this sense it is noteworthy to recognize that the embrace of Mexican art at this moment would have also followed a pan-American, anti-European impulse, when Europe represented the Fascist and the Stalinist threat from which the Central- and Latin-American satellite states had to be protected in the ideological gesture of the democratic pan-American embrace.

We do not know the history of this exhibition (and this is not the place to exhume it) but any exhibition that proposed to make twenty centuries of a particular culture available has already betrayed its imperialist subtext (unlikely that any American museum would have suggested to install *20 Centuries of French Art*, for example). Perhaps its motivation was similar to other projects of the then primarily Rockefeller-controlled museum that on other occasions had traded educational institutions and exhibitions of Latin American culture for contracts guaranteeing Rockefeller's Standard Oil Corporation exclusivity of drilling rights in Venezuela. Or perhaps the exhibition enacted embrace as the best control in a manner similar to the more notorious occasion when the same Rockefeller had commissioned Diego Rivera to paint the decoration of the Rockefeller's architectural complex in New York, and the patron intervened by personally censoring the revolutionary politics of the Mexican avant-garde artist.

3. Shoshana Felman and Dori Laub, *Testimony: Crises of Witnessing in Literature, Psychoanalysis, and History* (New York: Routledge, 1992), p. 58.

4. Once again, the strategy of transforming a surface into a purely passive receptacle of merely accidental pictorial and indexical mark-making has a complex and largely unexplored history in the twentieth century: from Duchamp's *Elevage de poussiere* to Rauschenberg's *Night Blooming* (a painting series that Rauschenberg produced ca. 1951 during his sojourn at Black Mountain College in North Carolina), to the typical epigone gestures of Yves Klein when he produced a painting in 1961 recording all the imprints made on a white canvas installed on the rook of his car when traveling from Paris to Nice. Although sculpture typically has been far less disposed to open itself up to a similar degree to these concepts and processes, Bruce Nauman's *Flower Arrangements* of the late 1960s or Richard Serra's extraordinary *Hand Catching Lead* (1969) would come first to mind as examples of random sculptural imprinting in the search for predecessors of Orozco's peculiar intervention.

The Sleep of Wakefulness: Gabriel Orozco (1993)

Jean Fisher

> Someone said to me: You have not woken into wakefulness but to a previous dream. That dream is within another, and so on to the infinite, which is the number of grains of sand. The path that you will have to retrace is interminable and you will die before having truly woken up.
>
> —*Jorge Luis Borges*[1]

We are on a beach at Chacahua, collectively engaged in the process of realizing a work by Gabriel Orozco. Before us is an ocean of infinite horizon and beside us a wall of craggy rocks, a site carefully chosen by the artist. We have instructions to make balls of sand and to place them in whatever little hollows we can find in the rocky surface (fig. 6). The balls are to be made by gathering a handful of wet sand, forming it into a sphere, and dusting it with dry sand. Miraculously, this works. There is, of course, a childish pleasure in this activity, but it also carries an erotic charge—the weight of the ball of sand in my hand is sensual, like cradling breasts or male genitals. I lose sense of time in my preoccupation with making a perfect sphere, and it is only after several attempts that the impossibility—absurdity, even—of this becomes apparent. Nevertheless, my best efforts are born from an attentiveness to the relation between the volume of sand and the space that my cupped hands can encircle; with too little sand, the hands are too clumsy to get sufficient purchase on the material and it falls apart; with too much, the fingers grope over a surface too large for them to mold. One could say, therefore, that the "most perfect" sand ball is an

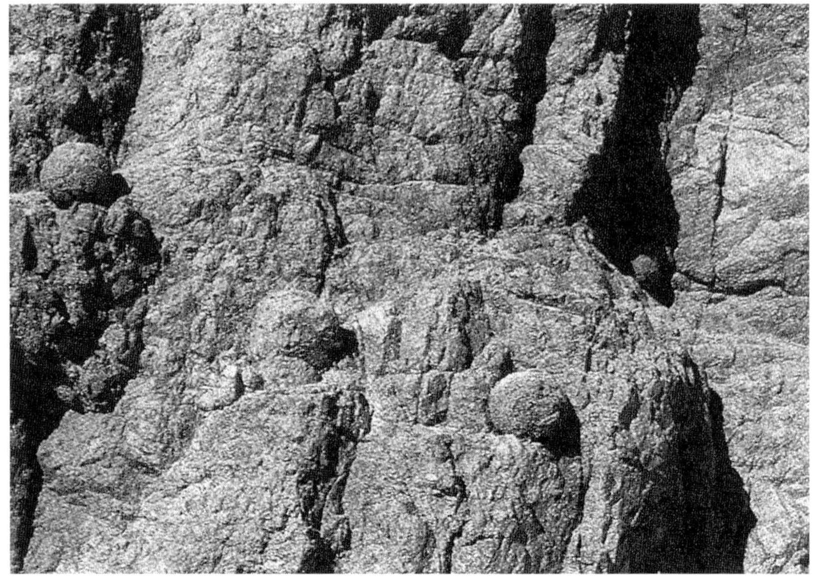

6 *Sand Balls*, 1991 (detail).
Silver dye bleach print.
16 x 20 inches.

index of the interior space of my cupped hands, and thus becomes their extension into the world, just as we, in making the balls, are the extension of the artist's hands. (Later: a group of small boys take equal delight in smashing our little spheres with their own sand missiles, accelerating the process of disintegration.)

I recount the event on the beach in an attempt to convey, however inadequately, something of the intimacy of the encounter with a work of Gabriel Orozco. The work is sometimes so discreet that it almost seems not to be there—the inattentive might easily miss it; yet it insists as a quiet presence inhabiting, rather enigmatically, a space and a moment of negotiation between the world and the viewer. The absence of a readily identifiable content gives the work an opacity: it does not surrender itself instantly to the analytic demands of language. Rather its immediate appeal is to the emotions and senses, producing a somatic resonance often approaching the synesthetic: one might almost hear the sigh of his inflated rubber ball, *Recaptured Nature* (1990); might almost feel in the fingertips the boniness of the fired brick clay of *My Hands Are My Heart* (1991); or generally sense the dangerous implications of the conceptual marriage of flesh with iron in *Open Body* (1991). The body, its tender vulnerability, seems never far away in this work. And yet, to emphasize this aspect without qualification is to trap the work in aesthetic frameworks to which it does not belong: the body as unmediated "nature" is not the veiled subject of representation here; nor is the artist himself made "present" to the viewer in a transferred moment of epiphany from one transcendental ego to another.

Two works of simple elegance, *My Hands Are My Heart* and *My Hand Is the Memory of Space* (1991) (fig. 7), suggest what is at issue. The former is a small heart-shaped sculpture made by the pressure of the artist's fingers on a ball of brick clay held in his hands. It evokes a number of opposing qualities simultaneously: the hard protective carapace of an invertebrate creature and the vulnerability of internal human organs, the soft pliancy of the heart and the hardness of bone. The conjunction of hand and heart also contains that generous gesture of touch and emotion by which one human being offers him- or herself to another. *My Hand Is the Memory of Space* also begins with the hand; spread flat on the ground, its boundary becomes the point of departure for a radiating wave, extending approximately five meters, of wooden ice-cream spoons, now transformed into golden scales like those of a butterfly wing.

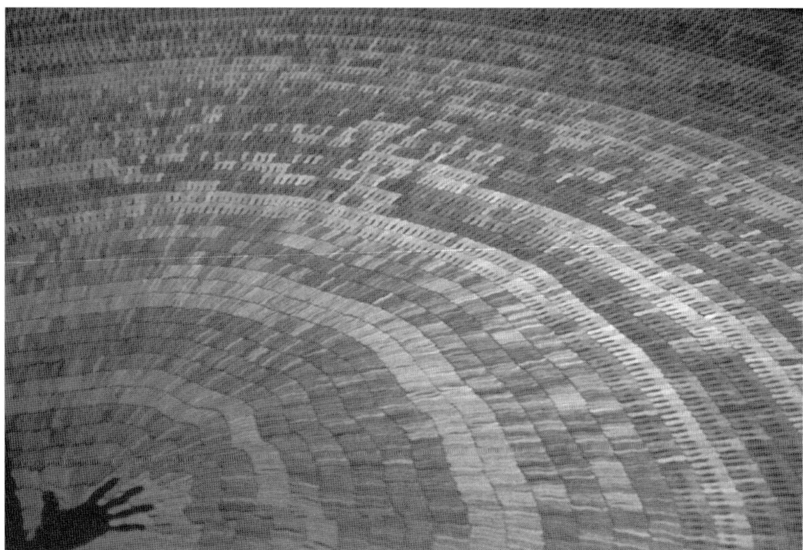

7 *My Hand Is the Memory of Space,* 1991.
Wooden ice-cream spoons.
Dimensions variable.

As with the sand balls, these works do not represent the body as such but present a kind of cast or impression of the space it occupied and the possible limit of its extension. In the former work, an evisceration or a turning inside out takes place where an impression of the exterior of the body (the hands) becomes a projection of the interior (the heart); in the latter, the spoons extend the fingers to touch the limit of what might be an inhabitable space. The body—the hand—is no more than a trace, yet it is precisely this that gives a sense of continuity to the self in the place of its absence. This extension, moreover, implies a search for an orientation in the world, a reaching out toward the other, toward the limits of the knowable; or, like the magician in Borges's tale "Las ruinas circulares" (The Circular Ruins),[2] an attempt to dream into being a reality beyond the uncertainties of the self. The hands have a crucial function here, not simply as basic human tools, but as signifiers of the creative act and its movement from the singular to the collective. As such, Orozco's work may best be described as a profound meditation on the act of making and the psychic impulses that generate it: a vigilance to the processes by which the benthic pulsations of desire, an inchoate mental representation, an act of the imagination, find a tangible form.

That the sentient body remains a referent in Orozco's work goes against the grain of the dominant Euro-American aesthetic debates of the past decade, in which "reality" disappeared into Jean Baudrillard's hyperreal to emerge as the infinity of mirrors that is simulation.[3] All fabricated images and objects are, to some extent, surrogates for the body in what Elaine Scarry proposes is a necessary disembodiment—an impulse toward the transferral of and release from the pain and discomfort of physical existence through the agency of the sign.[4] As Karl Marx insisted, in making the world man remakes himself. And yet, among the privileged sectors of overdeveloped societies, an excessive proliferation of signs of signs—Baudrillard's "precession of simulacra"—becomes self-defeating, since these "sublimated versions of themselves . . . systematically eliminate from their interior the picture of the human body, make progressively more unrecognizable their resemblance to the site of their own creation."[5] The confusion arises when these signs come to be perceived as "reality" itself and not as provisional tools for ordering it. If the object or image ceases to function as a referent to the "real" and the act of making-real a mental representation, then it loses its efficacy as an agent of transformation of human reality. The anxiety tormenting Western discourses on mediated realities is not only that the deterritorialization of symbols from popular memory—specific histories and places—distances them from lived experience and their capacity to establish a communal identity, but that, in a hermetic circuit of signs, there can be no space for "individual" human agency. In Michel Foucault's assessment, institutionalized forms of knowledge, of which mass culture may be an example, stifle popular memory and impose interpretations of reality, such that "people are shown not what they were but what they must remember having been."[6] In this way people lose a sense of participating actively in the processes of life: history and destiny.

In terms of cultural politics, it is commonplace now to say that the economic and political control exerted by the capitalist metropolis on the production and distribution of signs also means the imposition on others of its system of signification and concomitant construction of simulated and commodifiable cultural identities. In the case of Mexican culture, this has no doubt aggravated the pervasiveness of "Mexicanicity": a marketable and institutionalized national "identity," invented from a sentimentalized past, to which Orozco and others of his generation stand in critical opposition. Nevertheless, the existence of profoundly heterogeneous populations with widely varying economic and political realities, and a diversity of histories, has meant that the development of mass culture and its relationships to other forms of cultural production have not followed the same trajectory in Latin America as in the northern metropolis.[7] Mexico remains an intensely visual culture, retaining vernacular and popular expressions of knowledge of immense variety and inventiveness, which, although clearly not immune from commodification, offer a context in excess of the globalized homogeneity of Western-generated mass media. Western distinctions among different forms of cultural production (kitsch and high art, mass and popular culture, and so forth) are not easily applicable here, where "high" and popular cultures may plunder signs and symbols from both the folkloric and the mass media. The streets and markets possess a multitemporal vivacity, juggling such cultural expressions as indigenous weaving and pottery, *fotonovelas*, plastic representations of the personalities of the Lucha Libre wrestling, and magic potions, or the rustic stone wheels to grind maize for tortillas and the doormats and shoes recycled from old rubber tyres.

Orozco's aesthetic strategies of salvage and recycling, of improvization and taking advantage of immediate situations, while seemingly close to those of European Fluxus or *arte povera*, are nevertheless the conditions of lived experience in Latin American societies, and therefore spring from a sensibility and life-world not wholly appropriable to Euro-American categories. His work opens onto not only contemporary art practices dominated by the Western metropolis but also the local practices of his native country.

Orozco's reclamation of defunct and discarded objects or part-objects is an act of reanimation. New life is breathed into the broken rubber inner tube, cut and rewelded to form the air-filled sphere of *Recaptured Nature*. In the installation *Encountered Bodies* (1991), the *objet trouvé* takes on new but unstable identities in a reverie on what is for the artist a rare allusion to the doubling complexity of Mexico's historical identities. Replicated cast-iron parts of a plough become the scales or "feathers" of a sinuous serpent, the spirit of Quetzalcóatl in *Serpent* (1991). Both the plough and the feathered (flying) serpent are powerful mythic symbols uniting Earth and sky; but at the same time, the work draws out the occulted relationship between the blade ("culter" in Old English) that cuts (or cultivates) the Earth and the savage incision that an imported culture and civilization made in the Americas. In *Open Body*, a piece of iron from a truck suggests the hips and open legs of a woman or the helmet of a *conquistador.* As in *Tip of Tongues* (1991) (fig. 8), an iron sheath filled with animal tongues—a direct visual allusion to the relationship between the power to speak and the possession of the phallus—the intimate connection between sex and violence points, in turn, to the trauma of Conquest, of the imposition of one symbolic system on another, one body on another, that haunts history in the Americas.

There is a chimerical quality to these and other "bodies"—bodies like *Nude* (1990), which consists of an upturned chair supported on a workbench by a palm trunk, or *Sleeping Leaves* (1990), in which the opening of a sleeping bag reveals a sheaf of palm fronds. The chimera is a perplexing figure; neither one thing nor another, it occupies an uneasy space in language—a namelessness, suggesting that an understanding of reality is not to be found in the world of objects alone. Closer to the workings of dream than to rational thought, the chimera is drawn from the enigmatic and archaic strata of the mind–body, from the melancholy memories of an evasively present past that includes those figures of the dreamwork—the puns, portmanteau words, and rebuses emerging from the dream's visual and verbal condensations—by which the unconscious manifests desire despite the psychic maneuvers that constantly strive to suppress it. Insofar as the dream springs from psychosomatic impulses it can be no less "real"

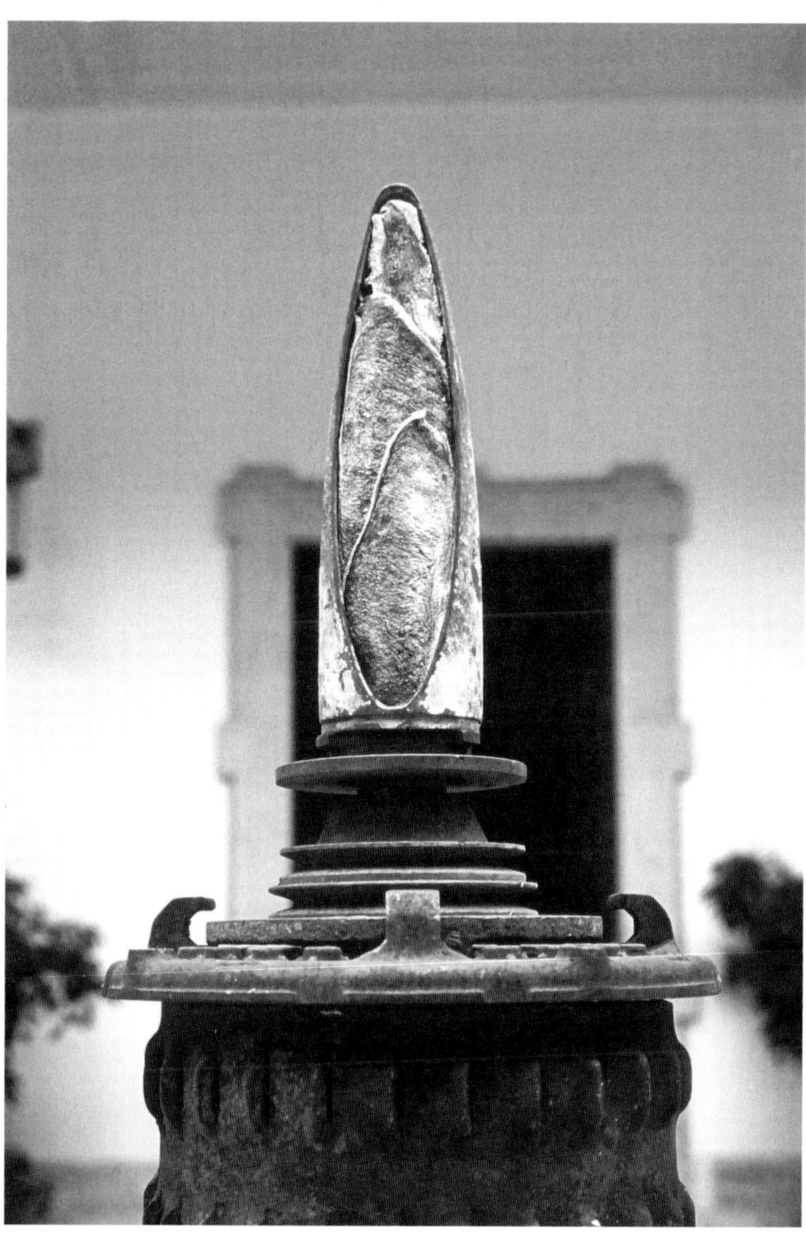

8 *Tip of Tongues*, 1991.
Metal and cow tongues.
78 × 11 3/4 × 11 3/4 inches.

than the world of rational thought. The dream is in us even as we are in the dream, and, together with rational thought, is part of the material universe from which our physical being emerged. Straddling both worlds, the chimera signals the impossibility of establishing certain boundaries between dream and wakefulness, between one identity and another. It is tempting, of course, to assign the chimera to the melancholy that inscribes the stereotype of the Mexican character. And yet there is a wit and sense of optimism in Orozco's chimeras: an implication that time does not follow an inexorable linear path; that other spatiotemporalities can be drawn upon to make the world anew, to forge new combinations and meanings from the residues of the old—which is perhaps the significance of the chimera and, in turn, the cultural *mestizaje* symbolically figured by these "children of Malinche" in *Encountered Bodies*.

Orozco's is a practice of considerable reticence; it expresses a reluctance to impose on the viewer an already framed, prepackaged meaning. On the contrary, the artist often makes minimal interventions in the life of the object, sufficient to extend the form and context of the materials without either disturbing the reality that attracted the artist in the first place, or closing off the imaginative space of the viewer. The question arises of what may constitute the limit of recognizability of a work—that unstable border between something and nothing, order and chaos; and, in the absence of closure, or of already established systems of signification, the suspended moment between the possibility of a coming-into-being of language (an ordered reality) and a slippage into incoherence (incoherent perhaps insofar as we do not have the tools to recognize an order). The latter recalls Umberto Eco's meditations on the ambiguity of what he called the "open work," whose threshold as a work was "not a function of aesthetics, for only a critical act can determine whether and to what extent the 'openness' of a particular work to various readings is the result of an intentional organization of its field of possibilities."[8] Thus, for Eco, the "open work" was, like Orozco's, one that was in-formed yet did not display a specific content, thereby allowing an imaginative play of several possible realities.

Testing the limits of the work through an "intentional organization of its field of possibilities" would seem to be an apt description of Orozco's shift from a purely studio-based practice to one that engaged with the contingencies of the streets and environs of the city. For the moment, the street—with its rituals and objects of daily life, its spontaneous poetry—seems to answer a demand in the work for a space unfettered by the conventions of the studio and the gallery, one more open to a fluidity of meanings, to the possibility of chance encounters between the artist and images and materials, or between the work and the casual passerby. Orozco trawls the streets looking and listening, not always certain what for, but alert to a sense of place and ready to grasp the opportunity to act in response to it. *Crazy Tourist* (1991) was just such a spontaneous response to the experience of Cachoeira market (in Bahía, Brazil) as it closed for the day: the piles of broken and discarded oranges on the ground, the rows of now empty tables, the vendors standing around having finished work. Orozco reassembles these elements: one orange placed on each table, momentarily creating a new constellation from the prevailing disorder, a different vision of familiar everyday objects, much to the amazement of onlookers.

Transient and contingent but without the romantic and touristic colonizing gaze of a Richard Long, Orozco's outdoor pieces are informed as much by the confusion and chaotic energy, the constantly changing states of decay and renewal characteristic of the daily life of Mexico City (and also, as it happens, of New York), as by his knowledge of recent art history. In Mexico particularly, cultural artifacts, from architecture and domestic furniture to pottery, traditionally possess a sturdy geometry that organizes form and space in relation to the demands of the human body rather than to an Ideal of pure form independent of any concrete reality so characteristic of the Euro-American tradition. Anthropomorphic without being anthropocentric, this cultural "corpus" takes on board the impossibility of perfection, like Orozco's rubber ball, whose resting, slightly sagging, and vulnerable form is still a sphere despite its lack of geometric precision, like the Earth itself. Moreover, for the artist, the illusion of permanence and invulnerability cultivated by "First World" countries is unthinkable in the unpredictable conditions of the "Third World," where structures, like people, acquire the skin—"sensualized through time," as the artist commented—of a body inhabited by, yet also inhabiting, the world. Orozco's desire to find material form for this opaque movement of existence takes shape in the metaphor of erosion—which returns us to the cycles of making and unmaking the world. *Rubbed Bricks* (1991) (fig. 9) presents this process through the texture of little piles of red dust made by rubbing together old bricks found on a plot of wasteland following the Mexico City earthquake in 1985. Like the relation of sand balls and rock, erosion here alludes to the interaction between the surfaces of things, between

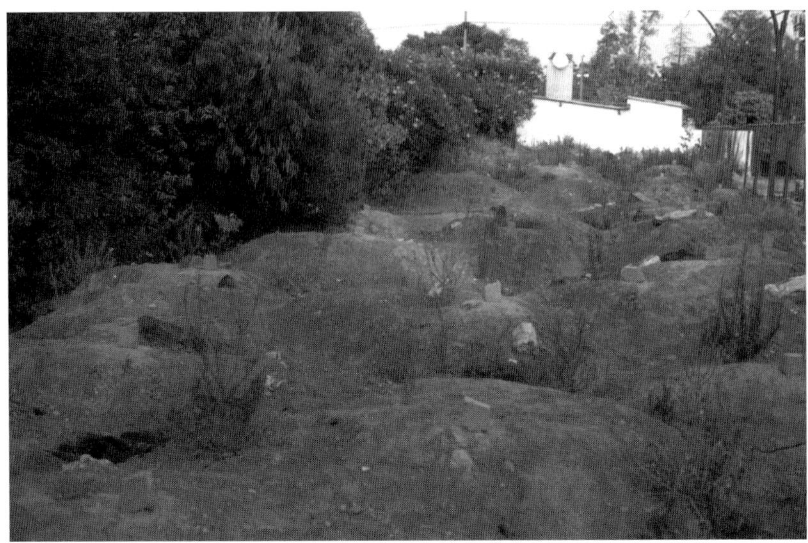

9 *Rubbed Bricks*, 1991.
Fuji crystal chromogenic archive C-print.
16 x 20 inches.

bodies, in a movement that is at the same time disturbing and erotic. Perhaps the most poignant expression of this idea is *Yielding Stone* (1992), a black plasticine ball, the weight of the artist's body, which had been gently rolled through the streets, its softness yielding to the impressions of the ground, its surface acquiring a stonelike patina as dust and debris adhered to it. *Yielding Stone* is above all an object of touch: a surface that invites probing fingers, a mass that compels the more brutal viewer to test its inertia with their feet.

Dust and stone hold a special significance in this body of work; on this connection, the artist commented that "a new building is like an image, but a building covered in dust is like a stone." Perhaps this is because they both possess an enigmatic materiality that resists representation and the closure that it imposes on the act of dreaming or imagining. What this further suggests is the difference in experience between distance and an intimate proximity; between, on the one hand, the gaze—that all-consuming vision that demands the subject seek itself in the image or death of the other; and on the other, a refusal of its totalizing power—a blinding of the gaze that turns the eye from an organ of exteriority to one of interiority and touch, in which the other is felt in the reciprocal resonance of bodies. Here the opacity of Orozco's work might be understood as a refusal to present an image or identificatory mirror that would guarantee and situate a coherent subjectivity. Instead, the work demands that the viewer approach the condition of Borges's incarcerated priest in "La escritora del Dios" (The Writing of God): that, in the implication of work and viewer, all subject–object polarities dissolve and what emerges is the movement of consciousness itself.

The demand of the work is *vigilance*, which is not a state of consciousness that stands in simple opposition to sleep. We might try to approach this ambiguous condition through Orozco's own avowed fascination with watching sleeping bodies or objects, like the rubber ball, dwelling in the quietude of an impenetrable reality. This is the subject of several works such as *Sleeping Leaves, Sleeping Boundaries* (1991), and the quite astonishing image *Sleeping Dog* (1990). What is the fascination here if not that of witnessing a being entrusting itself to what Maurice Blanchot calls "an act of fidelity and of union [with] the great natural rhythms, to the laws, to the stability of order";[9] or a being enfolded back into what the physicist-philosopher David Bohm describes as an "undivided wholeness": reality as an "unknown and undefinable totality of flux that is the ground of all things and the process of thought itself"?[10] Blanchot concludes that vigilance is more the property of the sleeper than the person awake:

> Vigilance is sleep when night falls. Whoever does not sleep cannot stay awake. Vigilance consists in not always keeping watch, for it seeks awakening as its essence. . . . [S]leep is intimacy with the center. I am, not dispersed, but entirely gathered together where I am, in this spot which is my position and where the world, because of the firmness of my attachment, localizes itself.[11]

For both Blanchot and Borges, to dream is to touch the unknown totality; but it is also to risk inertia, for to stay in the dream is to dwell in the interminable where the self no longer recognizes itself. It is essential, therefore, that the sleeper be vigilant even as he dreams. "Whoever has glimpsed the universe," says Borges's priest, "whoever has glimpsed the powerful design of the universe, can no longer think as a man. . . ."[12] Sleep, on the other hand, is that moment in which "in order to act it is necessary to cease acting."[13] And in this moment when acting ceases, creative thought catches its breath.

Here perhaps we might grasp the significance of Orozco's play of interfaces, of sensual encounters and collisions, of mutable realities: the street as the boundary between private and public space; the outline of the hand in *My Hand Is the Memory of Space* as the difference between the absent body and its extension into the world; the rubber skin of *Recaptured Nature* as the interval between inside and outside; the small stone that sits on the horizon between sky and pyramid at Monte Albán; the rustic table at Chacahua as the space that both separates and unites the sand pyramid on its surface and the sand on which it rests; dust and stone; the chimera hovering in the space between dream and wakefulness. Where is the interface located? It cannot be said to belong properly to either an inside or an outside, functioning rather as a vacillating interval between states. Perhaps, however, it does not "belong" at all to the dimension that it appears to occupy.

In speculating about the installation at Kortrijk, Orozco considered "reflecting something of the outside of the brewery building on the inside," a notion that implies more than a simple mirror reflection (at the very least because it would involve shifts in real time and space in the perception and memory of the viewer). Another possibility was to install a photograph of the interior of the Kortrijk building incorporating an insert of a similarly derelict space from the Lobos Hospital in Bahía, as if a hole had been punched through space and time and one place folded onto another. Perhaps we can speculate, then, that Orozco's chimerical interface is linked to what Bohm calls an *unfolding* from the "implicate order" of reality—the "undivided wholeness" whose nature is unknown but whose rhythms we may sense before rationalization is possible—to an "explicate order" which is the familiar one of space, time, language, and so forth; in the way that a telluric movement may throw into relief previously hidden strata, or as the unconscious manifests the pulsations of desire through fissures in the shield of psychic repression. What the interface seems to figure, therefore, is the process of creative thought as it strives to give communicable form to new intuitions of "reality."

Orozco's spheres and "sleeping bodies" are worlds in themselves, but they also interact and participate with others in a larger whole, receptive to the transformations that such encounters engender. *Dial Tone* (1992) is such a world: it consists of the complete entries of the Monterrey telephone directory, cut and pasted onto a roll of fine Japanese paper, and presented as a wave in the process of unfolding.[14] As Orozco remakes the world of the telephone book, so we, bringing our own memories and imaginative intuitions to it, may make it anew. As I re-mark the contours of the work, so it inscribes me within its own dimensions. In this encounter, the one may glimpse itself within the totality and the totality within itself, even as the world is in a grain of sand.

Notes

1. Jorge Luis Borges, "La escritura del Dios," in *Nueva antología personal* (Buenos Aires: Emecé, 1968), p. 211. Translation by the author.

2. Jorge Luis Borges, "Las ruinas circulares," in *Narraciones* (Madrid: Ediciones Cátedra, 1990), pp. 97–103; published in English as "The Circular Ruins," in *Collected Fictions*, trans. Andrew Hurley (New York: Viking, 1998).

3. In addition, several objects that Orozco has used in his work have a direct relation to the body's posture and comfort: tables, chairs, sleeping bag.

4. Elaine Scarry, *The Body in Pain: The Making and Unmaking of the World* (New York: Oxford University Press, 1985).

5. Ibid., p. 325.

6. Michel Foucault, "Film and Popular Memory," in *Foucault Live (Interviews 1966–84)*, ed. Sylvère Lotringer, trans. John Johnson (New York: Semiotext[e], 1989), pp. 89–106. This interview was originally published as "Anti-Rétro" in *Cahiers du Cinema* 251–252 (July–August 1974), pp. 5–15.

7. For an analysis of this subject, see William Rowe and Vivian Schelling, *Memory and Modernity: Popular Culture in Latin America* (London: Verso, 1991).

8. Umberto Eco, *The Open Work*, trans. Anna Cancogni (London: Hutchinson Radius; Cambridge, Mass.: Harvard University Press, 1989), p. 100.

9. Maurice Blanchot, "Sleep, Night," in *The Space of Literature*, trans. Ann Smock (Lincoln: University of Nebraska Press, 1982), p. 265.

10. David Bohm, *Wholeness and the Implicate Order* (London: Routledge, 1980), p. 59.

11. Blanchot, "Sleep, Night," p. 265.

12. Borges, "La escritura del Dios," p. 212.

13. Blanchot, "Sleep, Night," p. 266.

14. The telephone directory has a paradoxical significance: it refers to location and communication, but the telephone itself is a medium that separates even as it seems to connect people.

Gabriel Orozco: The Sculpture of Everyday Life (1996)

Benjamin H. D. Buchloh

> Why should it be that advertising, which has endowed the modern world with so many unexpected creatures, has yet to have entered the domain of statuary: advertising, whose billboards bestow such grandeur on the landscape and whose presence accentuates the majesty of mountains, meadows, oceans. I would love to see a Cadum baby in porphyry rising from a marble basin . . . or the little Meunier Chocolate girl in granite and ivory, leaning against the walls.
>
> —*Robert Desnos, "Pygmalion et le Sphinx," 1930*[1]

All sculptural production in the last thirty years finds itself knowingly or naively suspended between two realms and registers of articulation. On the one hand, it is positioned within the institutions of the bourgeois public sphere, as an object either in the museum or in the mythical domain of "public space," where it claims to assume all of the traditional functions of the "monument" and pretends to enable acts of simultaneous collective reception and historical commemoration.

On the other hand, sculpture is positioned within the equally mythical but more powerfully "real" dimensions of the culture industry and of spectacle, the world of industrially produced "objects" and "signs," and as such it operates in the field of ideological interpellation. While it seems evident that the conflict between the two spheres of object experience has been intensified in the contradictory structures of postwar sculptural production, the fundamental differences between these two models and their respective spheres of reception have hardly been recognized.

Rather than presuming a unified, transhistorical experience of sculpture as a discursive object, it appears necessary to propose two opposing models of reception. The first would argue that sculpture continues to function in a space of relative discursive and institutional autonomy. As such it would generate seemingly neutral forms of aesthetic experience, determined primarily by problems of sculptural specificity and the phenomenology of perception (e.g., the work of the minimalists up to Richard Serra). The second model would recognize that sculpture in the public sphere—like all other discursive forms—operates within the spaces and institutions of ideology and as such communicates not only (if at all) in a field of pure perception but also (if not exclusively) in a space of interpellation.[2] If we use the term "public," we refer to the tradition of theorizing public experience developed in the writings of Jürgen Habermas: an argument that institutions and discursive practices in democratic societies construct subjectivity as much as they determine the subject's forms of perception, articulation, and interaction. Evidently, avant-garde production—if only hesitatingly considered by Habermas—would be the first to be affected by structural transformations occurring within the public sphere. This, then, would apply all the more to those practices of cultural production that had been traditionally assigned to function as public display, instruction, and commemoration (even if mostly as the commemoration of rule).

If we use "mythical" in the discussion of the terms "public sphere" and "public space," we define it at first as the more traditional concept of myth, hinting at the rapidly disappearing forms of simultaneous collective experience traditionally associated with definitions of the public sphere, and at the vanishing models of communication, conventions of perception, and institutions of social interaction. If we use the term "mythical" in the discussion of the sculptural sign, however, it refers to a more precise concept, encompassing both Roland Barthes's linguistic and semiotic definition as a particular structural and ideological form as well as Jean Baudrillard's insertion of an economic dimension into the concept of the sign, redefining it as "sign exchange value."

In this text I will attempt to sketch out a discussion of the work of Gabriel Orozco, based on the hypothesis that these three concepts of the public perception of object production—myth, exchange value, and interpellation—could in fact clarify the specific forms of sculptural production emerging in the last decade of the twentieth century.

It is difficult to ascertain the exact historical circumstances during which the splitting of the sculptural body into the two opposing halves of residual, perceptual object and emerging sign of interpellation first occurred. It is less difficult, however, to describe the wide variety of symptoms within the history of twentieth-century sculpture that attest to the actual crisis between the two spheres. The first such instance would obviously be the moment when sculpture increasingly assimilated itself within the body of the commodity, eventually becoming congruent with it: we know that this articulation is one of the great achievements of Marcel Duchamp's readymades. But how do we identify the subsequent historical moment when sculpture itself is completely transformed from the object into the sign of advertisement, even if the object advertises only itself as pure and traditional sculpture supposedly existing outside of the commodity and the advertisement sign, as in the countless recent examples of trivial, traditional sculpture?

Obviously Duchamp had already tested the viability of the advertisement image (for example in *Apolinère Enameled*, 1916–17) as a matrix or *template* for painting within which each and every feature of aesthetic intervention would be contained and suspended like a fossil of a past life in its petrified incarceration.

Yet it is undoubtedly one of the most crucial aspects of Andy Warhol's *Brillo Box* (1964) to have superimposed two opposing sculptural traditions and to have hybridized them at the same time with the inexorable logic of the advertisement sign. First of all, the *reductivist* (geometrical/stereometrical) paradigm appears here once more—at the height of minimalism's re(dis)covery of that tradition, but it appears as one that is always already fused with the structural logic of an industrially produced container.

Second, the *readymade* paradigm (the industrial box) is converted into a design/sign that challenges the myth of sculpture's seemingly guaranteed conditions of weight, mass, and corporeal tangibility altogether. What is at stake here—as in Warhol's work in general—is in fact not just the shift from readymade object to (graphic/photographic) sign, but moreover the sign's role in the process of *interpellation*. For if it is the structure of the commodity fetish and the principle of sign exchange value that primarily determine collective object experience at this point, then the following questions arise: in what other forms of object—and image—relations could sculptural production take recourse in order to communicate with its presumed spectators? In what way could sculpture provide the innate resources of critical opposition against the universality of the commodity object's reign and the sign of interpellation without relapsing into a claim for a purely phenomenological object or without reclaiming a discursive specificity and autonomy for sculpture? And lastly, and more difficult yet: in which institutional space and in which discursive register could the sculptural object articulate critical opposition to these universally valid principles without reclaiming a mythical sphere of a "naturally" given public space?

The precariousness of object experience and its tenuous existence within residual or ruinous forms of the public sphere are *actual* and common conditions of everyday life at the sites of economic and political marginality, whereas they are only *symbolically* articulated in the high-art discourses of the avant-garde in the centers of economic and political power. This condition alone could explain the fatal bonds that link almost all European and American radical sculpture of the postwar period to its utter opposite: while one could suggest that one of the attractions to *arte povera* was its invention of a new assemblage aesthetic that promised to overcome both assemblage's historical obsolescence as form and procedure as much as it seemed to abolish sculpture's fundamental alienation from the natural object, the *poverty* of *arte povera* teetered from the beginning along the boundaries of the most luxurious design gadgets. Similarly, the suggestion of a proletarian public sphere in Serra's work seems to have always anticipated its future subservience to the postmodern corporate architect's *diktat* of spectacularizing radicality.

Even the bricolage of damaged goods (from Arman and John Chamberlain right down to the present) inevitably acquired an instant air of calculated artificiality. What appeared still possible in the moment of surrealism—namely, the redemption of sudden acts of memory in the discovery of obsolete spaces of fashion and consumption—can hardly operate any longer under the circumstances of an accelerated obsolescence. Enforced obsolescence eliminates these acts to the extent that it cannot permit the aging of objects even through usage. Thus the very signs of obsolescence, and the actually extant spaces of the outdated themselves, are instantly recuperated by sign-exchange value to compensate for the disappearance of yet another experiential form that had to be colonized by consumption control (e.g., that of use value or that of the temporality of deterioration). It is significant to notice that this dimension is most clearly articulated in the transition from the objects of surrealism to the *nouveaux realistes* of the postwar period, especially when it comes to the radical transformation of the assemblage aesthetic in the work of Arman. What Arman has achieved in his *accumulations*, and more programmatically in the *poubelles*, is precisely the articulation of a disappearance, namely, the spatial destruction of an interiority of commemoration that gradual obsolescence and the natural deterioration of objects (for example, in the work of Joseph Cornell) had still allowed for.

The work of Gabriel Orozco provides an exacting account of the fragile conditions of object experience and sculpture's tenuous existence within them. His work does not assume sculpture's guaranteed access to both historical reflection and public experience, and it could be discussed as a model of object production that responds critically to the loss of the commemorative dimension as much as to the questions of whether sculpture can at all constitute itself any longer within a democratically defined, bourgeois public sphere.

At equal remove—or in equal proximity—to the American as well as the Italian modalities of sculpture of the late 1960s and early '70s, Orozco continues and alters, inverts and counters all of the fallacies that hindsight and history have made apparent in the sculptural practices of the past four decades. Drawing with equal ease upon Serra's processual definitions and Gordon Matta-Clark's interventionist performances in architectural fragments, Orozco has considered with similar care and historical interest the synthesis of the cultural and the natural in the work of Michelangelo Pistoletto and Giuseppe Penone. Yet Orozco's sense of hybridity does not solely result from his clear observation of these fragmented conditions of public spatial perception and object experience in postwar sculpture since his work emerges from an aesthetic, but even more so from a geopolitical and historical, distance. Thus Orozco confronts us with a surprising insight: namely, that the impact of high cultural practices emerging from different centers can be particularly productive when they are (mis)read from a considerable distance and hybridized in a geopolitical margin, outside the strictures of local discursive orthodoxies and conventions.

Orozco's sculptural work shifts continuously, applying various strategies of discursive, temporal, and institutional dislocation: from the precarious, yet still manually produced object, the result of an almost ritualistic gesture of sculptural modeling (*My Hands Are My Heart*, 1991), to the performative slicing of the debris of a glorious industrial past (*La DS*, 1993), and from the bricolage for a minimal consumption of the future (*Crazy Tourist*, 1991) to the mnemonic image of a public sculpture cast in the body of an object of consumer design (*Habemus Vespam*, 1995, and *Until You Find Another Yellow Schwalbe*, 1995).

Each object and installation emerges from a contextually specific analysis, yet at the same time transcends the limited range of site-specific definitions from the '60s and '70s by freely employing all available genres and conventions. Sometimes the work remobilizes esoteric conceptions of plastic experience long thought outdated. Sometimes it reaches the dimension of a universal legibility through its explicit inhabitation of commodity design. The multiplicity of sculptural definitions (playing out the utilitarian against the mnemonic, puncturing the aesthetic with the ritualistic, defining the language of commodity design as the sole site of simultaneous collective perception) even increases the instability of Orozco's practice. This multiplicity of functional modes finds its exact correspondence in an equally complex range of sculptural procedures: on the one hand, it leads Orozco to the invention of automatist procedures of *modeling* in works such as *Yielding Stone* (1992), a plasticine sphere that indexically records the anonymous imprint of particles absorbed in the process of being rotated in the street. On the other hand, it leads to the anchoring of the impulse to model in the purely corporeal activity of an indexical imprint (*My Hands Are My Heart*). In a third case, it is the emphasis on the mere mass and weight of wet papier-mâché cast into old socks that models itself by process alone to Brancusi's ideal of biomorphic perfection.

Similarly, the procedure of *cutting* reappears in Orozco's literalist deployment of sculptural conventions; instead of cutting stone or wood, however, he splits and slices industrially produced structures. This strategy appears for the first time in *Recaptured Nature* (1990) when Orozco cut a found, industrial object (a truck tire's inner tube), a strategy culminating—at least for the time being—in the large-scale project of *La DS* in which Orozco subjected an entire car to the procedure of a spatial splitting.[3]

The third of the sculptural strategies redefined by Orozco is that of the *distribution* and/or *doubling* of found materials and objects. Distribution as a device to arrange found objects or readymades in noncompositional formations derives most explicitly from the legacies of Duchamp and surrealism and their reemergence in Arman's accumulations. Subsequently, it reappeared in the chance arrangements of postminimalist distributional sculptures, such as Carl Andre's and Richard Serra's various scatter pieces of the 1960s, Bruce Nauman's *Flower Arrangements* (1966), Robert Morris's

Continuous Project Altered Daily (1969), and Barry Le Va's untitled scattered glass pieces of the early 1970s.

Yet, in Orozco's installations the performative dimension of distributional process is foregrounded by the same degree that the site- and context-specificity of the object as much as its framing conditions are explicitly reflected upon in the arrangements. One such example would be the peculiar dialectic Orozco develops around his use of seemingly nondescript objects such as fruit in several installations, and in the corresponding photographs documenting those performative interventions. The first one, *Crazy Tourist*, displayed single oranges on the emptied tables of a street market in a small Brazilian town, arranged after hours by the artist in order to generate an almost formalist, linear perspectival recession of orange points along the axis of tables at the abandoned market (fig. 10). A complementary installation would emerge two years later in a work Orozco produced for the Museum of Modern Art, New York, entitled *Home Run* (1993). Here the artist asked the museum to negotiate with its adjacent residents to place oranges in a grid formation on the interior windowsills of the apartments and offices that faced the museum's north facade and overlooked its sculpture garden.

If the oranges in *Crazy Tourist* were distinguished by their artificial rarefaction (after all, an orange on an empty table in an outdoor market gains exceptional visibility only as a result of the peculiar formal intervention of isolation), the oranges at the Museum of Modern Art, by contrast, appeared as a serial linear arrangement (fig. 11). They linked diverse and separate private and semipublic spaces, generally not known to display fruit on their windowsills in an almost ornamental fashion (like a festive garland), but the objects remained in an enigmatic condition of illegibility since they clearly could be explained neither as decoration nor as vending display.

While the singularization of a serially produced object is as integral to the concept of the readymade as is the alteration of the framework of display, in Orozco's work both strategies generate a rather different range of readings as a result of the shift from the industrially produced object to the common, "natural" object of everyday life. The seemingly anodyne character of found fruit as readymade object distinguishes Orozco's work in particular from the earlier examples of distributional sculpture whose claim to "pure" materiality and whose insistence upon an exclusive concern with perceptual structure and sculptural form had remained relatively abstract regarding their reflection of context (how could one

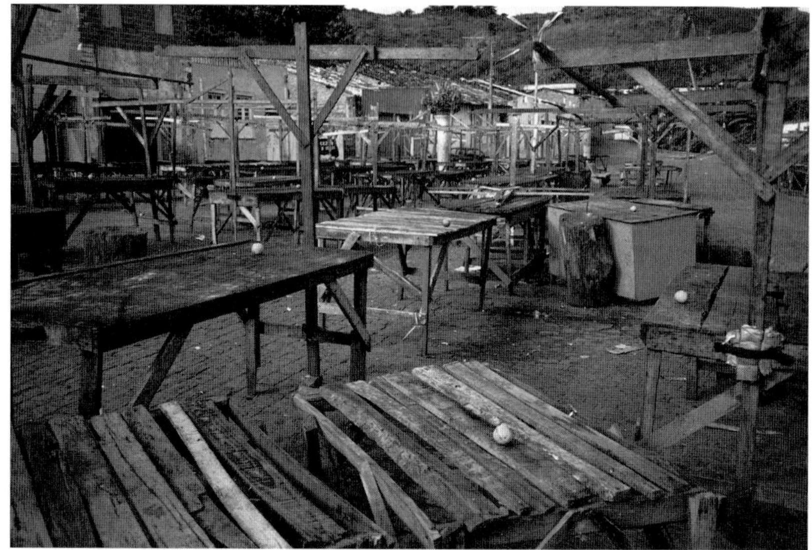

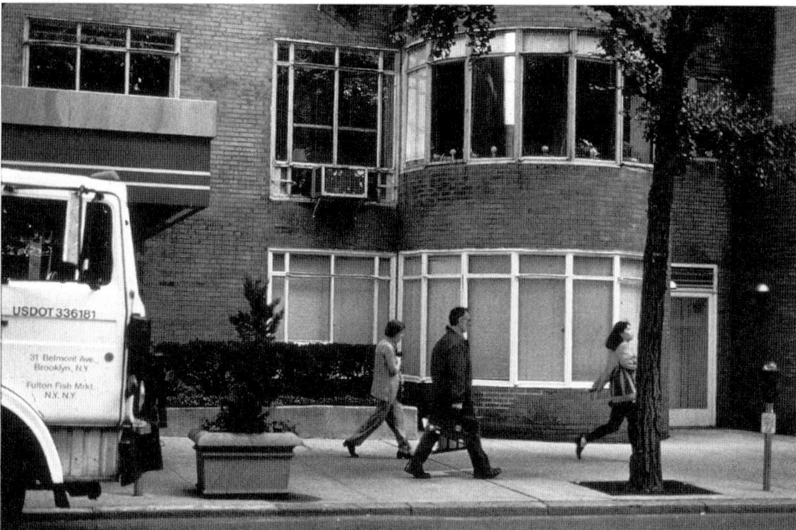

10 *Crazy Tourist*, 1991.
Chromogenic color print.
16 x 20 inches.

11 *Home Run*, 1993. Installation view of oranges placed in apartment windows across the street from the Museum of Modern Art, New York.

construct a compelling logic to place molten lead, pieces of felt, glass, or flour on the floor of a gallery or museum?). Orozco's distributional sculpture deliberately reconventionalizes this supposedly "radical" principle of the late 1960s by reinvesting the object with an iconic dimension. Thus he recognizes them not as primarily defined by morphological or phenomenological structure, but as always already participating in the spaces of sign production and thus inextricably bound within the acts of ideological interpellation. Equally, the principle of spatial organization in Orozco's work differs from the emphasis on randomness in traditional distributional sculpture. *Crazy Tourist* and *Home Run* develop a more explicitly structured yet still highly ambiguous relation between a seemingly arbitrary scattering of nondescript materials/objects and the focused reflection on the relationship between site-selection and object choice.

These works foreground the contextual interaction between specific framing conditions and their effect on the readings of the specific object on display. Yet paradoxically—and it is perhaps in this aspect that Orozco's works depart most dramatically from the practices of institutional critique that had evolved in the wake of postminimal distributional sculpture (such as the work of Michael Asher)—these objects now appear as strangely animated agents, simultaneously subservient and subversive to the institutional framework. This peculiar dialectic between an artificially constructed specularity and a seemingly benign banality of displayed objects generates the force field of the installation. Fusing three types of radically different spaces, Orozco's intervention invites the spectator to recognize that these objects—suspended between the public and the private—articulate the fundamental condition of sculpture and its inability to resolve these contradictions. First of all, the spectators perceive themselves as positioned within an indoor museum searching from the authorized institutional perspective of public exhibition and its objects. Subsequently they contemplate the display of structures in the sculpture garden as an *official* institutional site where sculptural objects would generally be exhibited according to their discursive classification. Lastly, the spectators realize that they have to stare—somewhat illicitly—into the spaces of private homes and offices, where the *actual* installation takes place in the facades of the buildings that now function as a vitrine outside the showcase of the sculpture-garden itself.

It is here that—intensified by the illicit act of staring into a private home—the oranges and their intimate banality as readymade objects achieve their goal: in the momentous withdrawal of privacy, in the negation of the grand sculptural gesture, and in the paradoxical appeal to a minimal collective endeavor in arranging a still life of oranges on display.

Thus all three spaces and their correlating object types appear as insufficient for, yet integral to, the constitution and the reading of the sculptural work: the institutional spectacle, the discursive convention, and the private fetish object. None of them alone generates a sense of compatibility and finite correspondence between viewer, object, and institutional framework. Instead, a principle of circulation between all three spheres remains operative, and it is precisely in the manifest incongruence of these objects/spaces that the work articulates the actually existing fragmentation of the experience of public space and the concomitant annihilation of simultaneous collective conditions of reception. Orozco's work articulates the paradox of having to construct sculpture as public experience under the conditions of interpellation that prohibit the self-determination integral to traditional theorizations of the public sphere. It is in this paradoxical constellation of sculpture's necessity to function as a public structure and to simultaneously denounce "public" experience proposed by aesthetic means alone that Orozco's installation gains its credibility. Orozco's sense for the precarious status of the sculptural object between private fetish and public spectacle seems to have alerted him to those objects whose public perception and historical memory are located precisely within the languages of design: the field of interpellation by specific objects of consumption and the rapidly changing ideological identifications they generate. Three projects of the last three years make this interest an astonishingly consistent focus in Orozco's work, in spite of its continuously changing approaches and procedures.

The three works, *La DS*, *Habemus Vespam*, and *Until You Find Another Yellow Schwalbe*, are linked first by their careful object selection: as a series they constitute a typology whose "public" status appears to be already guaranteed by its mere affiliation with transportation, urban circulation, and consumer-culture design. Thus the works' common iconographic and technological structure seems to suggest that urban transportation and circulation are, in fact, the last domains in the vernacular fields of everyday life where residual "publicness" in its spatial, social, and discursive intersection can still be traced. Here, collective social communication and interaction supposedly do still occur—even if only in the most banal and catastrophic forms. But the promise of an accelerated temporality through public mobility and the recognition of an entropy of planned obsolescence are intertwined in these structures in the same manner that vehicular circulation and commodity circulation are inextricably fused with each other. The proclamation of a purely technological utopia of accelerated mobility—pronounced as a future resource of unlimited glamour and power and made by the futurist avant-gardes and Dadaists like Francis Picabia at the beginning of the century—returns in Orozco's work at the end of the century as a melancholic contemplation of the condition of waste and ecological destruction, futility and loss, and the exhaustion of resources by violently enforced, planned obsolescence. To the extent that all objects of traffic circulation are also objects of commodity circulation, the three objects chosen by Orozco occupy a particularly important place in the design histories of each country in which they were produced and exhibited (France, Italy, and Germany, respectively). Thus it becomes evident that the artist considers the sphere of consumer design and its languages not only as another intricate form of experience where "publicness" is buried and latent—but also as the domain where a dimension of temporality (and by implication one of historical experience) can still be detected, even if only through the perverted form of the deterioration of objects of consumption. Accordingly, all three objects, while still in use, are, in fact, manifestly outmoded, and as such they introduce a reflection on obsolescence into Orozco's work, linking it with those strands in the surrealist tradition that had attempted to spark a mnemonic dimension through the obsolete objects and fashions of the recent past.

The strategies deployed in these works inscribe the classical conventions of twentieth-century sculpture onto the very bodies of the design object itself. Thus the principle of the cut appears here not just as a radicalized sculptural procedure, but as a gesture that activates the entire spectrum of spectacularized modernity. First performed by Lucio Fontana in the field of the pictorial in response to Jackson Pollock, it had been transferred by Arman onto the daily objects of domestic culture and consumption, finally reaching architectural scale in Gordon Matta-Clark's interventions in public and private spaces of obsolescence. Forty years after its appearance, Orozco slices, trims, and sutures a Citroen DS (*la déesse*)—a car designed during Fontana's first cutting of the picture plane, and which represented the French claim to a new futuristic car culture (figs. 12 and 13). At the height of its performance in Parisian streets, the *déesse* generated a collective desire for a specifically French car, a feminized car as the object of *luxe, calme, et volupte*, which would thus fence off the masculinist American threat in the domain of car consumption. By 1957 it had already become the almost exemplary subject of a

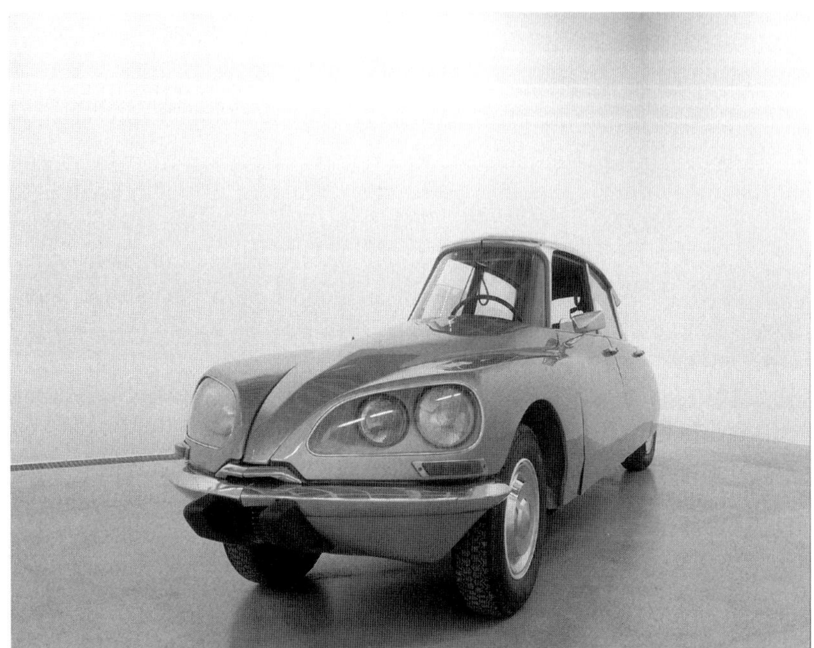

12 *La DS*, 1993.
Modified Citroën DS.
55 1/8 x 190 x 45 3/8 inches.
Image courtesy: Galerie Chantal Crousel, Paris.

semiological analysis of myth in Roland Barthes's *Mythologies*. Orozco's monstrous hybrid, carefully sutured back together after a good third of its body had been removed, confronts us not only with a strangely outmoded image of luxurious ambition on the level of mass culture, but also as a strangely disfigured memory image of a crucial moment of the recent past: namely, the moment when identity construction through interpellation by the design object had been grafted onto the more traditional models of forming subjectivity and identity through interpellation by the ideology of the nation-state. Disfiguring the body and the sign of the *déesse* generates, however, yet another sudden insight: that it is a quintessential strategy of postwar design to inscribe and bind in its sinuous promises precisely those structures of utopian desire that had once been articulated in political claims and oppositional struggle but have now been absorbed and extinguished in the shift from the political public sphere to the collective enforcement of private consumption.

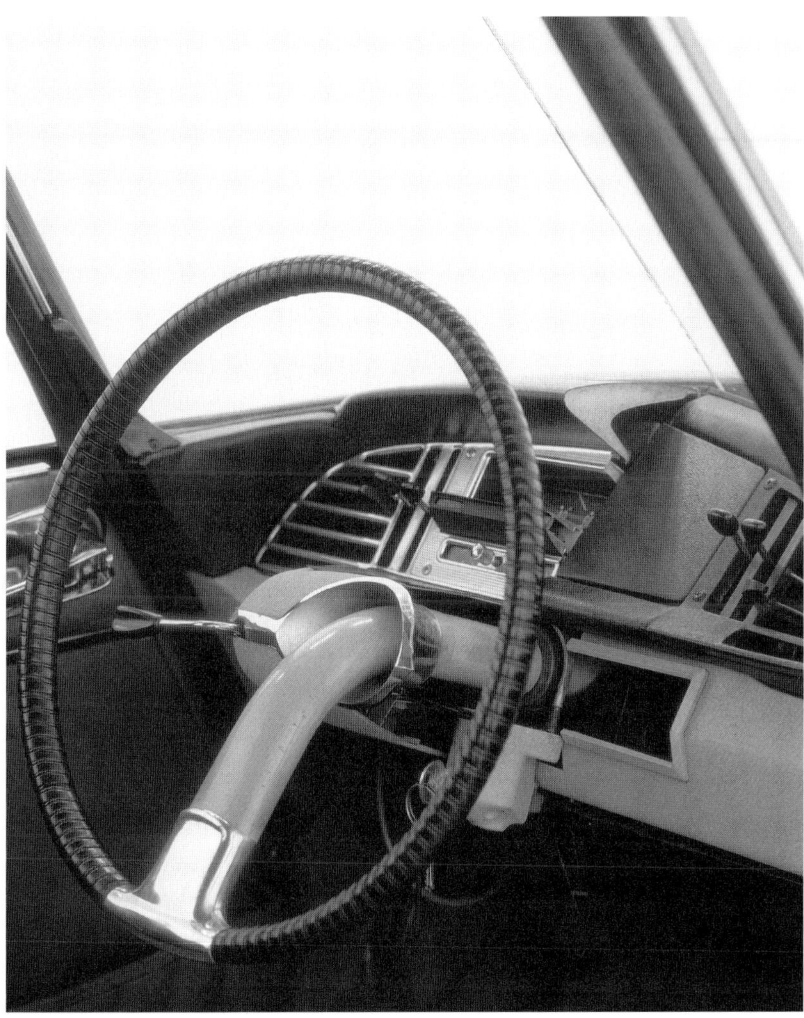

13 *La DS*, 1993 (detail).
Image courtesy: Galerie Chantal Crousel, Paris.

Orozco's cut through the *déesse* thereby performs not only the shifting of a classical sculptural procedure onto the body of the commercially designed object, it also retains some of the destructive impulses that had motivated the gesture of cutting in its original enactments (such as Hannah Höch's *Cut with the Kitchen Knife through the Last Weimar Beer-Belly Cultural Epoch in Germany*, 1919–20). Inasmuch as the slicing of the car's shell mimetically traces the very undulation of its sinuous design, it also drives it to the level where the hidden agenda of all design culture and its inherent betrayal of desire are revealed. In the act of suturing the two halves, that hidden agenda appears in all its monstrosity: merely the carcass of promises, between coffin and projectile.

The critical pessimism of *La DS* finds a dialectical reversal in a work that Orozco conceived and executed while living in Berlin in 1995. Entitled *Until You Find Another Yellow Schwalbe*, this performance/installation work situated itself once again in the sphere of design and circulation, yet it differed already by the peculiar choice of a design object from the recently disintegrated German Democratic Republic, a country that would have prided itself in its resistance (and its failure) to produce an "adequate" advertisement and design culture (fig. 14). Typical of the objects for consumer culture in a socialist country, the vehicle chosen by Orozco was a strange breed between a scooter and a motorcycle, euphemistically entitled *Schwalbe* (the swallow). The design of the scooter can barely conceal the desire of its makers to offer a vehicle that promises to be as prestigious (i.e., Westernized) as it would be functional (i.e., economically affordable). Yet at the same time, it suffers all the pathetic shortcomings of hypertrophic engineering and excessive luxury that consumers of the Western world consider by now to be part of their birthright and that would entitle them in their view to make equipment such as the *Schwalbe* the easy target of mockery and supercilious disdain. It is precisely from the opposite perspective—and certainly enabled by his contemplation of the object from the position of a subject with ample experience in comparing standards and expectations of the so-called Third World to those of the so-called First World—that Orozco deals with the peculiarly charged remnant of a recently vanished socialist state.

Here the obsolescence and historically retarded technology suddenly appear as exemplary cases of an approach that socialist culture had once claimed among its central concerns: to construct an object whose priority would become its universal accessibility as much as its use value (fig. 15). Obsolescence thereby suddenly acquires the opposite reading as well: it appears no longer as the inevitable complementary formation to the overall process of reification but emerges as the temporal dimension of a forfeited aspiration, one that still contains the nucleus of a reflection on the wasted opportunities of a socialist countermodel of consumption that had been once at hand. Accordingly, in this work the procedures of structural organization were also radically different from the gestures performed on the *déesse*. The work's formal principle consisted of recording all the necessarily random instances when Orozco would discover another Schwalbe motorcycle parked on the streets of Berlin in order to pair it with his own model for the production of a photographic record of the encounter. Typical of the careful structuring in Orozco's work in general, a peculiar chromatic restriction (the color yellow) limited the otherwise excessively large number of potential object encounters and the occasions to perform their public reunion, as much as it also unified the accumulation of randomly encountered vehicles and their photographic records according to a strictly formal criterion.

By introducing a carefully chosen, *specific object* (in continuation and in opposition to the principle of the *readymade*) and matching it with the principles of *doubling* and *serial repetition* in the random chance encounters of these vehicles in a vast urban territory, this work not only introduced a complex variation (and critical revision of three formal paradigms of Dadaist, surrealist, and minimalist procedures), but it also shifted from the dramatic performance of an act of public fissuring (in *La DS*) to an act of public fusion.

Resonant with the complex political implications of territory, and given the city of Berlin during the immediate aftermath of German reunification, the work's subtle but insistent mnemonic dimension seems to ask for more than the mere retroactive contemplation of possibilities in a socialist object of consumption.[4] As an already obsolete object of socialist consumer culture and an example of a modest yet fully functional object of utilitarian value, it seems to hold out quite well against the violence of waste that the new capitalist order announces and will from now on impose. Yet in its performative doubling of an object from a culture whose memories and legacies would now be erased as rapidly as possible, the random and ludic "unification" of these two color-coordinated objects opposes precisely the impulse to repress which the grand "unification" enforces.[5]

Thus it becomes evident that Orozco's insertion of specific objects from the languages of advertisement and consumer culture into his

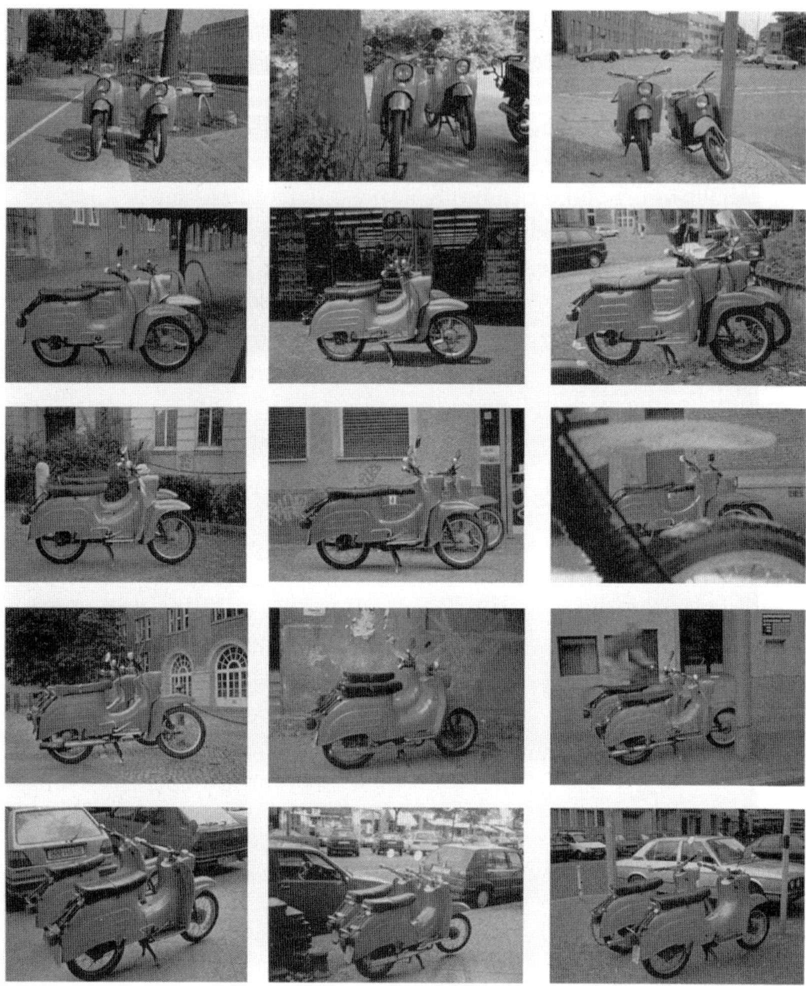

14 *Until You Find Another Yellow Schwalbe*, 1995 (detail).
Set of forty Chromogenic color prints.
Each print 12 7/16 x 18 5/8 inches.

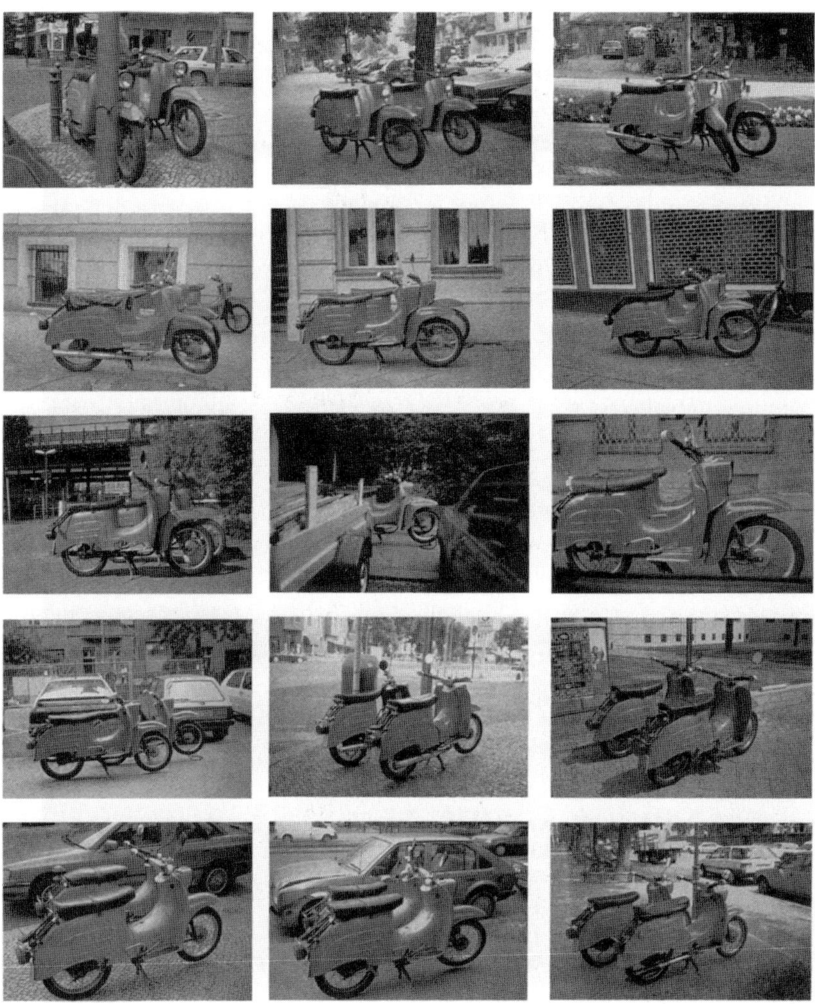

15 *Until You Find Another Yellow Schwalbe*, 1995 (detail).

installations simultaneously analyzes the larger political and ideological implications of the social spaces where these objects operate. And while a work such as *La DS* could be criticized for its peculiar conventionality in radical gesture by inserting a readymade object from public urban space, and the public sign-exchange system of advertisement and product design, into a semiprivate space of discursive practice, experimentation, and commodification (the classic dilemma of all readymade interventions critically denounced by Daniel Buren in the early 1970s), a subsequent work seems to take precisely this dilemma into account and reverse the principle.

In such a sudden conflation of the public urban space of traffic and the public institutional space of the art gallery, Orozco's work *Parking Lot*, installed in 1995 at Galerie Micheline Szwajcer in Antwerp, confirms our earlier observation that the dislocation of the sculptural object and the destruction of the experience of public existence are the central questions of Orozco's project. In a gesture that seems to respond critically to, and at the same time perform, an act of allegorical sublation of the famous installation by Jannis Kounellis at the Galleria l'Attico in Rome (when the artist transformed the exhibition space for the duration of his exhibition into a stable for live horses), Orozco transformed the gallery space for the duration of his exhibition into a functioning parking lot to be used by any passing vehicle in search of a convenient parking space in midtown Antwerp.[6] Here the result of the artist's performative intervention disappears altogether by inscribing the activity totally within the creation of a "situation"—a "situation" that indicates that what is even more rapidly disappearing are precisely the boundaries between traffic and exchange and the exempted public spaces of discursive reflection and critical historical insight that the institutions of the bourgeois public sphere once promised.

Notes

1. Robert Desnos, "Pygmalion et le Sphinx," in *Documents* 2, no. 1 (1930), p. 36, as quoted by Yve-Alain Bois in "Kitsch," in Yve-Alain Bois and Rosalind Krauss, *Formless: A User's Guide* (New York: Zone Books, 1997), p. 119; originally published as *L'Informe: Mode d'emploi* (Paris: Editions du Centre Pompidou, 1996).

2. The concept of interpellation as a principle of subject formation in ideology was first defined by Louis Althusser in *Ideology and Ideological State Apparatuses* (1969). See the English translation by Ben Brewster in Louis Althusser, *Lenin and Philosophy and Other Essays* (New York: Monthly Review Press, 1971), pp. 23–70.

3. For a more extensive and detailed discussion of *Recaptured Nature*, see my essay "Refuse and Refuge," originally published in *Gabriel Orozco*, ed. M. Catherine de Zegher (Kortrijk, Belgium: Kanaal Art Foundation, 1993), pp. 38–51, and reprinted in this volume, pp. 1–15.

4. Reflections on the question of what features the socialist object of consumption could display to differentiate it from the capitalist consumer object and how artistic production would engage in the questions posed by its design and distribution were, to my knowledge, addressed extensively for the first time in Christina Kiaer's dissertation on Alexander Rodchenko, since published in a revised form as *Imagine No Possessions: The Socialist Objects of Russian Constructivism* (Cambridge, Mass.: MIT Press, 2005). I owe the term and most of my discussion to Kiaer's arguments, delivered in two lectures at Columbia University in 1995 and 1996.

5. It is quite telling, and it speaks to the success of Orozco's work, that when he approached the National Gallery in Berlin with the idea of concluding his *Schwalbe* project with a biker-style reunion of all the owners of yellow *Schwalbe* scooters, the curator refused to have the reception take place inside the National Gallery, arguing that "Orozco had not understood anything at all about Berlin culture." Thereupon Orozco decided to hold the reunion in the parking lot of the National Gallery.

6. The comparison with the installation of Jannis Kounellis at Galleria l'Attico was suggested to me first by Catherine de Zegher, who first exhibited the work of Gabriel Orozco in the exhibition America: Bride of the Sun in Antwerp in 1992.

Between Work and World: Gabriel Orozco (1998)

Guy Brett

The two historical streams which seem to me to converge in Gabriel Orozco's work are those of sculpture (a category still holding together despite many changes in practice) and that desire, underlying the experimental impulse in so much twentieth century art, to "dissolve art into life." These streams were astutely summed up in two sentences that Jean Fisher applied to Orozco in her 1993 essay about him, "The Sleep of Wakefulness."[1] In his work can be felt, she wrote, on the one hand, "a profound meditation on the act of making"; and, on the other hand, "the question of what may constitute the limits of recognizability of a work." Conventionally, these categories would seem to exclude one another. But the inherent paradox may be very much to the point.

Take, for example, Orozco's *Sand on Table* (1992) (fig. 16). I see it simultaneously as a modest, random occurrence of everyday life, and a sculpture. It seems to be very much a proposition within recent sculptural trends, beginning perhaps with *arte povera*: the "poor" material (sand), the everyday support (table), and the beautiful equalization between the material displayed on the pedestal (the maximum that gravity will allow to stay there) and the surrounding world, fused with the ancient figure of the pyramid (a form common to Egypt and to Central America). But I immediately realize that this sand and table would not have nearly the same effect if displayed as an object in an art gallery. The warm sunlight, the random impressions of people's feet in the sand, give the poetic inflection of the "world," "life," which enables one to internalize the image in a different way. In particular we seem to shortcut the institution of art, and to be placed directly in that common area of experience we all share. The lightness of touch by which Orozco does this is what we especially enjoy.

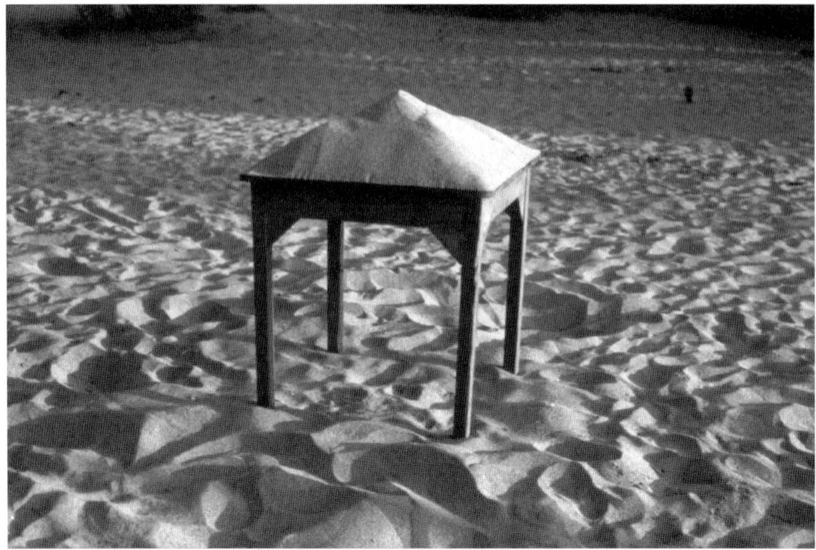

16 *Sand on Table*, 1992.
Silver dye bleach print.
16 x 20 inches.

At the same time I cannot help but realize that I am looking at a photograph. This photograph is the sign of a perception taking place in the midst of life (albeit stimulated by previous works of art), but it is also an object that may be displayed in a gallery, bought and sold. Where does the freshness of the perception, which is basically a prolongation of the act of pointing, as if we were walking with Orozco and he saw the object in front of him, or put it together from what was lying around—where does this moment begin to cede to the demands of the marketable object? If Orozco simply kept his perception to himself in the act of walking around, thinking, and feeling, there would be no communication. But nor would there be if the institutionalization of the object obliterates that act of perception.

Looking for antecedents, Orozco's interventions have most often been interpreted in the stream of European and North American sculpture. Benjamin Buchloh, for example, in the course of two probing, deeply thought-out essays on Orozco's work, has seen it as a derivation from, but radical "inversion" of, positions reached by the likes of Bruce Nauman, Richard Serra, and Tony Cragg.[2] While true, this seems to me to be only a part of the story. Orozco can be related to another stream, already flowing for many years, which connects artists originating outside the European–North American mainstream, and which has been profoundly concerned with questioning the art–life boundary, the "act of making" and the "limits of the work." In fact, a practice as specific as walking the streets and designating portions of reality within the conceptual framework of a political-poetic vision can be found among these artists. It would include the activities of the Argentinean artist Alberto Greco (1931–1965), a rebel against every form of institutionalization, who, in 1962, proposed his *Vivo Dito*. Marcel Duchamp dedicated one of his aphoristic approbations to it. Partly inspired by the example of Yves Klein, Greco would carry a piece of chalk with him to draw a line around an object or person in the street and sign it with his name (*Vivo* = living; *Dito*, derived from *dedo*, a finger, = the act of pointing). About the work, Greco wrote: "The artist will not show any longer with the picture but with the finger." In the early 1960s such behavior still had the implications of madness or effrontery and involved Greco in some narrow scrapes. In the mid-'60s, Brazilian artist Hélio Oiticica (1937–1980) carried out, among other projects, his *Appropriations*, designating various found objects within his generic category of *Bolides* ("fireball" or "energy-center" in Portuguese). Some were given the qualifying subtitle of *Estar*, "to be" as a quality of things, and the artist explained their rationale: "There is complete accessibility here for whoever arrives; no one is constrained by being in the presence of 'art' . . . 'things' are found, which are seen everyday but which one never thought to look at. It is a search for oneself in the 'thing.'"[3] Oiticica also had a general notion of inspired findings in the flux of the streets, which he liked to call *Delirium Ambulatorium*. Then, as a third example, there is the Filipino artist David Medalla (b. 1942), with his ongoing nomadic series of *Impromptus* (c. 1979–), seizing in the photographic instant a hidden meaning in a particular place/time.

My intention is not to make divisions between artists of different geographical origins, but to provide a reorientation of connections. In fact, the positions just mentioned in turn rebound and reveal a tradition within European art, even within sculpture, which revolved around the polemical negation of established canons of value and permanence, and an ironic embrace of the worthless. For example, Giacometti, at a certain moment in his "surrealist" phase, produced what he called *Disagreeable Objects*, "objects without base and without value," in his words. What Giacometti had to say about the wooden carved plane with two protuberances called *Object To Be Thrown Away* (1931) is very interesting:

> It was no longer the exterior form of things which interested me but rather what I felt in my own life. . . . I didn't want to create a figure which looked realistic on the outside, but wanted to experience life and to create only those forms that really affected me, or that I desired.[4]

Giacometti set "experiencing life" against the traditional practices of art, and his talisman of this desire was a sort of ugly thing that would not fit or function within established, expected protocols, "mobile and silent objects" as he also called them.

The conundrum is that life and art are not two separate entities but are continually creating one another. Subject–object, active–passive, are similarly pairs of opposites that cannot exist without each other. There are the objective facts of the environment around us, but there is also our subjectivity and deep individual psychic response that makes us alive to one aspect and blind to another. "Life," in this sense, is as much fantasy and dream (which may be shared of course) as solid reality. Jean Fisher's encapsulation of Orozco's process as "a meditation on the act of making" could be expanded and reciprocated to include "a meditation on the act of being made." All the objects or situations in the street that seem to be objectified by the artist are simultaneously creating him. This indication of the importance of reciprocal relationships would be highly appropriate, given the yielding, "feminine" aspect of Orozco's sensibility that delights in imprints.

Yielding Stone (apt oxymoron!), Orozco's "disagreeable object" from 1992, is one obvious example: the plasticine lump that rolls and picks up imprints and debris wherever it is, a clear self-image since its weight has been made the same as the artist's. An earlier work, *My Hands Are My Heart* (1991), conjoined the active and passive when the heart-shaped piece of clay was made by the clasping impress of his two hands. Indeed, the metaphor of the heart (centrality, feeling, life, "what really matters") is made a nexus where earth, body, the will to form, and the surrender to being formed meet equally.

It is a precarious matter, on the edge of dissolution. The beauty of another work, *Pinched Ball* (1993), lies in its light touch, its marriage of sculptural reference and psychic makeup (fig. 17). We all know those punctured footballs that have been kicked about the streets and then abandoned. A cipher of activity, competitive play is made into a yielding receptacle which has passively received some rainwater that now calmly

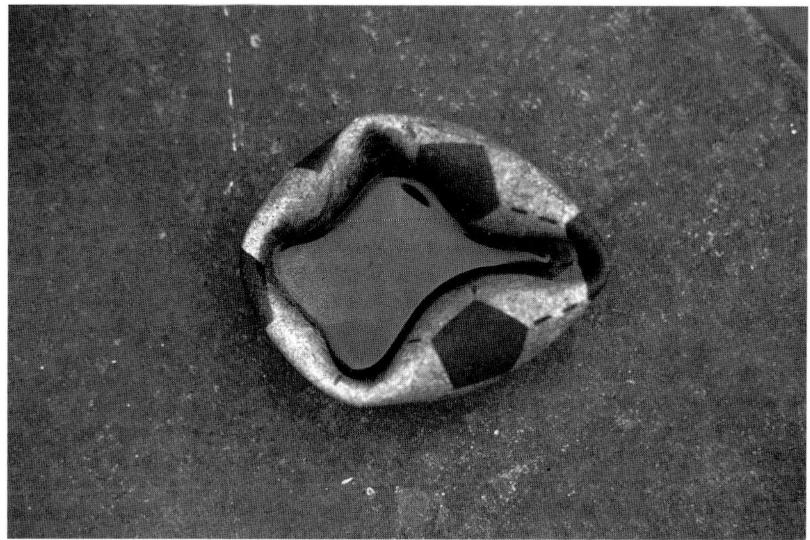

17 *Pinched Ball,* 1993.
Silver dye bleach print.
16 x 20 inches.

reflects the sky, a delicate image in subtle tones extending (accidentally? deliberately?) to the pale blue-green-gray of the asphalt on which the ball has been photographed.

The nagging contradiction waiting in the wings is that the light touch that captures an instant of perception out of the flux of life can be reduced to boredom and inertia by repetition. The image becomes emptied and exhausted by consumption, just as a fashionable word, so fresh when first coined, comes to signify nothing but the pretension or conventionality of its users. This hardening inevitably misses the life-experience—the process of walking, thinking, feeling, experimenting with the environment—that is vividly recorded, for example, by words and pictures in Orozco's series of ongoing notebooks. One way out of this impasse is to make the consumer also a producer. This would be another aspect of thinking in relationships and reciprocities rather than either/or categories, and admitting that every person is multifaceted. Many of the participatory and collaborative proposals by artists in the 1960s and early '70s (which have yet to be given their due in art history) provided structures in which active and passive, individual and collective, producing and spectating, ephemeral and durable, were woven together. They leave a powerful and demanding legacy, summed up, for example, in writings by Oiticica in the 1960s where he spoke of "the quest for individual liberty, through increasingly open propositions, aimed at making each person find within themselves, through accessibility, through improvisation, their internal liberty."[5] Can we follow this call for "increasingly open propositions," in today's inevitably changed conditions? Clearly, there must be many models for reciprocity, as a means to avoid the dogmatic and formulaic and stay close to life-experience.

One of these models may be to explore with greater subtlety the reciprocity—and disjuncture—between the "art" space and the "rest of the universe." A motive that runs like a thread through many of Orozco's works—found, made, or a combination of the two—is the desire to find figures of cosmic generality, astronomical/mathematical figures of movement and space, within the accidental and the everyday. This was seen in *Crazy Tourist* (1991), the planetary system of single oranges arranged and photographed on the stalls of a ramshackle, deserted popular market; and its metropolitan variant, *Home Run* (1993), where the public looked out from the Museum of Modern Art in New York to see the work in the windows of neighboring apartments.

Our earlier mention of the extreme selectivity of any view of the "accidental" and the "everyday" (a testimony to its immense flux), leads to the observation that in Orozco's "everyday," people, at least until very recently, have rarely appeared. Orozco's is a sculptural everyday. There are sometimes animals, but mainly objects. In fact it becomes part of the poetics of a light touch to evoke the human through inanimate objects. It stresses that we exist with objects in a state of interdependence and reciprocity, for better or worse. In one of his notebooks, Orozco speculates about "social space/time in the form of an object" (*The Oval Billiard Table*, 1996, could be an example, one in which the hand is invited to intervene). This is only a device, of course, which could and perhaps has started to change, although the introduction of the human image in Orozco's work remains an intriguing problematic.

The boundary between the "art" space and the "rest of reality" is a very mobile thing as its exact placement is continually being contested between the liberating forces of imagination and the stultifying tendencies of the institution. When I think of this contest, I think of two of Orozco's works in particular, which are themselves mobile and silent (to borrow Giacometti's terms), and in an important sense, "empty." Both *Empty Shoe Box* (1993) and *Parking Lot* (1995) are marvelous instances of lateral thinking—illuminating the field by taking a position to one side of habit—and of the application of a Zen, or guerrilla, tactic: turning to one's own advantage already existing systems of powers that be.

Empty Shoe Box has frequently caused considerable annoyance when it has been exhibited (fig. 18). Directors of busy public museums despair of the consequences of insuring as an artwork a nondescript open box that Orozco insists on placing on the floor or in a corner where it could easily get kicked or thrown away. There has sometimes been the complaint (not least at the Venice Biennale in 1993) that Orozco has lowered the tone of a would-be important mixed show by submitting a slight piece of work, whereas, paradoxically, the modest empty box can become in one's mind the opposite: an expansive figure of receptivity, openness, possibility, especially by contrast with some of the more labored efforts around. In the atmosphere of "artistic jousts" that these group exhibitions have become, rather as in the poetic jousts of the past, to accomplish much with minimum effort counts for a lot, and raises the pitch of the vitality that all are seeking.

Parking was the title of a recent Orozco exhibition at the Galerie Micheline Szwajcer in Antwerp. He simply opened the art gallery as a

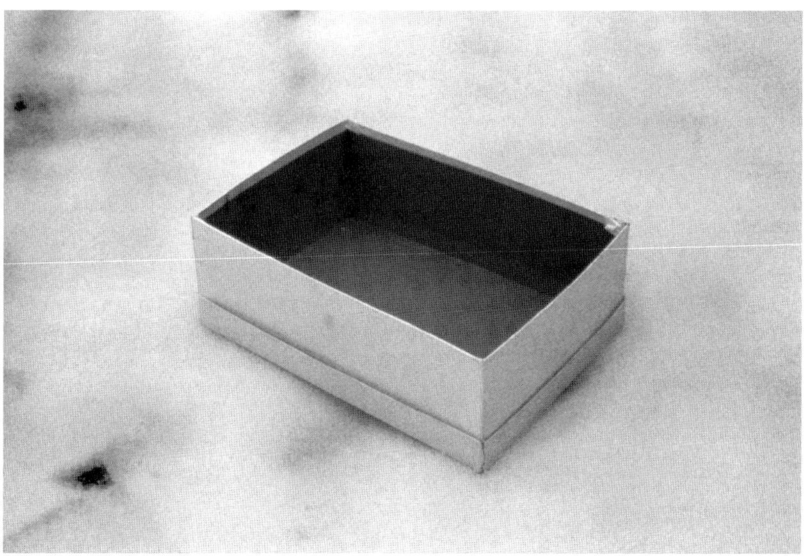

18 *Empty Shoe Box*, 1993.
Shoe box.
4 7/8 x 13 x 8 1/2 inches.

parking space to any passing motorist who happened to be cruising the city center looking for a convenient place to stop. "Lateral thinking" is perhaps synonymous here with a "light touch"! As well as a sophisticated addition to his "yielding" images—opening oneself and the art space to the random intrusions of the anonymous city—Orozco produced an allegory of the deflation of artistic pretension that includes the essential ingredient of a self-deprecating humor. In fact, he perpetrated a joke far funnier and more pointed than any satirist of the absurdity or the "emptiness" of modern art has managed to produce. It was encapsulated in the idea that an anonymous passer-by, in the act of blithely solving a banal problem of everyday urban life, could unconsciously contribute to the elucidation of a crisis in the direction of contemporary art, a choice of alternatives that can either lead the way to a pointless, self-referential trap or open up possibilities for a vitality of art–life interrelationship that is yet to come.

The anonymous motorist and his symbiotic car slip into the role of protagonist by crossing a threshold between one context and another, contexts that are as much mental as physical, which may be as invisible to one person as they are loaded with meaning to another. This is the reality in which we live, the multifaceted simultaneity of our social being in which we continue to insist on our unique individuality. What but an agile, ironic, and tender consciousness can negotiate between the two?

Notes

1. Jean Fisher, "The Sleep of Wakefulness," in *Gabriel Orozco*, ex. cat. (Kortrijk: The Kanaal Art Foundation, 1993), pp. 16 and 19. Reprinted in this volume, pp. 17–29.

2. Benjamin H. D. Buchloh, "Refuse and Refuge," in *Gabriel Orozco*, exh. cat. (Kortrijk: The Kanaal Art Foundation, 1993), and "Gabriel Orozco: The Sculpture of Everyday Life," in *Gabriel Orozco*, exh. cat. (Zurich: Kunsthalle, 1996; London: Institute of Contemporary Arts, 1996; Berlin: Deutscher Akademischer Austauschdienst Berliner Künstlerprogramm [DAAD], 1997). Reprinted in this volume, pp. 1–15, 31–49.

3. Hélio Oiticica, "Position and Programme" (1966), reprinted in *Hélio Oiticica*, exh. cat. (Barcelona: Fundació Antoni Tàpies, 1992), p. 105.

4. Alberto Giacometti, letter to Pierre Matisse, 1947, quoted in *Alberto Giacometti 1901–1966*, exh. cat. (Vienna: Kunsthalle; Edinburgh: Scottish National Gallery of Modern Art; London: Royal Academy of Arts, 1996), p. 146.

5. Hélio Oiticica, "Appearance of the Supra-Sensorial" (1967), in *Hélio Oiticica*, p. 127.

The Tempest (2000)

Molly Nesbit

The sprite sang of yellow sands and hands, with refrains of barking dogs,

Full fathom five thy father lies;
Of his bones are coral made;
Those are pearls that were his eyes:
Nothing of him that doth fade
But doth suffer a sea-change
Into something rich and strange.[1]

The refrain became a bell.

The lines of verse, a movement, passed through materials, elements. The tempest inhabited every little thing. The storm broke. The tempest inhabited everything inside and out. Shakespeare broke its spell, but not its movement. The tempest still exists. It is neither an object nor a space exactly, it cannot occupy the definition we have settled upon for sculpture. Perhaps that definition is arbitrary.

Is it necessary?

Benjamin Buchloh and Gabriel Orozco have had an ongoing conversation about sculpture for years now, dating to the time of the *Yielding Stone*. Generally they cede to lunch. Once, in 1998, they let their conversation reach print. Buchloh was wanting to know more about the relation between photography and sculpture as Orozco saw it; Orozco did not see them as distinct activities, nor as ends in themselves, but rather each one serving the purpose of activating a space or of showing a space that had been activated and left. "The space," he explained, "is not about a physical white cube; that's why I was interested in abolishing the link between the outside and the inside, the noisy, dusty street and the white, clean space of the gallery and the museum, the private and the public and how they are all always interconnected, collapsing."[2]

Buchloh gathered all this and asked again about separation. These were points he felt important to clarify, since they were, to his mind, the way to see how this work of Orozco's could be understood, compared, to its precedents. But were the precedents prototypes? Buchloh pursued the matter.

> From Henry Moore to Richard Serra you can say that sculpture, as much as it might be hybridized and contingent upon others, it has its disciplines and discourses. You have approached it from the beginning as a return to hybrid objects, to hybridized space; your work does neither inhabit the discursive space of sculpture nor that of the street; it is not located within the space of the museum, yet it does not share the space of the readymade or the commodity object, nor is it merely the object of phenomenology: it is all of these and in between all of them. Is that correct?[3]

These were questions that followed from the frames Buchloh had already constructed earlier in his essays for the Kanaal Art Foundation in Kortrijk, Belgium, and for the Zürich Kunsthalle in order to think about Orozco's objects within the frame of the world. There he had focused on the business of the object, its ability to escape the simple projections of national or ethnic aesthetics, or modernist aesthetics. He saw a silence coming from the objects themselves. He saw this silence bespeaking an awareness.[4] The greasy thick black plasticine of the *Yielding Stone*, a most imperfect sphere, a child's material expressing the artist's actual weight, was incapable of maintaining surface clarity. This was a stone made to be rolled in the street, receiving the dust and refuse into itself as an outer layer of fluctuating grime, impersonal trace, a sphere of dense nothing, a space without point. The stone relayed the outside impress of a changing world, the kick of the spectator, the paw of the dog. It shrugged off pictures. Orozco speaks of it variously. He told me that it was like the stone in nature on which animals sit.

Orozco made the stone in 1992. The next year he had his show at the Kanaal Art Foundation in the spring. In the Aperto of the Venice Biennale, he put an empty shoebox on the floor across the room from the *Yielding Stone*.[5] It too was kicked. In Mexico City another *Yielding Stone* turned up in the parking lot of the Museo de Arte Moderno for the exhibition *Lesa Natura, Marred Nature*; inside was another plasticine ball showing off half an orange skin and on the wall a drawing made from toothpaste spit.[6] For the Institute of Contemporary Art (ICA) in London as part of a group show called *Real Time*, he made a series of supermarket interventions in Covent Garden, rearranging the stock on the grocery shelves, and brought back a melon to sit on the very top bookshelf in the store of the ICA.[7] He made the project space at MoMA in New York expand into episodes that erupted quietly around the museum and then outside it. He tried hanging a hammock from two skyscrapers and then settled for two trees in the sculpture garden. He asked the occupants of the apartments across the street to put fresh oranges on tumblers in their windows.[8] And when they did, the oranges sat behind the glass windows, living up to their title, *Home Run*. Here was a game beyond baseball, a game that could score without breaking windows or surfaces, a game that left museum aesthetics behind. There was no stylistic thread linking all of this, no consistency that could be packaged into the kind of commodity we call a line of work. The year would end in Paris at Chantal Crousel with the cut compressing the DS. It was accompanied by the sound of softly squealing brakes taped into a rhythm in collaboration with his friend, Manuel Rocha. They called it *Ligne d'abandon*.

Objects rolling away from models, from purchase, objects uncontrolled, uncaged. John Cage. Gabriel Orozco had discovered his work in Madrid in the late 1980s. Cage's *Silence* had explained things, partly. There was the "Lecture on Nothing" and the "Lecture on Something." All of it helped Orozco develop his sense of the expanded space in which he still works. Cage was quite clear about the fact that life overrode art's social privilege. "WHEN WE SEPARATE MUSIC FROM LIFE," he wrote,

> WHAT WE GET IS ART (A COMPENDIUM OF MASTERPIECES). WITH CONTEMPORARY MUSIC, WHEN IT IS ACTUALLY CONTEMPORARY, WE HAVE NO TIME TO MAKE THAT SEPARATION (WHICH PROTECTS US FROM LIVING), AND SO CONTEMPORARY MUSIC IS NOT SO MUCH ART AS IT IS LIFE AND ANY ONE MAKING IT NO SOONER FINISHES ONE OF IT THAN HE

BEGINS MAKING ANOTHER JUST AS PEOPLE KEEP ON WASHING DISHES, BRUSHING THEIR TEETH, GETTING SLEEPY, AND SO ON.[9]

Was this music sculpture?

Was this sculpture music?

Later in this lecture, "Composition as Process," Cage spoke of interpenetration and unimpededness, quoting the Zen master D.T. Suzuki. How to understand that every human being and every thing is at the center in all of space? How to understand that to see that is to see no impediment? And then with interpenetration, each being and thing is moving out in all directions in both time and space.[10] There will be no cause or effect, no real difference between spirit and matter, or matter and movement. These were lessons that Cage had worked to absorb. He did not see art as a professional activity. He did not observe the strict divisions of labor between the arts. He and Robert Rauschenberg would ink the tire of his truck and drive it down Fulton Street one day in 1953. Twenty pieces of paper placed on the street recorded one long track.

"Beware," Cage had cautioned, "of that which is breathtakingly beautiful, for at any moment the telephone may ring or the airplane come down in a vacant lot." All of this was said pausing. He liked silence. "A piece of string or a sunset, possessing neither, each acts and the continuity happens. Nothing more than nothing can be said."[11] There is a contact with the world being made here, but it does not englobe. There is thought. But no presumption that thought or art can hold or bound a world or an age's version of a world.

This flies in the face of so much. In Cage's time, as in ours, there was a sense that art was meant to carry a global image on its shoulders. The role of modern art was being defined by a criticism based in America, a criticism that sought mandarin status for itself and set about proposing general, international definitions, total master models, for the course of modern art. They would think of art as a progress, as a refinement, as a lineage, as a politics. A tale of countries. One tale or another of fathers and sons. Their picture of art had much in common with the idea of the world picture that Martin Heidegger had proposed in his essay of 1938. Of course all of them owed something to Hegel. The idea of the picture had to be big.

"Metaphysics grounds an age," Heidegger had said at the outset, "in that through a specific interpretation of what is and through a specific comprehension of truth, it gives to that age the basis upon which it is essentially formed. This basis holds complete dominion over all the phenomena that distinguish the age."[12] In the modern age this metaphysics would find truth lodged in science, and the metaphysician would come to understand his business to be falling in line with that of the research worker. It is under these conditions that the metaphysician can see that the world has for the first time become "a picture." Certainly thoughts like these were made possible by picture magazines bringing the world forward in photographs and circulating its image as never before. Heidegger, however, wished to discuss the matter in terms of an enhanced position of subjectivity; in other words, a certain sense of Man has made this Picture or *Weltbild* come forward. This picture is more than an image; it is a structured image. We might say that it is a picture that carries an idea not only of structure but of composition within itself.

That composition becomes a priority in art historical analysis in the twentieth century is a parallel phenomenon. In many ways the different models put forward in modern art criticism proceed from the assumption that their general model can function as a world picture and that it can be revealed by attending to composition as it involves both internal pictorial structures and a relation to a beholder. Heidegger did not predict this. He had ended his essay with a discussion of scale. The world he saw was gigantic, and not to be understood through the mere trope of America. It was the scale of achievement, of victory over matter, of the mass media, quantity achieving special quality, he said. Heidegger sought to endow the gigantic with the force of a concept, to make it have the properties of mental existence. His gigantic had the form of a continual not-having-been-here-yet and was incalculable.

Cage wrote, as many did in the '60s, about how to improve this world. "We are getting rid of ownership, substituting use. Beginning with ideas. Which ones can we take? Which ones can we give? *Disappearance of power politics.* Non-measurement." The world is dismantled unscientifically into portions and considered piecemeal. "Begin again," Cage said, "assuming abundance, unemployment, a field situation, multiplicity, unpredictability, immediacy, the possibility of participation."[13] This was quite another world picture. In many ways it was not a picture.

His example, not Heidegger's, was important to Orozco, who would open the pages of *National Geographic* and lay little balls or worms of gray plasticine on top, to give another layer to the picture, weigh on it and add inscrutable blobs of confusion. But Orozco would not be specifically referencing John Cage when he plunged into New York and rode his bike through the puddles, making circles that reflected the cold winter

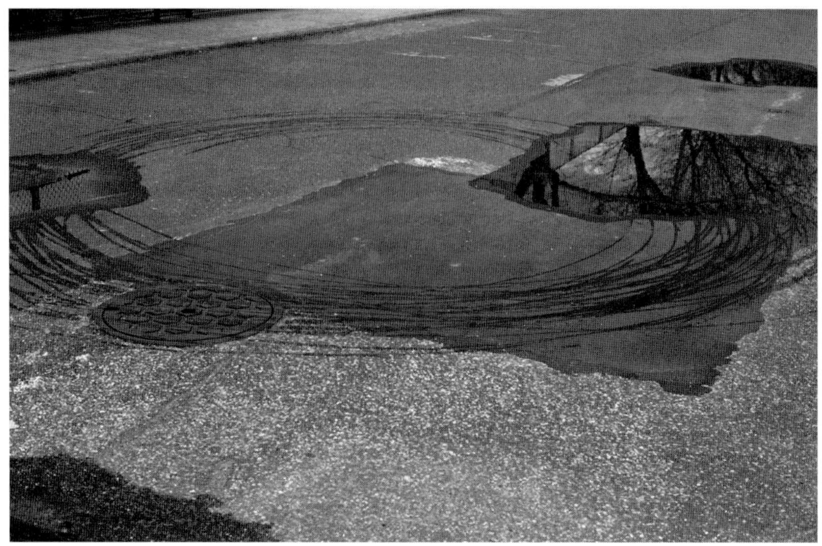

19 *Extension of Reflection*, 1992.
Chromogenic color print.
16 x 20 inches.

sky. He photographed that result too and named it *Extension of Reflection* (fig. 19).

When is a reflection a shine?

When is a reflection a thought?

There is the tendency on the part of those who follow contemporary art to look in the puddles for a link to a precedent, a tradition, a master model, and to let tradition structure the discussion. As a result, Orozco has had to be clear about his use of precedent. "I think it is a side aspect," he told one curator.

> I was aware of these connections. When you are transforming and trying to generate your own experiences, you have all this information which is very influential in how you act. Also you have a particular phenomenon which is present right there at the time and it is not about history. I can tell you for every piece why I made that piece and it is not because of another artist. It's not that I was making a homage or because I was trying to connect with anything. Like that bicycle. I bought a bicycle because I need a bicycle. I was in the East River park with my camera and it had just rained and the light was very beautiful

> and it was full of reflections . . . then there were all these cycling guys going really fast and I was there with my $100 bicycle, and they were fast and avoiding all the puddles and I was thinking that they didn't need to avoid the puddles. They are accidents, it is the residue of something. I also have this photo of *Island within an Island.* I like puddles. What I did was just to cross them and instead of avoiding them, I made a personal situation absurd, connected it to the puddle. And it is an extension of the reflection because you see the reflection of the branches in the water and the extension of the lines. It was a very basic thing, very stupid. I didn't plan it at all.[14]

He said all of this in 1997, the year of *Documenta X*, the Documenta that did without mandarin models of modernism entirely, seeing them to be either academic or absolutely obsolete[15]—seeing the definition of a world picture proceeding without a central authority, moving its idea of art out through built space, subject to thoughts that range from a poetics to a politics. It would happen that Orozco made a work for that Documenta calling up the Day of the Dead. In *Documenta X—The Book*, it is called *Skullpture.* It would eventually have another title, *Black Kites* (fig. 20).

A picture flew.

Stupidity has its intelligence. Puddles follow tempests. Orozco, the lover of puddles, often speaks of falling back on turbulence in the absence of anything else. *Black Kites* will have no specific reference that will aim and target interpretation. Buchloh, for different reasons, would have to ask Orozco about this, "is it that no model seems to be quite right anymore?" And Orozco would tell him, "That's the first thing, it's true."[16] His kite skull holds no idea at its center, nor is it to be controlled by an idea from the outside. A bone surface of mind is lifted to death kites by lead. That the skull was bought in Soho from a store called Evolution makes for comic detail. That Orozco tried out the idea on a monkey skull was a practical detail. He would build the drawing into a precision web that fluctuated with rise and fall of a head, moving into the unit circle at the ear, drawing the web deep into the eyes. Was this web a human sight?

The strict but mobile pattern of the kites was an extension of his computer drawings, one of which was illustrated in the *Documenta X* book. In the interstices one read words: "EMPTYING THE MIND ON ITS WAY TO THE VOID FULLNES [*sic*], WHICH IS EMPTY OF ANY EXISTENTIAL THOUGHT."[17] This was matched by a page from one of Orozco's notebooks.

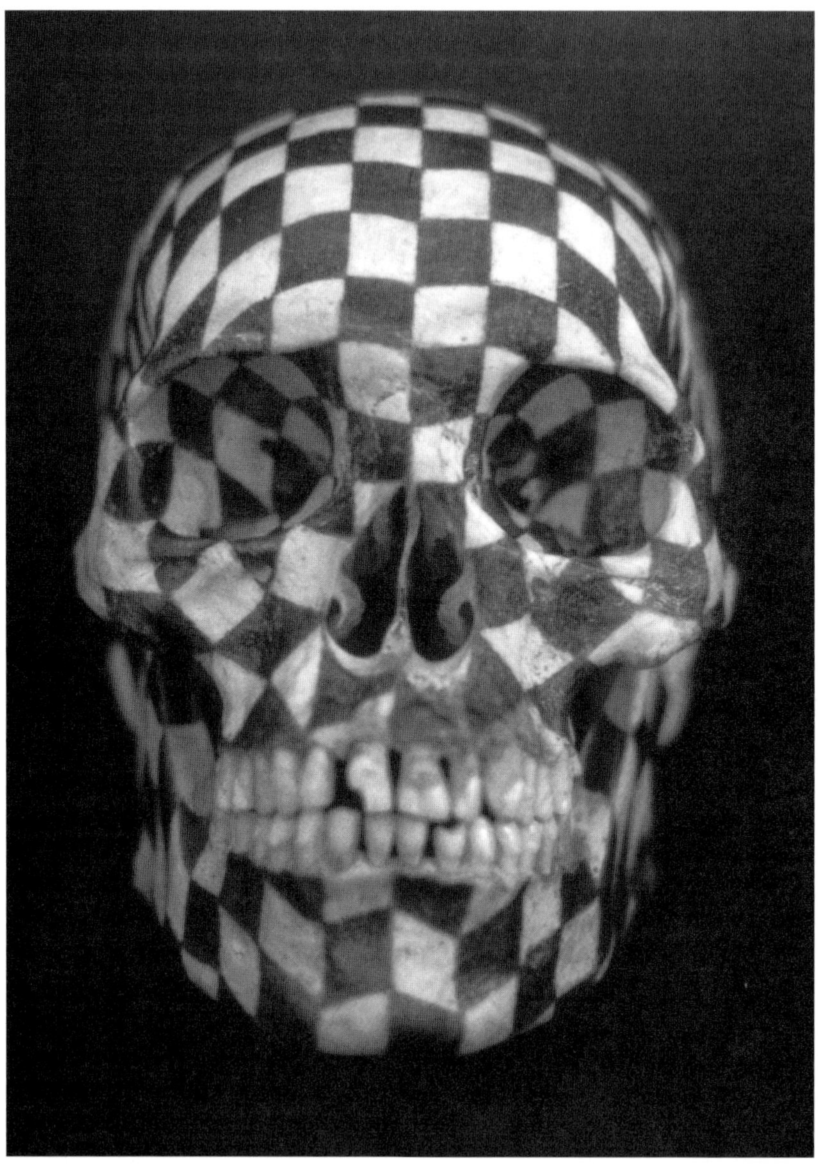

20 *Black Kites*, 1997.
Graphite on human skull.
8 1/2 x 5 x 6 1/4 inches.

TO DRAW ON A BONE STRUCTURE DESCRIBING THE THREE-DIMENSIONAL IDLENESS.
LINE OVER VOLUME. TOPOGRAPHY OF THE CRANIUM. ENTERING THE EYES. LOSING ITSELF. PORTRAIT OF A SPACE. A SPACE THAT HAPPENS. SUCCESSION OF LINES. SPACES AND TIME. TO KILL TIME.
GRID OF THOUGHTS. CONNECTIONS. AWARENESS AS A GRID OF PERCEPTION
A DRAWING OF NOTHINGNESS. THE VOLUME OF NO. EMPTY RECEPTACLE. LIKE A SHOE BOX.
THE GAZE AS SPACE. RECEIVING.
THE GAZE AS SPACE THAT RECEIVES.
AS RECEPTACLE
TO SPEND TIME WITH NOTHINGNESS. TO WASTE TIME.
LINES ON WATER.
PENCIL AS SCALPEL

SKULLPTURE.

WITH THE DRAWING WE FLATTEN ~~THE IMAGE~~ THE OBJECT. VOLUME MADE GRAPHIC.
OBJECT MADE IMAGE[18]

This was his response to the demand for both world picture and for composition. In place of it all something flies over the mind. Is it the kite or the shadow of the kite?

Is it Borges?

Early on, in 1922, Borges wrote an essay dedicated to the subject of the nothingness of personality. He repeated his proposition throughout, "There is no whole self." More programmatically, he stated his intention and his course of action: he hoped to cast aside all strict and logical schemas and instead to make a pile of examples.

> I aim to prove that personality is a chimera sustained by habit and conceit, with neither metaphysical support nor intrinsic reality. Therefore, I want to subject literature to the consequences flowing from those premises. On those premises, I wish to elaborate an aesthetic principle that will oppose the psychologism left to us by the last century.[19]

He lamented the fact that Walt Whitman tried to carry the world on his shoulders; he mocked Picasso and his pupils; he pointed out another way of seeing contemporary painting as simply "the gorgeous unicity of a king of spades, a gatepost, or a chess board." "Reality," he asserted, "has no need of other realities to bolster it." He himself was not to be confused either with his seeing, hearing, smelling, tasting, and touching; he was not to be confused with his body. He would eventually put these ideas more succinctly in a story. There he submerged the problem of the self. "Time," he wrote, "is the substance I am made of. Time is a river which sweeps me along, but I am the river; it is a tiger which destroys me, but I am the tiger; it is a fire which consumes me, but I am the fire. The world, unfortunately, is real; I, unfortunately, am Borges."[20] "The Argentine," he would write elsewhere, "feels that the universe is nothing but a manifestation of chance, the fortuitous course of Democritus' atoms; philosophy does not interest him."[21] He would remark that Heidegger's philosophy put each of us in a dialogue with nothingness or divinity, but that in the end this fomented the illusion of the ego. That illusion, Borges explained, had been censured by the Vedanta as a capital error.

This way of making reference turn to paradox, a wall, is useful. Knowledge does not become meaningless, but it does not ground; it shifts. It becomes just a window through which we see something else. Sight is a pile of examples turning into other examples. One can find the windows of Borges throughout Orozco's work, but Borges's figures do not control its forking paths. They sit like shadows on the inside of a process. Sometimes in Orozco's notes he quotes from them. He copied out the programmatic passage on the nothingness of personality.[22] "THAT DESTROYS SOME IDEAS WITH OTHERS," he wrote on another page, quoting now a favorite of Borges, Alfonso de Reyes, "TOTALITY OF UNITIES."[23]

To see the world as a totality of unities, moving, in friction, is also to see knowledge fragmented, dispersed. But neither Borges nor Orozco would see themselves to be culturally limited, shell-shocked, or deprived. Neither would see knowledge as a progress, only as something to touch and leave. Borges would say, when describing the Argentine writer's relation to tradition, that many traditions were accessible to him and that he could equally well touch them, like a table, with his left hand or his right. It is within this impossible tradition of traditions that Orozco proceeds to make a work with two hands, one holding the line of a kite, the other the camera. His kite and view flew over Varanasi, over the smoke of the dead rising from the shores of the Ganges. That same year he would make a video of the kites in Jaipur, dipping and soaring in the air currents, an arcing swarm of colored, shadowed diamonds. The movement of the camera's focus would catch and blur them; they became distant confetti, motes filtered by blue. The kites seem to participate in the dynamic of matter, as if they belonged more to it than to those grasping the string on the ground.

It is time to go Greek.

Democritus frequently wanders kite-like into the thoughts of Borges, who gave much thought to the problem of figuring totalities and much energy to refuting Nietzsche's concept of the eternal return, which he understood as a circular but mistaken variant of atomism.[24] Democritus had been instrumental in developing the idea of atomism for the ancient Greeks. Atoms, he had posited, would be indissoluble indivisibles, moving, requiring an infinitely empty space for their work. Thought could be understood as the motion of fire; the atoms of fire are spherical.[25] Borges liked to tell the story, probably apocryphal, of Democritus tearing out his eyes in a garden so as not to be distracted by the outside world.[26] To read Borges, like reading Democritus, will not give one a picture of the world, only a vision, and the unending problem of making it visual.

Borges and Democritus leave Orozco alone with the question: what does a totality of unities look like? It is not so much a question of appearances in images as the movement into and out of appearance. Things come and go. Things and people leave a wake behind them, a wake as track, as trash, as space. Something outside is generating circles and cycles. Any idea of a single, still world picture has been jettisoned. In 1996 Orozco let Democritus wander straight into the center of his work. All it took was a word. He titled a series of manipulated British sports photographs the *Atomists* (fig. 21). These pictures were part of a larger installation for his Artangel show that year in London set up in a vacant Piccadilly gentlemen's club, a place where gentlemen had played and dealt with the matter of global trade and political influence.[27] Atomism was being set into the larger than pictorial seat of empire. Could it sit? Orozco's pictures gave the atomists as circles and the empire as sport. That the atomists and the players could seem to cancel each other out both conceptually and visually appealed to him. All the circles were structural, extracted from the Benday dots of the page, their colors too, siphoned off into the cells of a computer drawing. He blew the image up to human life size as an Iris print. Atoms large and small were everywhere. The colors shifted across axes while men executed virtuoso kicks and strokes. There was a weave of action, a heroic

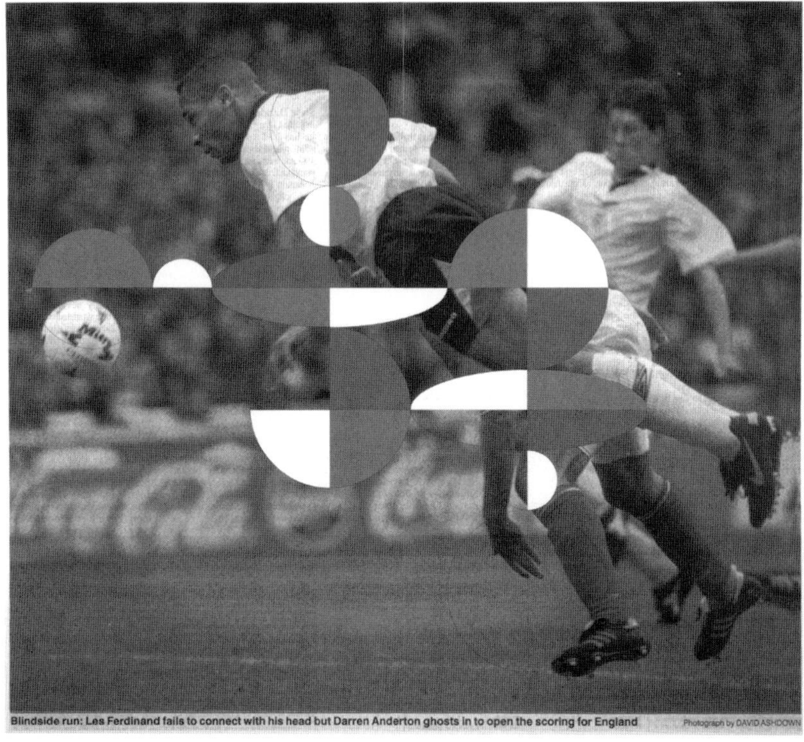

21 *Atomists: Blindside Run*, 1996.
Inkjet print.
79 1/4 x 87 1/2 inches.

clash of layers, freeze. No single layer of circles resolved matter into a composition. No thought would extract one from this sight.

Disks rotate as elbows draw back in unison. Time will not become this river. There is no single way to characterize the flow of the movements described in the *Atomists*. There is no single or single economic value, no pound, no coin of the realm. Orozco will point Buchloh to the markers in mandalas and the artist André Cadere's striped bars. Movement, he will say, generates a void. "You clean as much as you can with signs."[28] Later he would explain that the general logic guiding the shifts of color on the disks was derived from chess.[29] For him, to think in chess was instinctual because as a child he had been a chess champion. Deep in the heart of the *Atomists*, an inner circle provides the point from which three colors move out like the knight, straight up two squares and over one. The colors mark the absence, of course, of any knight.[30] Knights have touched and left. Knights have cleaned any residue of composition into the forms of void. Think of the awareness being generated by this complex of movement as "a floating impasse."[31] Those were his words of advice. He talked to me one day of the move as an *infra-mince*.

The *infra-mince* is more than a sign. It only begins as the word Marcel Duchamp came up with while trying to characterize a movement between two physical states, a transition expressing both difference and connection, a void empty and full that would never be defined. The idea came to him in Denmark in the summer of 1937 and he played with it in his mind for the rest of his life. It would help articulate his interest in what he liked to call gray matter. "The retina," he said once, "is only a door that you open to go further."[32] Forget pictures. This *infra-mince* was a kind of cut that took the idea of the mathematical cut out into the physical world of surface sensations and senses. His first notes speak of the matter as a separation between the sexes, something found in the sound made by velvet pants.[33] The gaps were physical, to be crossed but strangely. Who can be oriented by an exhalation, by the smell of a mouth in smoke, by echoes in a breath?[34] More examples of *infra-mince* would be worked out very sporadically in notes. The thought scattered into a pastel made of dandruff falling on a sheet of glue, a kind of caress, a color, a mold, an *allégorie d'oubli*. It would be the warmth left by someone else in the seat of a chair.[35] The idea itself would be largely withheld from the public.[36] To think of it as analogous to a chess move, as Orozco does, is probably not wrong. Duchamp was a chess champion too.

With his *infra-mince* Duchamp had attacked value, privately. He had stopped making readymades, the works made not to be works of art, in 1923. They had once been everyday objects detached from the regular economy and from sense, brought to a place where they could exist a little like Democritus's atoms, often hanging moving in a void without emitting qualities or taste. By 1937 they were largely memories known to a relative few through photographs. After World War II, Duchamp found himself in the strange position of seeing the modern art establishment go forward classifying the work of his youth, codifying it, bit by bit displaying it, embalming it and his earlier life. He had made reproductions of his work in miniature just before the war and boxed the ensemble into small suitcases, *Boîtes en valise*.[37] However, with the reproduction of his work by others and the incorporation of the readymade into their world picture, in effect he watched himself be buried.

In America this was accompanied by a new interpretation of his readymade as nothing more than a particularly difficult work of art. The readymade's great break with painting was ignored in favor of folding it into the imaginary continuity of avant-garde production. The new interpretation did not please him; he tried demurring and then took his distance.[38] "I never intended to sell them," he said to Calvin Tomkins. "The readymades were a way of getting out of the exchangeability, the monetarization, of the work of art. In art, and only in art, the original work is sold, and it acquires a sort of aura that way. With my readymades a replica will do just as well."[39] That the readymade ultimately could not escape the market's quantum growth in the mid-1950s would lead to the total demise of the concept in which he once took refuge. The change brought about by the speculation surrounding the new, flush modern art market was a topic Duchamp discussed with many of his interviewers. He was pessimistic. He called it a Wall Street affair.[40] Art, Duchamp thought, had become a product like green beans, something to be bought, like spaghetti.[41] He complained that there were too many standards, the gold standard, the platinum standard, the burlap standard.[42] The transitions of the *infra-mince* were made to resist precisely that kind of conversion. For one thing, the *infra-mince* was nothing that could be sold. It was a kind of field, but not a market. It was fluid, but not defined by an economy. It fluctuated but never had exchange value. It could do without capital. It did without capital. Attack value. Attack standards. Attack precedents with precedents?

Atomism has often been used as a weapon. Nietzsche, for one, spoke of Democritus admiringly. The ability to return to the field of atomism and the concerns of the pre-Socratics was something that he himself would seek to acquire. He singled out Pyrrhus, calling him a Buddhist for Greece, a latecomer who had seen Alexander and the Indian penitents and who was then seduced by everything lowly, everything poor, everything idiotic. Nietzsche remarked that in the heart of the crowd, such people feel a little warmth and need it. Their effort? "To disguise wisdom so that it no longer distinguishes; to cloak it in poverty and rags; to perform the lowliest offices: to go to market and sell suckling pigs—sweetness; light; indifference; no virtues that require gestures: to be everyone's equal even in virtue: ultimate self-overcoming, ultimate indifference."[43]

Atomism and the *infra-mince* came forward together in Orozco's work as he rose rapidly to prominence in the art market's world.[44] After the watershed year of 1993, he began to show regularly and frequently in international museum and gallery exhibitions and biennials. It was then that his work faced the high tidal pull of the market. He showed his work in fields that piled more examples, scattered points, opened striations. In the fall of 1994 Orozco had his first solo exhibition at Marian Goodman Gallery in New York. He attacked the vexing problem of the American center. He installed four yogurt caps in the white north room. If one looked carefully, one saw them, transparent, blue-rimmed, four vacant circles of garbage, plastic blanks. The container they had capped was gone. The yogurt eaten. Stamps and stickers gave a price, ninety-nine cents, and an expiration date, three from September and one from May, for in the spring Orozco had tried out the idea of the cap in his kitchen.[45] The gallery required four, like compass points, except that from any one point the viewer would only ever be able to see three. The fourth would have to nag behind, in the mind. But was this an address to the mind? Each cap was installed mouth high. As if there might be a memory of taste. Much later he told me he was interested in the orality of the vanishing point. What, by now, can one see from New York?

Eat me.

Another floating impasse. Neither the art market nor the food market had collapsed completely into these disks and metamorphosed. He and Buchloh turned these matters over and over again as they talked.[46] What was waste doing behaving like language, a letter, or an object, a commodity? Perhaps an art gallery could not protect art from ordinary economic conditions, the kind Marx and Engels described, where "all fixed, fast-frozen relations, with their train of ancient and venerable prejudices and opinions are swept away, all new-formed ones become antiquated before they can ossify. All that is solid melts into air, all that is holy is profaned, and man is at last compelled to face with sober senses, his real conditions of life, and his relations with his kind."[47] Ordinary capitalism has its own powerful, if harsh poetics. That is what allowed Marx and Engels to import the spells of *The Tempest* into their manifesto in 1848. They did not take on the entire spell; they did not see that we are such stuff as dreams are made of.[48] They preferred to elevate consciousness, not to present it a little life rounded with a sleep or with nothing.

Orozco kept writing to himself about the kinds of spaces he was generating. They, like the *infra-mince*, were spaces responding indirectly, obliquely, to the demands of other spaces. Circles to what point?

> (THE CENTER EVERYWHERE, THE CIRCUMFERENCE NOWHERE, THE PERFECT LABYRINTH IS THE DESERT)
> (THERE WILL ALWAYS BE A CAP OF YOGURT WE DO NOT SEE) (LIKE THE WAKE AFTER THE ACTION).

His notes quoted and summarized Borges quoting Pascal, but all of these thoughts were being made physical.[49] He was making things, not ideas of things. It became clear that an ordinary commodity was not going to be absolutely transformed by its entrance into the art market. It became clear that there were markets and markets, not a single world market, any more than there was a single world picture. Orozco varied his scale, began making the field radically change dimensions and suddenly go porous, something like the tooth marks Duchamp imagined puncturing Swiss cheese.[50] He would court inconsistency, experiment with very different kinds of processes and objects, sometimes working precious raw materials, like silk, into dandelions gone to seed, sometimes pinching and pulling beeswax into shapes that would be enlarged, cast in aluminum, and called stars. In 1998 he sowed three fields of work together in his solo show in New York. It was again Marian Goodman's gallery. The yogurt caps hung on the wall brightly as if they had never left. This show was titled *Free Market Is Anti-Democratic.* The idea of the free market seems to extend far beyond the art market.

The free art market still functions on the basis of commodities, even though the world's markets have long since abandoned gold and other such standards. To think an economy directly in relation to things, to materials, to sculpture, seems archaic. The free world market is driven by the production of super-profits, technology-based investment, merger and pure speculation, where value is attached instead to ever-new, ever-immaterial forms. The work of contemporary art does not yet represent this kind of wealth very well. It cannot come close to equaling the monetary value of the smaller super-profits; even the most successful work of contemporary art does not cost hundreds of millions of dollars. The scale by which contemporary culture is measured has had to shift to units of architecture and degrees of design. For the first time in centuries, the work of art runs the risk of a certain kind of obsolescence. But if the work of art is no longer well suited to represent wealth's accomplishments, this is having the odd effect of leaving it freer and poorer.

One wonders what Duchamp would have said. Orozco has quietly reached for the stars and the atomists. Markets are not his absolutes. Scale can be conceived at a grandeur larger than any world profit; the oldest thoughts of the ancients can open even larger distances; the mobility latent in poverty can be taken, like Nietzsche did, to be gain. If the work of art is freed from the duty of representing wealth, no particular reference need organize the field with a fixed exchange rate. No model of modernism need apply. No field need organize another field.

Imagine a field.

Imagine three.

The gallery showed three sets of materials put through cycles. There were the silk flowers from the Paris show of 1998, *Clinton Is Innocent*. There were the stars made for a show the year before in the d'Offay gallery in London, brought over to Paris to fall again into *Clinton Is Innocent*. Then there was the *Penske Project*, piles of someone else's garbage (fig. 22). In 1994 Orozco had made a work in the street out of litter and left it there, *Island within an Island*, a miniature World Trade Center, a parody. The Penske works abandoned mimicry. Each piece in the set was made

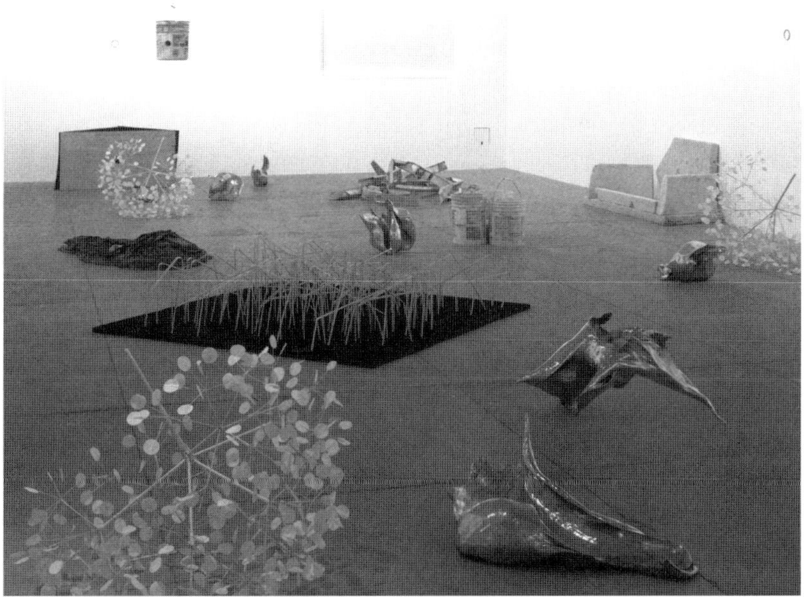

22 *Penske Work Project/Dent de Lion/Pinched Star*, 1988.
Installation view Marian Goodman Gallery, New York.
Mixed media, dimensions variable.

quickly on the street, the result of a fishing expedition in a dumpster. The work had to be finished there on the spot; it had to be light enough so that one person could lift it. Its scale would be personal, its reference the city initially, though as the work came back into the gallery its elements gave more pause. There were echoes of Duchamp, of Rauschenberg, of Serra, of so much more, of Orozco's old oranges. The past appeared as a space to be activated too. Often circles appeared to organize perceptions and disappear into material, nothing more complicated really than the edge of a bucket. This was the drift. Penske was the name of the yellow rental truck company, the container of all containers, that had, like the knight and the color, vanished.

Videos played away in another room. They showed sights from day walks through a city, from point to point, the movements of things and people in town caught and turned the lens. The sequence would never be edited in any other way except during shooting, and the title would simply begin with the first thing shown, say, dog shit, and the last thing, say, a picture of Maggie Cheung in the role of Irma Vep.[51] The space between was Orozco's concern, the physical spaces of material in the elements of earth, fire, water, and wind. The between, like the *infra-mince*, like the melting, filled frames with the simplest of movements. A page from someone's business philosophy class floated in a Dutch canal. Chocolate dribbled down the edge of foam in a spoon. Movements pushed into other movements and haunted the afterimages of movements. Movement pulled on movement. Movement pulled on moment. Time takes it all away. The *Penske Project* was the physical expression of this process.[52] The entire combination in the big gallery, the three fields deregulating one another, could be understood as levels in a universe of perpetual motion.

Insofar as no transformation is complete, no metamorphosis accomplished, these things are either more archaic or more advanced than the kinds of commodities with which Marx had been concerned. For Marx the commodity embodied values that had been transformed, labor had been buried, linen's value worked into the new value of the tailored coat, an exchange involving money blurred the identifications yet again.[53] This economy worked by erasing one value with another and another, by turning one material into another and another in a restless, relentless spin. The middle ground of transition, of between, did not especially concern him, just as it would not overly concern a capitalist. That would be the weakling's moment of panic, the nonbeliever's hesitation between profit and loss. But Duchamp had put the readymade there. An atomist could suspend such a moment in a completely different view of matter, the better to contemplate everything. Democritus and Leucippus, according to Aristotle, "say that the full and the empty are the elements, calling the one being and the other non-being—the full and the solid being being, the empty non-being (whence they say being no more is than non-being, because the solid no more is than the empty); and they make these the material causes of things."[54] The nature of nonbeing is explored by Orozco, but it is difficult to express now. We have come too late. We live in a time that wants nonbeing to have names.

Again and again Orozco is asked to call himself a nomad. Always he declines. To name this activity of his would label it into inertia, deprive it of its friction as well as its open path. It makes no difference that the nomad being offered is the nomad of Deleuze and Guattari, who in their *Mille plateaux* worked their transitional concepts and figures into swathes of perverse but optimistic possibility, slopes of miraculously anti-Oedipal slipped abyss.[55] To collapse all that into the mere name of the nomad actually goes against the grain of their thought, neuters the figure and ties it to a post. Orozco says he finds the prospect of this too glamorous. He asks instead that another, quite common word be applied. He calls himself an immigrant, one who travels mainly to follow the demands of work.[56] He puts himself back into the air of the world. This world is material.

In late April 1995 Orozco copied out the passage on *satori* from Borges's essay on Buddhism. It outlined the difficulty of understanding *satori*, the moment when, outside the bounds of logic, a sudden illumination occurs. Borges outlined a series of *koans*, the questions and answers that lead to *satori*. "What is the Buddha?" asks the student. "The cypress in the orchard," replies the master. "Three pounds of linen," said another master to the student wanting to know the meaning of the first patriarch's visit to China.[57] The same examples had been given by the Zen master of Cage.[58]

Ends become beginnings. The world circles. The cypress is a tree.

At one point while speaking to Buchloh, Orozco took the question of matter to the orchard. They were in agreement. "Precisely," he concurred, "matter is always perceived through social perception. Metal is not that close to some cultures. This complexity is represented for me by the image of the tree. In a way, my dream is to one day make a work that is as fantastic and perfect as a tree. Trees are perfect things, the perfect machine, the perfect body, the perfect exotic things, trees are so strange and always surprising, very mysterious. Then of course the relation with gravity and growing. If you want a model of what a sculpture should be, it could be a tree."[59] Questions swarm around the things that are not answers or values. Like kites, the trees catch and eat them.

Notes

1. William Shakespeare, *The Tempest*, in *Shakespeare: Twenty-three Plays and Sonnets*, ed. Thomas Marc Parrott (New York: Charles Scribner's Sons, 1938), act 1, lines 396–401. First performed in 1611.

2. *Gabriel Orozco: Clinton Is Innocent*, exh. cat. (Paris: Musée d'art moderne de la Ville de Paris, 1998), p. 31. My conversations with Gabriel Orozco took place in New York, Paris, and Tlalpan over the summer and fall of 1999.

3. Ibid.

4. Benjamin Buchloh, "Refuse and Refuge," in *Gabriel Orozco*, ed. M. Catherine de Zegher (Kortrikj: Kanaal Art Foundation, 1993), pp. 45–46. In this volume, pp. 1–15. Buchloh's "Gabriel Orozco: The Sculpture of Everyday Life," was first published in the exhibition catalog *Gabriel Orozco*, ed. Berhnard Burgi and Bettina Marbach (Zurich: Kunsthalle Zurich, 1996). In this volume, pp. 31–49.

5. See Francesco Bonami's account from the point of view of the curator, "Back in Five Minutes," *Parkett* 48 (1996), pp. 41–53.

6. *Lesa Natura: Reflexiones sobre Ecología* (Mexico City: Museo de Arte Moderno, 1993). See especially the essay by Cuauhtémoc Medina and Roberto Tejada.

7. *Real Time: Gabriel Orozco, Rirkrit Tiravanija, Lincoln Tobier, Andrea Zittel*, curated by Gavin Brown (London: Institute of Contemporary Arts, 1993).

8. Lynn Zelevansky, brochure for *Projects 41: Gabriel Orozco* (New York: Museum of Modern Art, 1993).

9. John Cage, "Composition as Process," in *Silence* (Hanover, N.H.: Wesleyan University Press, 1961), p. 44.

10. Ibid., pp. 46–47.

11. John Cage, "Lecture on Nothing," in *Silence*, p. 111.

12. Martin Heidegger, "The Age of the World Picture," in *The Question Concerning Technology and Other Essays*, trans. William Lovitt (New York: Harper, 1977), p. 115.

13. John Cage, "How to Improve the World (You Will Only Make Matters Worse," in *A Year from Monday* (Hanover, N.H.: Wesleyan University Press, 1967), pp. 3 and 157, respectively.

14. From Robert Storr's interview with Gabriel Orozco, "Gabriel Orozco: The Power to Transform," *Art Press* 225 (June 1997), pp. 25–26.

15. This is made clear in *Documenta X—The Short Guide*, ed. Paul Sztulman (Ostfildern: Cantz, 1997) and in the reader designed to accompany the exhibition, *Documenta X—The Book*, ed. Catherine David and Jean-François Chevrier (Ostfildern-Ruit: Cantz, 1997). The

grand and categorical model of modernism that Clement Greenberg's criticism embodied was supported by the institutional authority of the Museum of Modern Art and has been the subject of much criticism and emulation both in the United States and abroad. Its dissolution, however, is now more than evident, even in the most sophisticated of those projects seeking to bring a different coherence to the overview of modernism, most recently in the work of Yve-Alain Bois and Rosalind Krauss, *Formless: A User's Guide* (New York: Zone Books, 1997) and of T. J. Clark, *Farewell to an Idea: Episodes from a History of Modernism* (New Haven: Yale University Press, 1999).

16. *Clinton Is Innocent*, p. 151. See as well their discussion of *Black Kites* on pp. 95ff.

17. *Documenta X—The Book*, pp. 622–623.

18. The translation of this page is taken from Gabriel Orozco, *Photogravity*, exh. cat. (Philadelphia: Philadelphia Museum of Art, 1999), p. 148.

19. Jorge Luis Borges, "The Nothingness of Personality," in *Selected Non-Fictions*, ed. Eliot Weinberger, trans. Esther Allen, Suzanne Jill Levine, and Eliot Weinberger (New York: Viking, 1999), pp. 3–9.

20. Jorge Luis Borges, "A New Refutation of Time," in *Labyrinths*, ed. Donald A. Yates and James E. Irby (New York: New Directions, 1964), p. 234.

21. Jorge Luis Borges, "A Note on (toward) George Bernard Shaw," in *Labyrinths*, p. 216.

22. Gabriel Orozco, *Photogravity*, p. 26.

23. Ibid., p. 2.

24. See Jorge Luis Borges, "The Doctrine of Cycles," and "The Total Library," in *Selected Non-Fictions,* pp. 115–122 and 214–216, respectively.

25. See Nietzsche's sketch of Democritus's ideas, *Unpublished Writings from the Period of Unfashionable Observations*, trans. Richard T. Gray (Stanford, Calif.: Stanford University Press, 1999), p. 131; see also Bertrand Russell, *A History of Western Philosophy* (New York: Simon and Schuster, 1945); and Andrew Pyle, *Atomism and Its Critics: From Democritus to Newton* (Bristol: Thoemmes Press, 1997), p. 115.

26. Jorge Luis Borges, "Immortality," in *Selected Non-Fictions*, p. 485.

27. Gabriel Orozco, *Empty Club* (London: Artangel, 1996) documents the installation and includes essays on its different aspects: James Lingwood, "Circulation System"; Jean Fisher, "The Play of the World"; and Mark Haworth-Booth, "The Atomists."

28. *Clinton Is Innocent*, p. 113. Their discussion of the *Atomists* begins on p. 105 and is picked up again briefly on p. 159.

29. See Orozco's lecture on September 22, 1998 (organized by the Public Art Fund) for a different set of coordinates of explanation for the *Atomists*.

30. Robert Storr's interview with Gabriel Orozco, "Gabriel Orozco: The Power to Transform," gives Orozco's view of the knight: "To the art world, chess is related to Duchamp but chess is related with everything else. Duchamp is the least important thing about chess. Chess is a thing in itself. I was really just trying to make a new game because I was a chess player and pretty serious and then I left and I couldn't keep playing . . . [in text] so I wanted to make a game that nobody wins [*Horses Running Endlessly*; see fig. 59]. There is no winner, there's no reason, there's just space moving. The knight—the horse—is a very interesting invention in terms of space because of how it moves. It's like crossing a space that's impossible. All the other figures move diagonally or horizontally, but the horse moves in such a way that it crosses in between. All that is interesting, the basic banality of these

possible spaces—how much you travel between puddles, how much you travel or get transported playing with this landscape as a landscape with the knights and the chessboard."

31. Orozco, lecture, September 22,1998.

32. Dore Ashton, "An Interview with Marcel Duchamp," *Studio International* 171 (June 1966), p. 245.

33. *Marcel Duchamp, Notes*, ed. and trans. Paul Matisse (Paris: Centre Georges Pompidou, 1980), note 9. Craig Adcock has pointed out that the term may well have been derived from the mathematician Esprit Pascal Jouffret's sense that the point of view from the fourth dimension onto the third dimension passed through "*un couche infiniment mince.*" See his book for this and its extended mathematical discussion of the *inframince*, *Marcel Duchamp's Notes from the Large Glass: An N-dimensional Analysis* (Ann Arbor: UMI Research Press, 1983), p. 37. See also the section devoted to Duchamp in Georges Didi-Huberman's catalog, *L'Empreinte* (Paris: Centre Georges Pompidou, 1997). Here and elsewhere I have retained the French term. It is variously translated as infraslim or infrathin.

34. *Duchamp du signe*, 2nd. edition, ed. Michel Sanouillet and Elmer Petersen (Paris: Flammarion, 1975), p. 274. *Duchamp du signe* exists in an English edition, initially known as *Salt Seller*, and now as *The Writings of Marcel Duchamp*, ed. Michel Sanouillet and Elmer Petersen (Oxford: Oxford University Press, 1973), p. 194. It was first published on the back cover of the special number of *View* devoted to Marcel Duchamp, volume 5 (March 1945), in French, each letter in a different font:

> QUAND
> LA FUMEE DE TABAC
> SENT AUSSI
> DE LA BOUCHE
> QUI L'EXHALE,
> LES DEUX ODEURS
> S'EPOUSENT PAR
> INFRA-MINCE.

Les Quatre vents 8 (1947), p. 7, would publish it with a different array of typefaces. Reading this, Denis de Rougemont asked Duchamp questions that he recounts in *Journal d'un époque (1926–1946)* (Paris: Gallimard, 1968), pp. 567ff. in an entry dated August 7, 1945: "C'est quelque chose qui échappe encore à nos définitions scientifiques. J'ai pris à dessein le mot mince qui est un mot humain, affectif, et non pas une mesure précise de laboratoire. Le bruit ou la musique que fait un pantalon de velours à côtes, comme celui-ci, quand on bouge, relève de l'infra-mince. Le creux dans le papier, entre le recto et le verso d'une feuille mince. . . . A étudier!" (ellipse in original text). I have written about Duchamp's relation to language in an essay titled "Last Words (Rilke, Wittgenstein, Duchamp)," in *About Michael Baxandall*, ed. Adrian Rifkin (Oxford: Blackwell, 1999), pp. 84–102.

35. *Duchamp du signe*, note 4.

36. *Notes* (1980), notes 20, 28, 24, and 35.

37. For an account of the *Boîte en valise*, as well as one of the best assessments of Duchamp's oeuvre, see Ecke Bonk, *Marcel Duchamp: Box in a Valise* (New York: Rizzoli, 1989).

38. The arguments of "The Creative Act," first given at a session of the Convention of the American Federation of Arts, in Houston, April 1957, and published in *Art News* 56 (summer 1957), pp. 28–29, should be understood in this context. Anyone interested in pursuing this question will do well to read Duchamp's interviews carefully. See especially Georges Charbonnier's *Six Interviews with Duchamp for France-Culture*, Dec. 9, 1960–Jan.

13, 1961, published as *Entretiens avec Marcel Duchamp* (Marseille: André Dimanche, 1994); Richard Hamilton, *Marcel Duchamp*, BBC program "Monitor," which aired Sept. 27, 1961; Francis Roberts, "I Propose to Strain the Laws of Physics—Interview with Marcel Duchamp (October 1963)," *Art News* 67 (December 1968), pp. 46–47, 62–64; interview with Richard Hamilton, R. Kitaj, Robert Melville, and David Sylvester, June 19, 1966, in Hamilton's London studio; Pierre Cabanne, *Entretiens avec Marcel Duchamp* (Paris: Pierre Belfond, 1967); and Duchamp's lecture "Apropos of Readymades," given at the Art of Assemblage symposium, October 19, 1961, which was first published in *Art and Artists* 1 (July 1966), p. 47, and is included in Sanouillet and Petersen, *The Writings of Marcel Duchamp*.

39. Calvin Tomkins, "Profiles: Not Seen and/or Less Seen—Marcel Duchamp," *New Yorker* (Feb. 6, 1965), p. 65. The 1964 Schwarz edition of replicas provided Duchamp with a business opportunity and he took it. See Duchamp's discussion of the matter with Robert Lebel, "Marcel Duchamp, maintenant et ici," *L'Oeil* 149 (May 1967), pp. 18–23, 77, and "John Cage on Marcel Duchamp—An Interview with Moira and William Roth," *Art in America* 61 (November 1973), pp. 72–79.

40. See the following Duchamp interviews: "The Brothers," *Time*, April 8, 1957, pp. 74–77; [Geoffrey Hellman], "Marcel Duchamp," *New Yorker*, April 6, 1957, pp. 25–27; Mike Wallace's interview of Marcel Duchamp, December 12, 1960, aired January 18, 1961 on WNTA-TV, New York, on the program "Mike Wallace—Interviews and News," which was published in French translation by Naomi Sawelson-Gorse, "Sur le gril: Mike Wallace interviewe Marcel Duchamp," *Etant Donné Marcel Duchamp* 1 (1999), pp. 100–116. For other appraisals of the commercial change in the situation see Leo Steinberg, "Other Criteria," from his book *Other Criteria: Confrontations with Twentieth-Century Art* (New York: Oxford University Press, 1972), p. 55; and William Seitz, "The Rise and Dissolution of the Avant-Garde," *Vogue* 142, no. 1 (September 1, 1963), p. 182.

41. Georges Charbonnier, *Entretiens avec Marcel Duchamp*, pp. 15 and 87ff.

42. See William Seitz, "What's Happened to Art? An Interview with Marcel Duchamp on Present Consequences of New York's Armory Show," *Vogue* 141, no. 4 (Feb. 1963), p. 129. He had said the same thing to Alain Jouffroy, "Conversation avec Marcel Duchamp (December 1961)," in his book *Une Révolution du regard* (Paris: Gallimard, 1964), pp. 111–124. The interview was published, with audio compact disc, as *Marcel Duchamp rencontre* (Paris: Centre Georges Pompidou, 1997), p. 57.

43. Friedrich Nietzsche, notes written between March and June 1888, cited in *The Will to Power*, ed. Walter Kaufmann, trans. Walter Kaufmann and R. J. Hollingdale (New York: Random House, 1967), p. 241.

44. *Clinton Is Innocent*, p. 151: "And the space of Duchamp?" asked Orozco. "The Duchampian space is pretty abstract. It's physical, but it's abstract, it's *infra-mince*." For once they agreed. "I think," Buchloh responded immediately, "his concept of the *infra-mince* is the space that cannot be measured, instrumentalized, commodified, for example." It should be mentioned in this context that Laura Hoptman in her essay for the brochure printed to accompany *Options 47: Gabriel Orozco* (Chicago: Museum of Contemporary Art, 1994) brought in the *infra-mince* as a way to speak of absence and saw Orozco's work then as a kind of pure research into the concept of *infra-mince*.

45. See Catherine de Zegher, "The Os of Orozco," *Parkett* 48 (1996), pp. 55–67.

46. *Clinton Is Innocent*, pp. 163ff. At the time of the 1994 exhibition Matthew Ritchie described the problem of the space very well: "But the point about Orozco's work seems to be that any one reading will always be wrong. His work exists in the interstices, the negative

spaces which make up most of the world. In a deft process of misdirection, Orozco dips first one, then the other foot, into the rushing Heraclitean river and we can all briefly have the illusion that he's walking on water." Ritchie, "Gabriel Orozco," *Flash Art* (Jan./Feb. 1995), p. 96.

47. Karl Marx and Friedrich Engels, *The Communist Manifesto*, trans. Samuel Moore (1848; Harmondsworth: Penguin, 1967), p. 83.

48. Shakespeare, *The Tempest*, act 4, lines 148–158. Prospero speaks them:

> These our actors,
> As I foretold you, were all spirits, and
> Are melted into air, into thin air;
> And, like the baseless fabric of this vision,
> The cloud-capp'd towers, the gorgeous palaces,
> The solemn temples, the great globe itself,
> Yea, all which it inherit, shall dissolve
> And, like this insubstantial pageant faded,
> Leave not a rack behind. We are such stuff
> As dreams are made on, and our little life
> Is rounded with a sleep.

49. Orozco is quoting and summarizing from Borges, "Pascal's Sphere," in *Selected Non-Fictions*, p. 353. His notes are reproduced in *Photogravity*, pp. 6ff., 136–138, and 152–154.

50. *Notes* (1980), note 26.

51. Cheung stars in the film *Irma Vep* (1996), directed by Olivier Assayas.

52. Compare the interview with Daniel Birnbaum, "A Thousand Words: Gabriel Orozco Talks about His Recent Films," *Artforum* 36, no. 10 (summer 1998), p. 115, with the interview with Daniel Pinchbeck for the *Art Newspaper* 87 (December 1998), which was done in the truck while Orozco was actually working on the Penske project.

> To Birnbaum: "What I'm after is the liquidity of things, how one thing leads you on to the next. . . . The works are about concentration, intention, and paths of thought: the flow of totality in our perception, the fragmentation of the 'river of phenomena,' which takes place all the time. . . . Walking down, say, Sixth Avenue, I'll suddenly see something that intrigues me—a plastic bag, a green umbrella, an airplane tracing a line in the sky. . . . [T]he kind of connection that intrigues me is contiguity. . . . The connections themselves are real, not metaphoric. Borges wrote somewhere that all these things that are next to each other, we call the universe. It's this 'being next to each other' that appeals to me. . . . There could be some kind of resemblance between what I'm doing and John Cage's recordings, but Cage's work has so much to do with chance, whereas I'm really focusing on concentration and intention. . . . I trace certain intentions with the camera, and then suddenly the tension between my intentions and reality becomes too great and the whole thing breaks down." He speaks of the day as "a day of awareness" and ever so lightly quotes Borges, "*Las partes son el todo, el todo son las partes*." ("All these things that are next to each other, we call the universe.")

> To Pinchbeck: "I'm interested in the accidental, and I don't think stability anyway is a constant. What is really happening is always accident, accident, accident—that is the constant. If you really play with that it is like swimming in the waves and it becomes natural, you learn how to do it and you don't swim against the waves. What I think is going to be quite nice in this show is that all the pieces will relate to the body, what one person can lift. That will be the limit. . . . [He speaks of Schwitters.]

Probably the gesture is similar. Today was a weird day. I never used a literal quote of American products before, but I got attracted to the Coke bottles when I saw the liquid was still inside them. They were next to each other in the container and I reproduced that exactly in the piece. That's what was interesting to me. You know the word 'metonymy'? These objects are not related to each other, you walk around them and you can't put the relations together. I am really open about what I am looking for—you have to trust this very subconscious thing, you get attracted to something and you don't know why."

53. Karl Marx, *Capital*, vol. 1, trans. Ben Fowkes (London: New Left Review, 1976).

54. Aristotle, *Metaphysics*, as quoted by Pyle, *The Atomists*, p. 44.

55. Gilles Deleuze and Félix Guattari, *Mille plateaux: Capitalisme et schizophrénie* (Paris: Minuit, 1980). (Translated as *A Thousand Plateaus: Capitalism and Schizophrenia*, trans. Brian Massumi [Minneapolis: University of Minnesota Press, 1987]).

56. His interview with Ann Temkin for the brochure for *Museum Studies 5: Gabriel Orozco Photogravity* (Philadelphia Museum of Art, 1999) makes sure to cover the issue well:

> I travel because it is a way to be with myself. Sometimes you cannot be with yourself in your own city. But, it is not that I am the explorer or the anthropologist or the journalist. I have my own method, my own investigations, the things I am interested in through books, and through work. And then, my contact with reality, the street, the cities, the physical world, involves traveling and being outside, and not in my studio all the time.
>
> The most important thing is I am also an immigrant. It's not just that "I love New York," or "I love Paris." It's the reality of economic and political life, that you may have to move, to try to do work that you cannot do in your own country. So that's why when they say I'm a nomad, I don't like that word. I think that word is too romantic. Because I'm not a nomad, that's too glamorous, like Lord Byron . . . [ellipsis in text]. It is somehow important to contextualize the reasons why you travel or you live somewhere else—it's not just because you *want*. It is also because reality takes you there. It is important how reality affects my work. It is mostly what is happening to my life. To accept the accident of life and reality.

See also *Clinton Is Innocent*, p. 85, as well as Jean Pierre Criqui, "Like a Rolling Stone," *Artforum* 34, no. 8 (April 1996), pp. 87–93, and Nelly Richard, "The International Mise-en Scène of Latin American Art," in *Witte de With Cahier* 2 (1994), pp. 79–93. I have written at more length elsewhere on the relationship of the global artist to the new immigrant in an essay titled "The Immigrant," in *Looking Up: Rachel Whiteread's Water Tower*, ed. Louise Neri (New York: Public Art Fund, 1999), pp. 99–109.

57. Orozco's citation is given in *Photogravity*, pp. 124ff. For a slightly different version of Borges's thoughts see the lecture "Buddhism," published in *Seven Nights*, trans. Eliot Weinberger (New York: New Directions, 1984), pp. 58–75.

58. See the essay titled "The Reason of Unreason: The Koan Exercise," in *Zen Buddhism: Selected Writings of D. T. Suzuki*, ed. William Barrett (New York: Anchor, 1956).

59. *Clinton Is Innocent*, p. 69.

Lecture (2001)

Gabriel Orozco
translated by Eileen Brockbank

Shortly after finishing my studies at the art academy in Mexico, in the mid-'80s, I changed my working technique completely. What I had learned in art school was inadequate when I began to take an interest in what was all around me, walking down the street, experimenting with objects I would find, as well as picking things up and taking them into the studio to transform them.

During those years—from 1986 to 1989—my work was focused on the streets and area around my house and wandering around the city. Once I had abandoned the technique I had been taught, as well as its materials, I began to abandon the studio space as well, which is where those things are used. Since the materials were in the street and generally stayed in the street, what followed was a fairly natural process of abandoning my studio.

It was during this period that I began to use the camera. I hadn't studied photography; it didn't particularly interest me then or now, but I needed that tool for collecting and keeping my interactions in the streets. I also had the desire to record the time of my encounters: that is, to pass through and interact with the same site several times and see how each day differed from the following one. Sometimes I became involved in life on the same street, on the same corner, for several days.

Around that time I began to travel quite a bit. On my trips I deliberately didn't bring anything with me in order to participate in the reality I found in local places. An important trip was the one I made to Brazil in 1991. I was very impressed when I discovered the Brazilian landscape as well as Brazilian sculptural and musical traditions from the '50s on. Those months were influential in my life and on my work; for the first time, my travel and my work became complementary techniques and disciplines. That was where I created *Crazy Tourist*, the installation with oranges on tables at the market in Cachoeira, a city near Salvador de Bahía. I arrived at that market at about six in the evening, when I found it already empty, but with all the tables still in place. On one or another corner there were some rotten oranges that were no longer edible and had been thrown on the ground. I started to play with them. The light and silence of that time of day gave the place a special atmosphere. There were a few drunks who saw me walking among the tables to place the oranges and take pictures of them, and they began to shout: "*Turista maluco*!" "*Está maluco*," which means "He's a crazy tourist!" That's where I got the title for the photograph. In the orange book some of the activities of those years are documented, such as *Stones in the Fence* (on the calle de San Fernando, near my house in Tlalpan) (fig. 23).[1] I was constantly involved in this kind of activity on those trips in the '80s and early '90s, from Madrid to Cachoeira, as well as Mexico City.

In 1991, I created a piece called *Recaptured Nature*. Perhaps from having worked in the street so much, I took an interest in vulcanized rubber. I found a fairly beat-up trailer-wheel inner tube and cut it down the

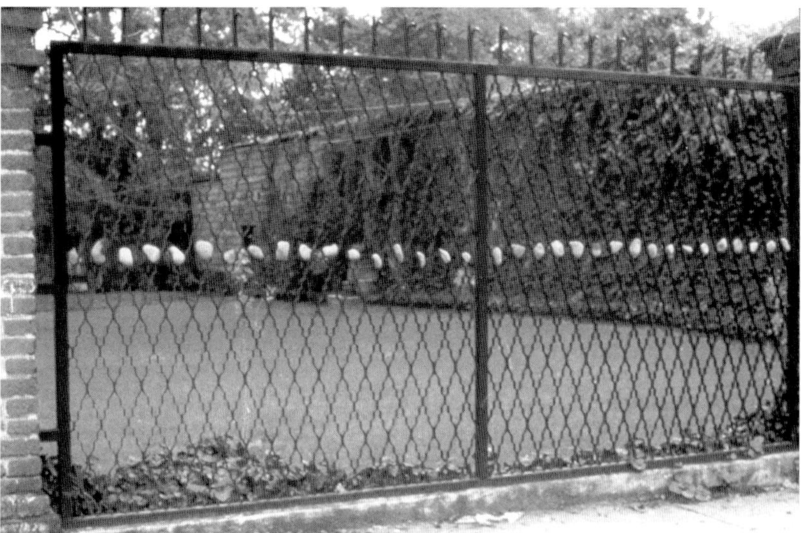

23 *Stones in the Fence*, 1989.
Silver dye bleach print.
16 x 20 inches.

middle, then opened it and cut two circular lid shapes from another inner tube and welded them at a tire repair shop. The result was an inflatable ball. I called it *Recaptured Nature* because I found it interesting to recover the original use of this vulcanized rubber. This was one of the first works in which I reconstructed an object, restoring its raison d'être and the original use of its material; so it became the prototype for other works such as *La DS* and *Elevator* executed two or three years later (fig. 24).

Nineteen ninety-three was a very intense year of work. I was invited to Kortrijk, in Belgium, to install an exhibition in an abandoned brewery. I spent two and a half months working on an installation at that site. I remember spending time sweeping and cleaning up the dust, which became a significant activity for me: to arrive at an abandoned site, start cleaning it, rediscover its sheen, its reflections, the time that had passed there.[2]

That same year, after that project was completed, I went to the Venice Biennale, where I presented *Empty Shoe Box*. I'd like to read you a few paragraphs from my notebooks:

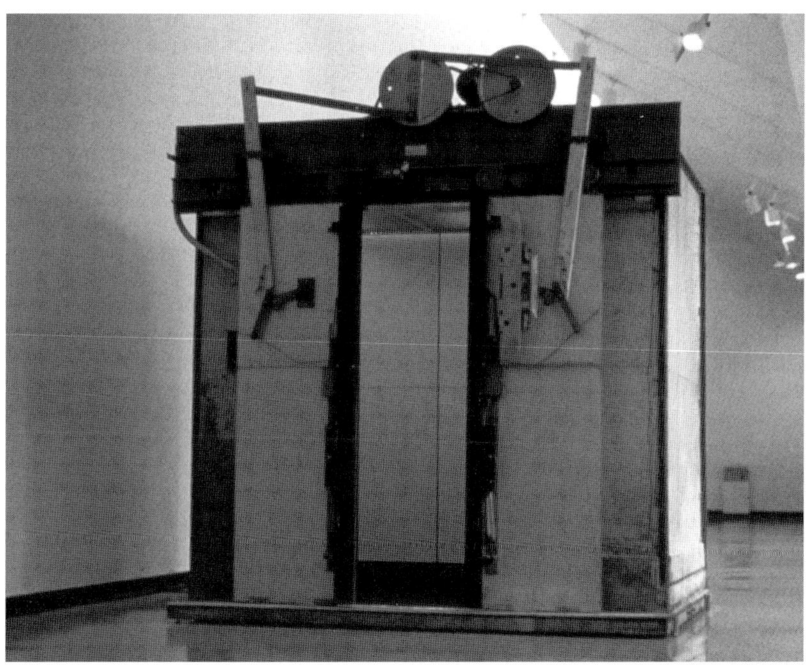

24 *Elevator*, 1994.
Modified elevator.
8 x 8 x 5 feet.

> Truly new art tends to be disappointing, especially for the public that already has an idea of what art should be.

This is because new art shatters the public, forcing it into a crisis based on the simple fact that there can be no public for an art that did not exist before. With the appearance of unfamiliar art, the traditional public disappears. New art shatters the public as a mass of believers and turns it into individuals. The artist is the first to be transformed, then a new public comes into being. This is a public that already existed but was in crisis when it stopped being a mass of believers and was turned into discordant individuals confronted with art that represents a new reality.

When I went to see the building for the exhibition in the Biennale, I found that in the corridor where the artists would be each artist had a very limited space. I realized that because it was such a large event, people were not going to spend more than three minutes on each work. So, working with the idea of containers and the void, as well as with found objects and the idea of what remains after an action, I decided to present a shoe box.

There are interesting stories about what happened to that box, like when it disappeared only minutes before the exhibition began, with the inaugural ribbon about to be cut and the multitudes waiting to enter, while all the artists who had just finished installing their work were on their way out. I was the first to complete the installation of my work; clearly, that wasn't a problem. But whenever I turned my back, it was carried off because they thought it was trash. So I spent my time taking care of it. I would place the shoe box, but whenever I wasn't watching, they would take it away and throw it out. First, I bought just one box. Later I had to go all over Venice looking for all the shoe boxes I could find to put them behind the wall and have them as replacements (an important artistic technique I learned that day). I also remember that the curator, who was very concerned, suggested that I fasten it to the floor so it wouldn't get lost or destroyed. I told him that that would be worse—and this comment made me think about the space between the base and the sculpture, that space we don't see where the sculpture rests and where the center of gravity exerts its force, where dust accumulates, but we'll get back to this subject later—because if I glued it to the floor, it would be destroyed by its own resistance. It would be better to let it be kicked and for the container to take the blows and ricochet all over the place. I ended up arguing that this way, it would be more likely to survive. When all was said and done, we did not fasten it down, and sure enough, it did get kicked around. Although what also happened was that people began to throw change for the poor into the shoe box. In short, it is a work that still continues to cause confusion and a certain amount of controversy. It is still one of my favorite pieces.

In 1993, I was living in New York without a studio, walking around the streets doing my work:

> Reality and realization: the maker [*realista*] who wishes for the accident. The object that arises in the world as a result of an unpredictable phenomenon and accident, but only when there is an act of consciousness—consciousness that is elicited by the reality of the body ready to receive it. The recipients: the surprise of the maker and the subsequent surprise of the realizer: he who activates the reality as a recipient of its future, he who realizes what is happening to him in the world. Acceptance of the real and its accidents. Acceptance of disappointment. Not expecting anything, not being spectators, but realizers of accidents, in which reality, when nothing is expected of it, gives us its gifts.

I am interested in disappointment. I believe that when something surprising happens in reality, it is generally when we least expect it. Reality is not surprising, but there is a moment when it seems to be. Reality is the continuum that is happening before us.

I'd like to talk about *Extension of Reflection*, the photograph of the action with my bicycle in some puddles in New York. It had just rained, and I went out for a ride. When I saw the other bicycles skirting the puddles, I began to go through them instead, taking pictures of what was happening. There was a bit of sun and some reflections, and the tire tracks would disappear very quickly. I had to jump off the bicycle and take the photograph before the stripes of water disappeared from the cement. I think that was how my fascination with puddles began. What is a puddle? It may be something disappointing, something to be avoided, a topographical accident, a bit of urban disorder, an accumulation of time, an imperfection. But it is also a space where something marvelous may happen. It is an element of reality that has generated lots of ideas in my work.

Going back to the disappearance of the public, of the spectators who wait for something to surprise them, I remember that expectations were high when I was about to have my first solo exhibition, in a gallery in New York in 1994. After my exhibitions at Kortrijk, the Venice Biennale, and the Museum of Modern Art of New York (which I will describe later) in 1993, I had my first exhibition in the fall of the following year at Marian Goodman Gallery.

I presented *Yogurt Caps*, four rings of blue plastic (with clear plastic centers); one was placed in the center of each wall (figs. 25, 26). One of the things I must say about this work was that I was fascinated with the idea of disappointing the public. I found it interesting to situate people in a void, to neutralize it, and with that power, start from zero to develop my work without expectations of the viewer who, tyrant that he is, begins to demand of the artist what *he* must be. The night the exhibition opened, when the invited guests arrived at the gallery with the caps installed, they saw them and left. They couldn't believe it, or they didn't know what to see. For the first hour of the opening, there was almost no one in that place. With time, they began to return, they began to understand or

25 *Yogurt Caps*, 1994.
Installation view, Marian Goodman Gallery, New York.
Four yogurt caps. Dimensions variable.

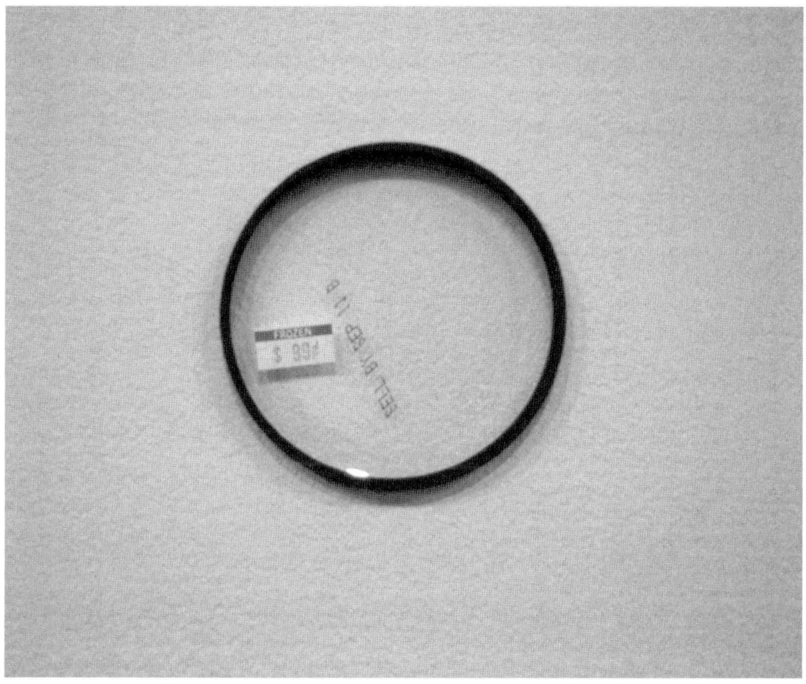

26 *Yogurt Caps*, 1994 (detail).

simply to relax into that situation, and finally they began to look. It was interesting to see people return after their first disappointment, when they began to consider the possibility of being surprised by or interacting with the space. With this work, perhaps a situation was created in which viewers felt they were disappearing, or felt that, since there was nothing to see, nothing could be expected. Possibly when a viewer returned with a different consciousness, with a new attitude toward what was happening—which was banal, which was real, which was nothing and everything all at once—a new surprise could occur:

> Acceptance of the disappointment, not expecting anything, not being spectators, but realizers of accidents. The artist is not working for a public that already knows what art must be. The artist is working for the individual who wonders what the reasons are that art exists. This art cannot be spectacular, since reality is not spectacular, except by accident or because the individual decides that that reality is

> spectacular. Intentional spectacles are made for the expectant public, and the artist is not working for that public. It is impossible to turn the public into individuals through a spectacle. Art is implemented when the individual is fulfilled by it, even for just a moment. Because, finally, art is a problem of time: of the art's moment in time.

I think about time for art more than about space for art. Time for art does not depend on the museum; the time of the work continues after the review is written or the building demolished. The idea circulates through the individual and his words and his relationship to the new reality observed through a new awareness. Thus the post facto controversy unleashed by a work is one possible measure of how that work was successful, how it transformed the viewers and, in turn, public expectations. A shoe box is a shoe box before, during, and after an exhibition. But as a physical and cultural accident that precedes the structure of the language that seeks to stabilize it and turn it into a rule, the shoe box continues to be a container empty of meaning and persists in memory as a banal, indecipherable sign: as an element of reality, a container of nothing, a container of dust.

Let's talk about *Yielding Stone*. In 1991 in New York, I was manipulating plasticine dough into a large range of shapes. A time came when the dough was so dirty and amorphous that I finally became aware that this was the essence of the material, material with which I could create something. This is a piece that includes several possible readings: the plasticine dough has the same weight as I do, it is oily and never hardens, which is why whatever happens to it is taken in and incorporated into its body. It was rolled in the street as a method of shaping it, and dust that adhered to it due to the oil as well as its consistency and weight (since weight is also what makes the material permeable). But in addition, after being rolled, it was important that it be exposed and continue to be permeated by the fingerprints of the viewers who touched it. It keeps on happening in the present; it has a natural subsequent activity; it contains time. It is not a work that happened and was later exhibited as a relic, which began and ended in that time of pure significance. It is not a physical thing whose temporal nature ended when it entered the museum and was kept static in a showcase or on a base where it could be seen but nothing could be done with it. *Yielding Stone* is a piece that was still functioning during the exhibition; what happened to it in the museum was as real as what happened to it in the street.

I decided that my weight should be the measure for that stone because I had to decide the maximum size of the dough. Without a clear limit, its possible dimensions could have resulted in a spectacular appearance. I understood that it was logical to show that through the force of my body surrounding it, added to the force of gravity, that other body would be formed.

I would like to continue the reading of my notes on sculpture, dust, and painting:

> I have always been interested in the tension between image and dust. On the one hand, we have a religious faith in painting: illusion and hope (horizon and sheen?). Painting is the art of faith and the spectacle that seeks to move us with its illusion of reality. Dust, its opposite, tends to cover the canvas and the image. That constant, eternal dust that darkens colors and becomes a thing, itself. From illusion to stone. From landscape to dust. The erosion of objects in the world covers bronzes devoid of body, shining marble and canvases, like a window that is never opened.

In this period of so much movement, so much travel, I find these ideas on objects in motion very compelling, as well as their relationship to dust. Dust accumulates where there is no motion, in the space between the sculpture and the base. I remember that during the time when I was frequently going to the Museum of Modern Art in New York to set up my exhibition what truly interested me was seeing the dust between the bases and the sculptures. In that impeccable museum, I was amused to find trash and dust hidden in intermediate spaces, missed by the eyes of the public. This relationship of force between sheen (illusion, the clean), which is what is visible, and dust, which is the dullness that covers and turns into a thing in itself (into stone), is one of my favorite motifs.

In Mexico, we have many sculptures in which the visual illusion is based on color, but we see how urban dust dulls them, flattens them, constantly darkening them. This reflects the problem of maintaining faith vis-à-vis inexorable reality. I am drawn to crossing the border between control and abandon, between the urban and the organic, the edges of the city where "order" is growing and clashing with the "disorder" of nature. Much of my work takes place in those border areas where that order (structure, language, urban faith) is confronted with disorder (the organic, the phenomenon, the wild), which simultaneously invades the city with its particular logic. These spaces of friction between the country and the city, between the organic and the inorganic, between the "artificial" and the "natural" are the wellspring of a great deal of my work; this is what I find on my journey.

It would be instructive to analyze, as artists, our particular idea of what is raw material: why we believe something still exists that is or is called a raw material, such as wood, marble, or clay. Pure raw materials are inconceivable; every material has its social and political baggage. It is impossible to seek a relationship of purity with what we call materials; clay, rock, and oil are unimaginable as neutral or virgin materials. These are useful materials with an implicit cultural significance, already prepared, already made; they are human and they are political. Materials already reasoned out and already functioning, materials with price and status. There is no such purity:

> The artist is first and foremost a consumer. The materials he consumes and the way in which he consumes them influence the development of his work and the subsequent implications. This consumption system is the first technique the artist has to define. Having abandoned my studio or workshop, I became a consumer of anything at hand and a producer of what already exists.

Clay is not just "clay"; it is clay for making bricks in *My Hands Are My Heart.* That piece was made in a brickyard in Cholula. I was never interested in clay, and in school, I never even signed up for ceramics class, but it happened that I found this traditional material in a specific situation. We have frequent encounters with those traditional materials through an awareness of what they mean today.

Regarding the materials I use to make my work, we can think about a continuity of materials: from the characteristics of rubber—which is still vulcanized rubber in *Recaptured Nature*—to the artificial stone in *Yielding Stone*, made of oil and dust and formed by rolling, which yields to multiple impressions. The four bicycles in *There Is Always One Direction* are from Rotterdam, and they were assembled in accordance with their own structure, removing the saddles and the handlebars and fitting the seat tube of one bicycle to the crossbar of the next, and so on (fig. 27). The elevator and the Citroën car also continue to be what they are after being cut up and reassembled; they keep on elevating and in some way transporting. They continue to function; we can live in their new configuration, we

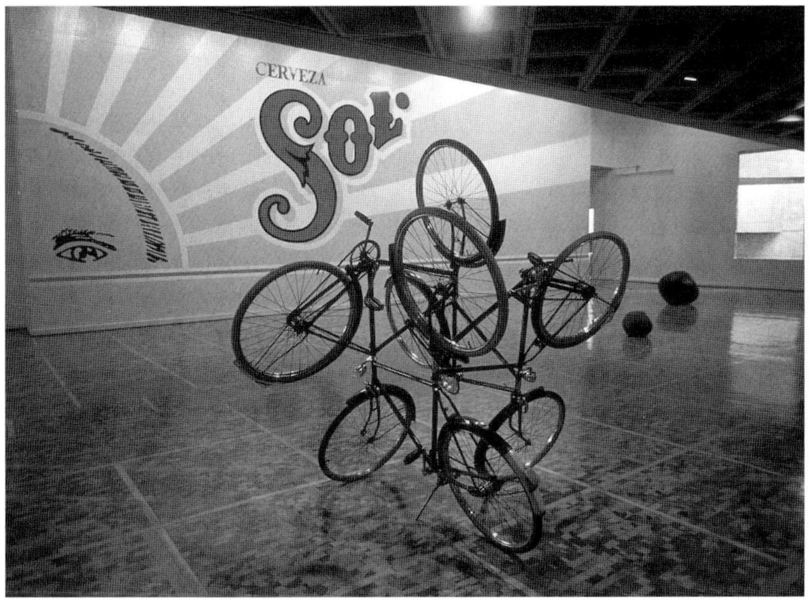

27 *Four Bicycles* (*There Is Always One Direction*), 1994.
Bicycles.
78 x 88 x 88 inches.

can get into them (although it may be problematic for the museum, but that's another matter). They continue to be means of transport, they continue to be vehicles for a body; their original function lives on. Billiard, chess, and ping-pong tables continue to be games and fields that may be traversed. Perhaps it is not understood why I created *Light Sign* in Korea (where I didn't understand what the signs made with light boxes were saying, either) (fig. 28). That limitation turned into an "illuminated phenomenon," and, as such, it is difficult to read, because it would be like trying to read a shaft of light. *Shoe Box* continues to be what it is—a container, just as almost all my sculptures are containers. *Working Tables* are what they are in their scale and in their use: like arriving at the table in a mechanical workshop and seeing the nuts and screws and the oily scraps, which are incomprehensible to the customer. Electric fans keep on ventilating.

It is important to understand the reason for each of these vehicles, for each of the materials I am using, where they come from and what they were designed for and how I try to give their intrinsic structure a

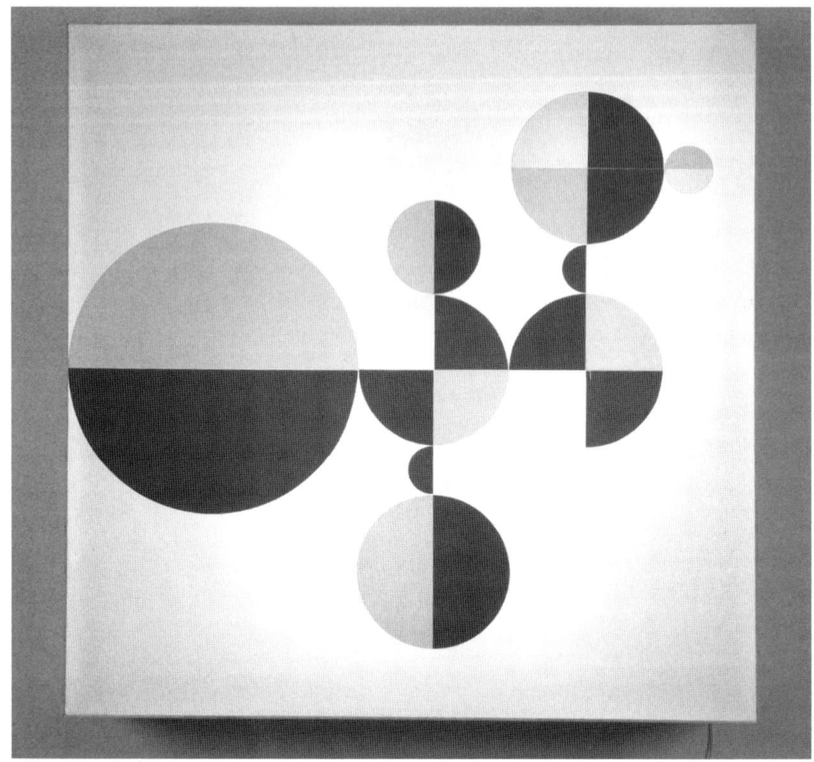

28 *Light Sign no. 1* (Korea), 1995.
Plastic sheet with acrylic paint in light box.
39 3/8 x 39 3/8 x 7 3/4 inches.

new way of functioning, metaphoric on the one hand, but also utilitarian and in some way real. To continue and extend the possibilities of the historical and mythic content of those objects and not just their mechanical structure. My works have a country of origin, and it is important to understand the reason for each object I use in terms of geography and history as well as for its function as a social material in our environment and our time. The bicycles are from the Netherlands; the elevator comes from Chicago; the vulcanized rubber, from Mexico; the pool table, from France; ping-pong, from all over the place and from Japan; chess comes from tournaments of my childhood; the sports, from wherever they are invented; and the atomists, from that most real of worlds, the world of our philosophical ideas.

The story about the elevator is a curious one. I thought it would be very easy to obtain a used elevator to cut it up; however, I spent a whole year finding it, because there is no such thing as a second-hand elevator. Elevators are made to order for each building, and when the building is destroyed, the elevators are destroyed. The Museum of Contemporary Art of Chicago, for which I made the piece, was looking for buildings in demolition until it found one with the elevator I had pointed out and asked them to please not destroy it. *Not* to destroy what was precisely in the center of a building turned out to be a lot of work. It was memorable to finally see the demolished building, the level ground and waste land, with an elevator in the middle, just like what we see now, because I didn't change it much: all I did was cut it and assemble it to my height.

In *Elevator*, something interesting happened with respect to the relationship between the interior and the exterior of the object. The interior of an elevator is its exterior, and when we have a "naked" elevator outside a building, the external part of the elevator is visible and we notice, or it turns into, that space I mentioned before between the sculpture and its base where the dust accumulates. That interior space of three-dimensional objects, the space that would normally be inside and that when you open it up, emerges from obscurity. In the elevator, the illuminated part, the clean part, is inside, and everything outside is dust and grease. Taking it out of a building is like turning the peel of a half orange inside out, pressing it out with your fingers so the peel is inside and the segments on the outside.

I mentioned that I was going to talk about the notion I have about time for art when I referred to my attempt to generate the time in which art occurs. Spaces for art, though they exist, and though there are more every day, are no guarantee that art will occur. I believe art does not depend so much on the creation of space for art, but rather on the creation of time for art. It is very important that that creation of time for art starts with the artist in his way of managing the time for creation. In that regard, part of my focus when I am working consists of playing with the speed or slow pace of the work time invested in each work.

MoMA in New York is a museum where you must decide precisely what you are going to do, in what space and how, at least one year before the opening of each exhibition. It is a sophisticated machine in which every centimeter is calculated and made use of to the maximum, not only for the collection, but also for the number of people who visit it every day.

For my part, today I still avoid decisions with so much lead time about what I'm going to be doing. It's impossible for me, because that space of time between the beginning of doing something and the final moment is a space I wish to explore. To have an idea about what is going to happen a year from now somehow gets in the way of my work. I prefer to be making the piece, thinking about the piece.

The most intense dialogue with the museum was about the appropriate timeframe for deciding on the project. I proposed the idea of the event with the oranges in the buildings across the street just two weeks before the opening. After a year of visiting the museum frequently, in the spring, in the fall, in the winter, the idea was clear. Finally, summer arrived, and it was interesting to observe how the climate might influence an exhibition: there are ideas for winter and ideas for summer. When the idea was defined, the work of the museum consisted of distributing oranges to the neighbors across the street, giving them fresh oranges every week so they could take them out of the window and use them, replacing them with other new ones. That was the museum's job for that exhibition.

I am interested in carrying my indecision around with me, or being in the middle of a decision, until the last minute, because I believe that places me in a situation similar to that intriguing space between the sculpture and the base, that place that is unimportant to everyone, where apparently there is nothing going on, where it is unnecessary to clean. The place that was not so visible in a museum, in this case, was the most visible in the whole museum: the buildings across the street. But it was outside the museum, in another dimension, closer to the real. Another important thing is that it was not so spectacular as people may have imagined; there were days when you couldn't see well. What was curious is that any person who suddenly looked at one orange then started to see all the others. I did not want to put up signs, though there were a few very discreet ones, because obviously, if there had been an announcement, "See, see the oranges!," the disappointment would have been worse. It would have been like trying to make something spectacular when it is not; it was much more important for it to happen naturally. The piece was not aimed at the museum's traditional viewers.

I believe it is more important to try to create a time in which the art occurs, a time that spaces for art are often unable to create. The artistic event and the individual event are highly orchestrated in spaces for art, and it is difficult for a surprise to happen, a poetic event, a moment in which the individual feels conscious, comprehending, realizing, or momentarily full in the apprehension of an idea. Art needs to generate the space for the individual perceiving the time, and not for mass consumption in an institutional space; time in which the viewer disappears as a public for that institution and becomes a person. The artist's task is to generate those moments in art, often working against the spaces of that spectacular corporate architecture designed by museums. One of the problems contemporary architecture has created for art is that the architecture is so scrutinized that it becomes difficult to create a poetic situation, an artistic state, for either the viewer or the artist.

In order to create the time in which art occurs in the viewer, we must change our own work time. Photographs and actions in the street gave rise to situations in which I had to make quick decisions, when, attentive to what was happening at that moment, I had to perceive it, develop it, think about it, and act. Obviously, I have taken a lot of photographs that didn't go anywhere. Still, faced with the phenomenon of reality, I developed a relationship of awareness and acted so as to avoid imposing my prejudices on what was happening, as well as to prevent the reality, possibly banal and spectacular (if I considered it spectacular) from creating an imbalance in that relationship. The relationship with what is real and its time is a very important factor every time I interact as a participant in the place where I am living.

Island within an Island is an example in this sense. There was a puddle in front of me, and I placed those sticks in relationship to the landscape behind it. For me, the scale of the object is very important, as well as the possibility for action in that moment when it is related to the entire landscape. Anyone can imagine putting oranges on the tables in that market or riding from puddle to puddle on a bicycle or throwing sand on that table or breathing on that piano. There is an object that acts, in its scale, in relationship to the landscape. The relationship of scale between the monumental urban phenomenon and the object acting and transforming it is a tension I find compelling: the possibilities of the real object, in this space and with this change of scale. That's why I don't need to bring anything with me, because the space itself will provide; this way I can carry on a dialogue and maneuver freely in the environment.

I am also interested in the scale of time for doing my work, such as time spent on the skull with graphite that I presented at *Documenta X*, which I intentionally worked on for several months. I didn't have the slightest desire to go out in the street; I wanted to be alone, closed in. So I created a work that had me sitting at a table for months. I wanted to render a drawing that was about thinking, time, volume, the labyrinth, the road traveled, which would require that amount of time and which was very concentrated and specific. I thought the actual time would become manifest in the work. I was very aware of what I was doing for that exhibition, and I had the impression that a single concentrated point of focus and time could have a greater impact and cause a certain disturbance for the viewer at a mass art event, where there would be spectacular installations and a great deal of information. I worked out the contrast, upon reaching a neutral point, a very concentrated point, where you could almost put yourself inside the eyes of that skull, and hence think about another possible space. That is what I intended with the drawing, and perhaps that is what it generated when it was later shown.

An artist often invests months of work in a piece, and the result is insignificant. Yet, on the other hand, sometimes a very simple gesture can have much more impact on reality and on art. For my work, it is highly important that the relationship between the size of the gesture and its consequences are not parallel lines, rather aiming for some random, minimal gesture to possibly have much greater consequences on reality than a mural or a building.

Another time-related concept I'd like to point out is that after doing something in an immediate way, it is generally assumed that we have to let time go by to know with greater clarity whether or not that gesture is interesting. I don't believe in that any more. Many apparently immediate works attract attention for a long time. That tension is important: to trust that rapid sensations and immediate action may have subsequent validity and thus to observe that there is no precise equation between the time we invest in doing a work and how long it later remains in memory. Because there is no guarantee that if we invest more time in rendering a work, it will remain in memory longer than other works. Sometimes a rapid gesture can last much longer. This turns out to be an interesting fact: time transforms the work of art more radically, and in a much more forceful way, than its physical vulnerability. Remembering or forgetting is more important for its preservation in history than the climate or the production of a work.

To make *Breath on Piano* took a few seconds; the photograph may last for a hundred years, but we do not know when the last person to remember it will die. Time will change ever more rapidly, and we will never know how this work will be seen in the future, in that accumulation of accidents to come. If we were granted the gift of seeing that photograph as it will be seen a hundred years from now, we would know what art would be like in a hundred years. Our way of seeing things changes much more rapidly than the object and its physical materiality.

Working Tables represents ten years of accumulated objects, mock-ups, and models, and their relationship with time is worth exploring (figs. 29, 30). Almost all these objects are vulnerable, incomplete, analytical. Perhaps they have no value in themselves, but as a record of daily sculptural activity, they generate a set of connections with other finished, public, synthetic works. It is important to learn to see these unfinished works as well. I believe it is important to see a work that was significant in order to reach that other result. As artists, we know it well: the relationship of durability of those works in relationship to the artist is truly infinite. On the one hand, there is the sure, synthetic, finished work, to which we relate as we would to an idea that turned out well; in fact, there comes a time when it is not so important to us, because that work has its own life when the recipient carries it on. On the other hand, there are the bad works, those that remain in process and do not turn out well. Those works are infinite for us, in the sense that they may still be something more, or there is still something else to be done, or perhaps something else will come of them. Those works are for the artist, they belong to him like his errors. These tables are a sample of that part. The viewer, passing through and observing that accumulated time, that trash and those models, may understand those possibilities and the multiplicity of their readings and may observe the different scales of work implicit in the object that is being made and the finished product. The objects on these *Working Tables* were kept in shoe boxes for ten years. They were transported in time.

For me, photography is like a shoe box. It is a container I use to transport what I pick up in my interactions. I am not especially drawn to photographic compositions; the object of my interest is almost always in the middle ground or the totality. As an image, it is fairly simple, directly tied to the event in reality; it is a record that focuses on the center of that object. I value the plane of the photograph in its description of the three dimensional and its possible space for storing time. I turn to the photograph as a sculptural space, and at the same time I am drawn to any object that may make an appearance in a photograph.

As I write in one of my notebooks, when I saw the photographs of *La DS* as a finished work, I became aware that the cut and assembled car looked like a three-dimensional photograph. Its new appearance and structure, with a portion of its volume removed (which nonetheless remains

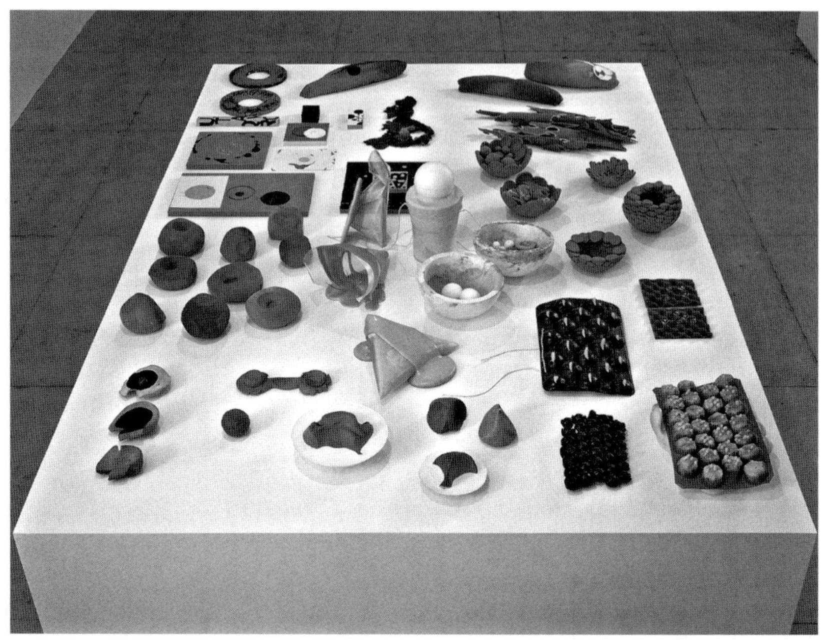

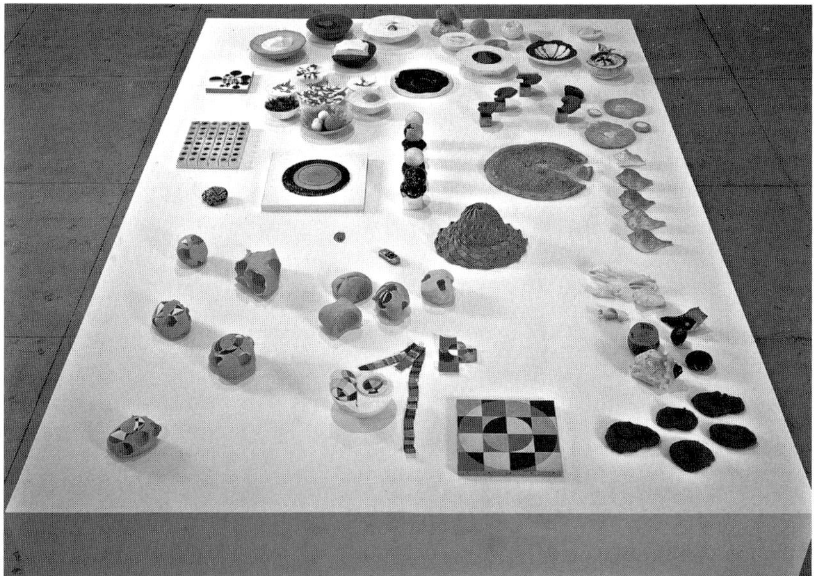

29, 30 *Working Tables*, 2005.
Unfired clay, straw, egg container, bottle caps, wiremesh screen, string, stones, shells, plaster, bark, polystyrene foam, painted wood elements, pizza dough, and other materials. Dimensions variable.

in our memory) creates a sensation of an image more than of an actual object. When we go over it and then back over it again, there are moments in which it flattens out, moments in which it has volume, moments in which it is a diagonal, and moments in which it looks like a photograph. By photographing three-dimensional objects, we discover the qualities of their iconic appearance, where they are not only sculptures, but they have or acquire an important visual quality. For example, although we know that the *Pinched Ball* contains a volume of water, it is nevertheless a very flat photograph, and the water seems to have turned into a mirror or a reflection. Often in my work we are dealing with an encounter between two empty recipients: the viewer and the object as recipients that have an encounter. I believe the best way of establishing contact with my work is when those two poles meet in the void between them, to be filled by the experience in real time, precisely at that moment.

Getting back to fruit, in 1993, in Belgium, I was cutting oranges and observing the peels. To create *Orange without Space*, I cut one orange, emptied the peel of its fruit, and then began to fill the two empty halves with plasticine. Starting with some object, we create a space in the middle that is infinite or that is no space at all. In *Orange without Space*, the plasticine dough covers that space between the two hollow halves and begins to cover its exterior and reunite the halves.

Thinking about fruit has been useful for me. It is a way to understand sculpture as a structure or as a means of transport or as a body that grows from a center and expands, forming an exterior appearance that is in turn related to what is going on within. The sculpture is a piece of fruit and a means of transport, with an interior and exterior structure related to the object it transports. The form of my sculptures comes from their center of gravity as related to the material and its resistance. That is their structure. They are implied by what they contain.

Finally, I would like to tell you that I see my drawings as puddles of specificity on the paper on which they occur. Apart from having a work notebook where I write down and draw my ideas, I am always drawing. This activity takes place on paper, which becomes in turn the platform for an act of consciousness in which, beginning with the center of the leaf, offshoots start to be generated. I call them puddles. Sometimes, I print a section on the computer; sometimes I take paper that already contains information, sometimes white paper, but it is always a way of focusing a moment of concentration and time in which I am thinking about what is happening. They are not drawings done to think about something else, about some project or to sketch what I see. I draw in order to think about that drawing. Normally, they are letter size, and I do them at any desk. I don't care much about the margins or the composition. They help me to create the space that has to do with the time of being there, doing that, on this field of action, on that playing field.

Just as my work is developed from possible centers that are the beginnings from which the structure of each work grows, my work also consists of finding new centers as new starting points for possible growth. I believe this is how artistic ideas, and the history of art, develops. We tend to believe that there is a genealogy, a history, as in families, in which ideas are handed down from generation to generation. But this is not how it is. Most of the time, art happens where it is least expected; suddenly there emerges a new name, a new recognizable artistic sign, a new star. And that new star, like every new star in the universe, exercises gravity. And that new center of gravity in the universe, which is growing in multiple directions, may in turn generate a constellation around it. The same thing happens in art. It grows as the universe grows, and an understanding of that is very rewarding for an individual who wishes to originate things and to be at the beginning of every work, before every possible star. That is the way new ideas arise; that is how new signs appear in different centers, in every country and everywhere in the world.

Notes

1. Orozco is referring to the exhibition catalog *Gabriel Orozco* (Los Angeles: The Museum of Contemporary Art; Mexico City: Museo Internacional Rufino Tamayo, 2000).—Ed.

2. The word "sheen" has been used to translate "el brillo" throughout the text.—Tr.

Gabriel Orozco in Conversation with Benjamin H. D. Buchloh (2004)

BENJAMIN BUCHLOH: Modernism has been a history of restraints, prohibitions, eliminations, exclusions, and subtractions, at least in those instances we take seriously. It's almost a rule in twentieth-century art that whenever you can define an epistemological shift within artistic production and within the theorization of what visual experience is, you engage in a systematic abolition of always previously available models of production of seeing, of thinking. When I look at your work I have the feeling that the restraints have come off a little bit, there's a certain plenitude of yielding that suddenly makes a multiplicity of positions available to all of us, positions that we had thought to be no longer accessible. I'm arguing of course from the position of conceptual art, which is my historical moment, as many people know, and the moment of conceptual art has been very important for you as well, so we both share this historical background even though we have differences in generation. So how do you explain the wealth, the generosity of your plenitude of yielding materials, positions, and practices after all of those have been denied, prohibited, devalorized? All of a sudden you make sculpture; in the 1960s and '70s nobody thought sculpture would ever be possible. All of a sudden you make photographs that have a certain narrative aspect, even though high conceptualist photography eliminated the narrative completely. All of a sudden, now you even make paintings—and we will get to this at a later point—and you occupy a whole range of production positions that had seemingly been shot down for good. Is it because you're an outsider in terms of the Western canon? Is it because you're a young artist in front of the generation of the '60s and '70s artists, and you oppose yourself to them and say "your prohibitions are unacceptable to me, I will show you that I can open up all of those positions from my perspective, from where I come from, from what I do"? Or is it simply a generational chasm?

GABRIEL OROZCO: Being an outsider would not be the answer because I've grown up in the Western culture. The education and information that I have as a Mexican is very much the same that a European kid would have. Of course there are differences, but I think those differences are of the same kind as those you find when comparing a Spanish boy with a British boy growing up. So I think the outsider explanation is not the answer.

I grew up in the art world and studied at the art academy in Mexico, learning what any student around the world would learn, including these prohibitions and what has been done in art history. But the most important step for an artist, at least for me, is to reestablish or to develop contacts, or bridges, in our relationship with reality—the real, whatever it is. That thing that is outside of us, that thing we need to know, that we want to explore in order to understand the world, ourselves, and the time we're living in.

I think one of the reasons that at some point some art methods are prohibited or becomes obsolete, is because in fact the art loses contact with reality, stops talking about real issues, and becomes a bubble on its own, something alienated, something that is just a mere game. It's interesting to observe how this has happened with any technique. But I would say that the problem is not so much a technical problem; it is not because you're doing terracottas, or paintings, or photographs. I think to focus on this would be misleading. In the case of my photography, for example, after I develop actions in the street, I need to take a picture, because it's the only way that I can keep or transport this action and show it to other people. I use it as a kind of bridge of communication.

BUCHLOH: Which is a very conceptualist strategy.

OROZCO: It is. But with the difference that I don't have texts with my images, and I don't totally trust the archival systematic documentation of events and objects. I like to document a specific phenomenon in which I intervened or that I witnessed. But there is not so much of a conceptual explanation or cataloguing of the event. I leave it quite open. I think it's visual the way it is transmitted. As I have mentioned on other occasions, I like the idea of the photograph as a shoe box in which you keep and transport objects or memorable events in your life.

BUCHLOH: The shoe box is an archive too, right?

OROZCO: It is not exactly an archive. It is a real object and a container. Sometimes I show it empty. The first time was in 1993 at the Venice Biennale. I had many of what I called my "exploring objects" in this shoe box in my apartment. After a few years I took the objects, put them on a table, and thought, "This is interesting all together," but then I looked at the shoe box and thought, "But this is better!" Then I decided to show the empty shoe box in the exhibition. I am not so much concerned with the archive as with how to get in touch with reality, to explore my landscape and my life. Those are the motivations for my traveling, or walking around the streets. That is the motivation for using different media, and it is through them that I have contact with the real.

BUCHLOH: Of course, it would be much easier for me to agree with that, and grant you the freedom of the individual, extraordinary artist, which would pretty much take care of the conversation, but I can't do that. [*Laughs.*]

So I do have to insist on playing the historian. There is a tradition and a trajectory of sculpture in the '60s that ranges from minimalism to postminimalism in the American context and, in the European context from Joseph Beuys to *arte povera*. That's the background of your history as a sculptor. Again I might be wrong, but for me you're primarily a sculptor, whatever this definition means or doesn't mean anymore.

Obviously the *arte povera* tradition and the postminimal tradition from Bruce Nauman to Eva Hesse to Richard Serra have been of crucial importance for you. You have looked at their work again and again, you've learned from their work, and you separate yourself from their work. So when you insist now on saying that artists lose the relationship to the real, and that you want to find the way back into your reality, how would you differentiate your reality from theirs? How would you differentiate your approach to sculpture from the development, let's say, of the work of the '60s, which started out with a very comparable insistence on reintroducing the somatic, the bodily experience, into the sculptural structure, which was very much opposed to the techno-scientist model that minimalism used?

In many ways your work is very close to that of Eva Hesse, which I think you admire very much; in many ways, you're close to some of the work by Nauman, least of all probably to Serra. But to use the body as an imprint, to use the body as a matrix for formal morphological production—as you have often done up to now—is a very common strategy in postminimal sculpture, in Nauman in particular. How would you define your reality as different from theirs?

OROZCO: When I work with objects, I focus very much on the object itself. I am not thinking about contemporary sculpture or traditions, or how to break with this or that. I am focusing on the material I have in front of me. When I did the inflated rubber ball (*Recaptured Nature*), for example, one of the things I was interested in was how to transform this object into something else, while also coming back to the reason for this material object to be. This rubber ball comes from an inner tube of a truck; I cut it, opened it, made two tops, and sealed it again, and it became this irregular sphere shape. So I'm using the material in the way it was made for: that is, to be inflated. So in every work, the first concern for me is a connection with what the material is, and that starts a process of analysis and posterior synthesis in which I arrive to a situation with the same object, without losing the essential characteristics, if we can say that, of the object and material itself.

Then of course, you can make connections with an artist who has used rubber, such as Serra. But I think his works are completely different. If I present a shoe box you can also connect it with Donald Judd if you want or with another minimalist, as a kind of joke about it. But also, and most of all, it is what it is. Of course you can say it's a readymade, but the fact is that it's not in a base, or that it's not even claiming to be a joke about art. It's really just a shoe box on the floor, which many people didn't even see it when it was shown, and which was kicked around. I have to insist on that point. When I did *My Hands Are My Heart* in clay, I was working with another artist in a brick factory in Mexico, and at some point this was a gesture that was kind of spontaneous, using this clay, which is made for bricks, it's solid. And then the title came afterwards, so it was not so much as if I'd been thinking, "I'm going to make a heart and it's about the body." It was a very immediate relation with that moment. After that piece I didn't work in terracotta for seven years, so it was very much something specific to that moment. I'm sure this is not answering your question, but I think that is very much the reason why I start many processes of working with different techniques and materials.

BUCHLOH: Since you mentioned the terracotta pieces, I was hoping to talk about them since three crucial new terracotta pieces are in this exhibition at the Serpentine. I consider them to be the most stunning of the entire show. They are very good examples both of the peculiar choice of process and materials, because, I am sure somebody in the audience might correct me, but I don't remember any artist using terracotta other than Lucio Fontana. That's the last artist whose terracotta work I know. We know that Fontana was important for you, but of course what he was doing was something very different. Again, you have a very peculiar hybridism between an artisanal process, a highly artisanal material, and an extremely strange morphology that is not artisanal at all. You explained it to me and, I am sure, it will be wonderful for the audience to know how they were made. They were very much the result of a chance operation, at least partially.

Also the pottery pieces (*Cazuelas*), which look like mortars to me (fig. 31). They look even more artisanal since they look like pottery that is unfinished, or mortars that are almost finished, and then they all have been destroyed or affected by pure chance intervention on your side, throwing clay balls into the wheel while the pottery was made. There again, you have this strange synthesis of a very traditional material, a very traditional process, and a very strong foregrounding of the process, which is coming out the 1960s postminimal process-oriented artistic production. At the same time, there's a very strange combination with the foregrounding

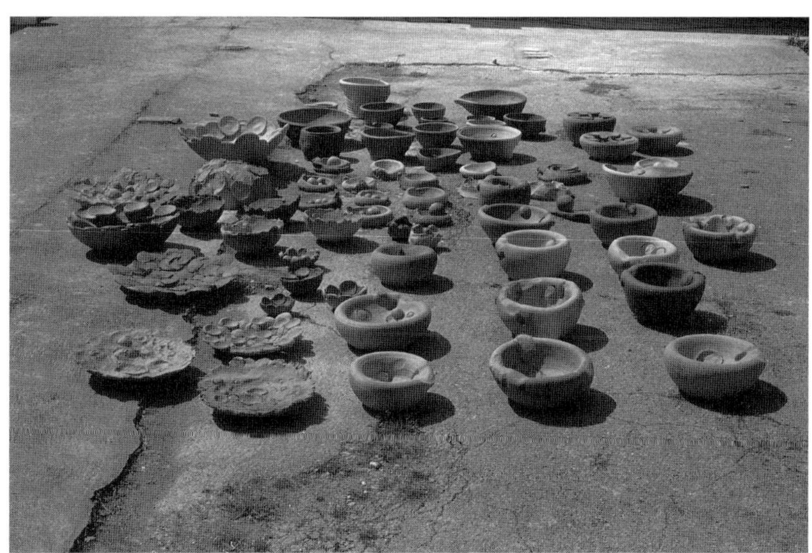

31 *Cazuelas*, 2002.
Fired clay.
Dimensions variable.

of chance operations, of utterly random or aleatory interventions. In the terracotta *Double Tail*, as you explained, you inscribe the shape of two wooden spheres at the end of this rolled structure, and it produces this utterly uncanny bodily quality, resulting in one of the most haunting works of sculpture that I have seen in a very long time (fig. 32). How does this relate to the body?

OROZCO: The body is important in all my work. But I don't think the representation of the body is enough. That means, the body's imprint or the body as a reference, or the space that the body occupies or generates, is not enough. Because this can easily become very anecdotal. I tried in the terracotta pieces. The movement of the making is very close to making bread, for example, when you start molding the mass on the table. The action of the body pressing this matter, it is a very primitive, essential movement onto the mass of the material. We have the body pressure on the mass and then the pressure of the wooden ball for the imprints of the

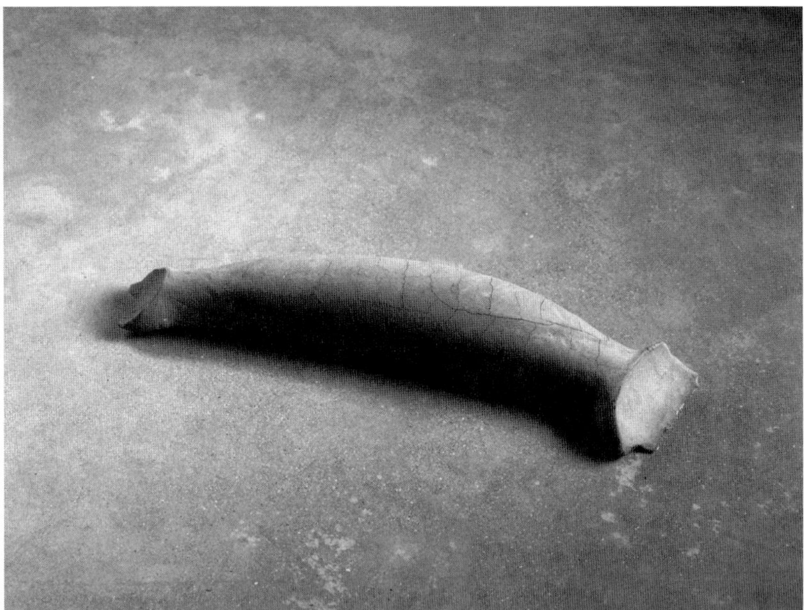

32 *Double Tail*, 2002.
Fired clay.
5.1 x 27.8 x 8.3 inches.
Image courtesy: Galerie Chantal Crousel, Paris.

spherical object. In these objects we have the pressure of an organic body and the pressure of the geometric spherical body into the rolled mass of clay.

Those two are the parameters that I like to include in every work: the organic, that is, the specific body doing something, and the geometric, the platonic or the abstract, mechanical and instrumental repetitive action on the same object. The confrontation of the two, the body and the mechanical, is very important. Even the cutting of the car (*La DS*) was a very bodily-like experience. At the final result you don't see the representation of the body making of the car, but it was not necessary because the car was already made for the body. We did this bodily-cutting exercise and then put it back, reduced, and it looked technical again. Part of the body of the car is missing, but it's still there, in our bodily-cultural memory of the object; it is now reduced but you can perceive that something strange had happened, even though it is still an industrial object. That is the balance I like to play with. What I'm trying to say is that, on one hand, minimalism and the nonpresence of the body in minimalist sculpture was not enough for me. . . . But on the other hand, if it's just the imprint or representation of the body and that's it, it's also boring. I think you need geometry and mechanism. Because our bodies are surrounded by geometry and structures that are part of them. They are not just organic.

BUCHLOH: Would you be happy if historians and critics adopted the reading that you just delivered and that seems perfectly complete, without wanting to touch it at all? Especially with the terracotta pieces in mind? Do you consider it impossible to go beyond that, in terms of asking the question of what type of body is articulated there? I mean, is this a utopian body? A fragmented body? A traumatized body? Would you allow those questions? Or do you think those have surpassed the pieces already? Because they're not happy pieces, they're not promising bodily plenitude at all; they're pieces of an extreme tension and fragmentation, and they complicate the conception of the body. It's not the body that is relieved or released in that context. The *Double Tail* looks like an amputated body part for example, at least it's one way of looking at it. There's no way to see this as a sign or a promise of bodily plenitude and happiness. It is a very fragmented structure, and it is very intensely present at the same time. It is very different in that sense from Bruce Nauman's cast *From Hand to Mouth*, for example, where we don't have that traumatic dimension at all. So what you have just said, that the pure cast of the body is not enough for you, could we not say that it is because you want to complicate the representation, or the articulation, or the indexical record of the body?

OROZCO: The terracottas look like body parts; they also look like shit or leftovers. They could almost look alive, but, of course, they look dead, too. Then there is one circular shape, which looks more like an industrial object, somehow. These bodies are representative but they're not representing. Those are the two parameters that I'm interested in: you are in fact representing something, a possible metaphor. Yet it's just a stone, or a shoe box, or clay.

This aspect can be connected with the finger-ruler drawings series, in which my finger obstructs the ruler in doing the perfect straight lines. This is a common accident, when the body is in connection with geometric mechanical instruments: you have this perfect ruler to make a perfect line, you have the hand, you try to make the line and suddenly the finger is in there and then you have this accident. So what I did is to make this accident a constant in the drawing. As a result, we have the trace of the seriality of these lines constantly interrupted by this finger-crossing. It is an organic and mechanical movement. That's why I installed them in this exhibition close to the terracottas. The mechanical drawing, the technical drawing, is not enough to express what it means to make a drawing. On the other hand, the pure organic drawing is not enough either. I prefer to combine these two extremes in any action. In drawing or sculpture this has many levels of interpretation.

BUCHLOH: Two artists keep coming to mind when one looks at your work. I mentioned one of them already, Eva Hesse, and the other is Piero Manzoni. I think both artists share with you, or you share with them, an extreme sense of the precariousness of bodily experience. That the body is actually something that is threatened, rather than fully available, fully present, fully redeemable. The choice of materials, in the *Lintels* piece, for example, which is such a extraordinary piece as well, points even more to the sense of the precariousness of bodily experience under the present circumstances. Because what is the lint? I feel obliged to ask, how do you relate it to Duchamp's *Dust Breeding*? That is the first work in the twentieth century where dust becomes a central matter. Now, this lint in its extreme fragility, in its extreme ephemerality, in its extreme kind of almost nonmaterial condition, is a sculpture, strangely enough. What type of bodily presence is articulated in that type of material, in that type of process of looking at that, which is both waste and a bodily expression of industrial nature?

OROZCO: The lint was taken from drying machines in a laundromat in New York. The lint is a combination of skin, hair, and fabric. It gets accumulated in the machines. You get these very flat "skins" industrially produced. When I discovered this and started thinking about the best way to express what it is in there, I was playing in many directions. But in the end I said, "well, this is basically a kind of cloth, it's a pattern, a chaotic pattern, but it's a pattern." So I decided to hang them like drying clothes, the way we do after washing our clothes. It's kind of obvious, but it took me some time to figure out the best way to express the qualities of that specific material.

Coming back to the essence of the particular object . . . it doesn't matter if another artist has used this lint or dust. What I was trying to express was that material, and a possible connection with other of my works related to light and dust. It is installed in a mechanical way. These straight lines are holding there. And you can also think of drying meat. But lint is banal, I don't think there is so much drama in it: it's just a simple industrial leftover that can be dramatic if we look at industrial leftovers as dramatic things. But the way these things are produced is not dramatic, it's mechanical. That, I believe, can be one of the strengths of the piece.

Talking about Duchamp's influence and about the dust in Duchamp, I always like the fact that, when he was doing *The Large Glass*, one of the things that intrigued him the most was to make this image in which you don't have a background, because it is in a glass that you can see through. More like a window. He was trying to make a mechanical representation of sex, life, and death. Then he left his studio and when he came back a few years later, there was all this dust over the object, making the glass opaque and looking like a landscape, a kind of field of dust, and then Man Ray took the photo of it.

When I started to work with dust, I was not so much thinking of Duchamp's work. I started to make the *Yielding Stone* when in 1992 I was playing with plasticine for another project. After a few manipulations the plasticine was totally gray, dusty, and amorphous. I accepted it somehow and it was liberating. After that I decided to make a ball of my own weight and roll it in the streets, to shape it and to see how it would absorb all the imprints. In that moment I started to work with dust, I started to accept dust. Dust, the worst enemy of painting.

BUCHLOH: Yes, it's a negative pigment.

OROZCO: It's a negative pigment and it's a totalitarian surface. Everything that gets dusty becomes just surface. A dusty window becomes a wall, a painting with dust tends to become a flat object again. Painting tries to create an illusion, the illusion of volume, perspective, or light. It promises a kind of enlightenment through color. But dust is the contrary force.

Dust means also that things are static. When there is no movement dust accumulates, which is gravity and cosmos being sedentary. To be alive is to undust things; to see light, you have to clean. These are two parameters I like to play with. I am interested in the confrontation of color and dust. We can see that confrontation in many public sculptures, how the maintenance of the illusion of shine gets covered by the dust that comes back again and again. In their usual state, all public sculptures look somehow abandoned to dust. In painting we can see how Michelangelo's Sistine Chapel was cleaned, for example, and it became a different painting: after being covered by years of smoke and dust, suddenly it was a very bright and light image. Our perception, or the memory of our perception, of that painting as we imagine it was shocked.

BUCHLOH: One inevitable topic that I really think we want to address is the group of brand new paintings that are shown at the Serpentine for the first time, which give me great trouble since I don't deal with painting now, as you know. But first let's get into the circularity and the sphere, which are such utterly central elements in your work. What would we call them: icons? epistemes? structures? forms? morphologies? instruments?

OROZCO: Instruments.

BUCHLOH: In your work throughout (drawing, sculpture, painting), circles come out from the very beginning. It's the most important, or one of the most important, model of process and production in your work, and once you start thinking about it—I'm sure many people have—you recognize that, of course, the sphere has a long genealogy, but it's an obscure genealogy. The genealogy of the twentieth century in terms of abstraction is rectangularity, scientific rationality, optical construction of perspective in space. Or its contradiction and its abolition, through the means of geometry, with the square, the utterly nondirectional pictorial space. Suddenly, the sphere and the circle enter into the fray. Of course they have been present throughout the twentieth century. If one starts looking for it, one can recognize that they have actually been present from the very beginning, in Malevich's work, in Delaunay's work, and then in Duchamp's work—most importantly—and so on. And they played a great role in Eva Hesse's and Jasper Johns's work. The sphere and the circle are really basically counterforces to the domination of rational Cartesian space throughout the twentieth century. But they have never quite reached the visibility or the comprehension that they deserve.

My question is: are we dealing in your work with an effort to dismantle and deconstruct the still governing principles of Cartesian rationality and spatial construction that rules up to minimalism? Are you introducing a dynamic model of spatial experience that is utterly different from the post-Albertian space that has ruled in painting up to the beginning of the twentieth century? Or is it once again the somatic dimension, since the body has orifices and circles but not squares and rectangles? Is the emphasis on the circle also yet another device of underlining, emphasizing the bodily experience of the making? Or the way our experience of the structure is determined by the body (visually and phenomenologically)?

OROZCO: All that. There was something I never liked about this Cartesian geometry in painting, this rigor, these straight lines. Even though I loved Mondrian, there was something that was a bit too religious in terms of geometry. The circle for me is an instrument very useful in terms of movement, in relation to gravity and erosion. It's the tendency of objects when they're in movement and are eroded by friction.

BUCHLOH: It has nothing to do with the ludic? Given that you are a soccer player, I thought that might be a dimension to consider as well, no?

OROZCO: Not really. That is one part, but generally we need circular objects when we move. Some of my work is a reflection on the circularity of objects in the everyday life, which in my opinion was not so much explored. We have the tables of Daniel Spoerri, for example, and we can see these circular elements (plates, bowls, cups, etc.) and claim that is the cosmos represented there. I think it's what he intended it to be. And I think he is right: the cosmos is there. The table is important to me also. The table as the platform for an action is important—the horizontal surface in which to make an action happen. I try to generate or construct platforms for different actions. My drawings, as much as objects like the boxes with plasticine (*Game Boxes*) are platforms for movement.

The circle for me is an instrument. It is not something spiritual; it is not a statement. It's just something that in my opinion represents better how the universe works. It started to come and come in many different ways in my work. And in doing these paintings I wanted to confirm that it was possible to generate a structure complex enough using this geometric system, without the help of a collage background, or a photograph added, like I did before, but just in terms of pure colors and geometry. I don't use a black line to divide the different fields of color. We have this division of colors that is growing, rotating, and jumping (like the knight in chess), and there are rules in the "game" of making the painting. At some point I even thought about calling these paintings *Board Games*. I decided to do them to see how much they could express geometry but also organicity. Also, how much they can communicate or represent gravity, because that is another point I am trying to make here.

BUCHLOH: How do they talk about gravity—how can a painting ever talk about gravity?

OROZCO: Dust, actually.

BUCHLOH: Traditionally, painting was simulating the absence of gravity; that's what the '60s was battling with, to really bring gravity into the foreground of experience by no longer concealing it. But now you're saying painting is gravity, so that's a bit of a provocative statement.

OROZCO: When I started to deal with painting problems, I had to forget that I do photography, I had to forget I do drawings, I had to deal with this flat surface and these four colors. In painting you confront various problems, you have balance, weight, and compositional problems in how to structure the plane. What I decided was first to start from the center of the plane, which I think is not very common. I started from the minimal point of the center, developing the structure toward the frame as the limit.

BUCHLOH: Like a Jasper Johns target?

OROZCO: I think the target is a complete visual idea that is immediately conceived as a whole. It is not something that Johns started from the center developing into an unknown shape; it's more like a logo or a flag. It's a complete image that you conceive in the brain and reproduce in the canvas. He was not starting from nothing, growing into an unknown kind of form, which I think is how organic creatures grow: they start from a center and there is no certainty about what kind of shape will be there at the end, and also how much they can keep growing.

BUCHLOH: Just like a crystal.

OROZCO: I think more in terms of trees. One painting is called *Samurai Tree*. I love the idea of how trees grow from a center. How they grow underground and on the ground from a center and a horizon and they start to develop all the branches. A tree is a metaphor for me. But it doesn't mean you see the representation of a tree. That would be very Mondrianesque. Mondrian's vision of a tree is from the point of view of someone standing on the ground looking at a landscape. Vertical and horizontal lines make the structure and representation of the branches. But if you look at a tree from above, you see the center from which the branches start to spread in multiple directions. In my understanding of how things work, it's not just one point of view toward the horizon, because we are also looking down, looking up. We have a peripheral view.

BUCHLOH: That is articulated in the paintings?

OROZCO: One is called *Spinning and Rotating* (fig. 33). There is a center point and when you have a center point you start to think in axes of possible directions. I am using just horizontal and verticals—I don't want to deal with diagonals for the moment—and they start to grow in different directions and the circles in different sizes. The center point is the one that is holding what I call the spinning movement of the painting,

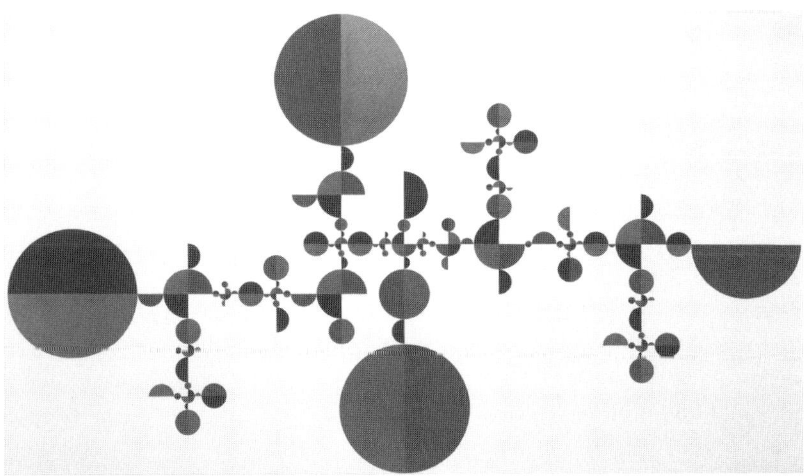

33 *Spinning and Rotating*, 2004.
Synthetic and polymer paint on canvas.
76 3/4 x 44 7/8 inches.

that is the centrifugal point of the field. But then, because there's a play with different sizes, there is a "play with scale" problem, and the spectator has to play with the distance approaching the painting. Minimalist abstract painting is an image that you see in one block, normally from one distance. You don't need to get closer to see the painting better. There is nothing much else to see in the details. In general, it is a one scale kind of thing. There's a problem with scale that I'm trying to deal with here, which means a problem of depth, not in terms of perspective but in terms of scale. The sequence of colors is distributed on the basis of the knight's move in chess, "jumping" two blocks and one, which I take as a representation of three-dimensionality in a two-dimensional field. In most board games you have diagonals or straight lines, and the way the pieces move is two-dimensional. But the knight in chess jumps, which insinuates or proposes a three-dimensional possibility; that's why I found this piece fascinating in chess. It is the only piece of the game whose movement is conceived to represent three-dimensionality. I am trying to apply that in the paintings, as much as I did in the *Atomists* series and in other drawings. I believe this system is representing the rotation of a body, in its growing or shrinking and in moving and rotating.

BUCHLOH: Why, then, execute such an extraordinary process with a very limiting and ultimately static structure? One of the key problems that the futurists failed to resolve, and it has been haunting the twentieth century ever since, is whether you can follow these ambitions for representation of the dynamism of the universe, or the dynamism of experience, or the flow of experience, with a relatively limited means of static representation.

OROZCO: One of the biggest needs in twentieth-century art was the illusion of movement and to try to represent the visual effects of movement and three-dimensionality. You have many examples of the worst failures in op art, trying to generate this kind of look—"Wow, it looks like three-dimensional," or Vasarely's kind of volume illusion. I mean, they are very nice tries, they were quite fantastic and I like them very much, since childhood. But I don't think it's a visual problem to try to generate a three-dimensional proposition, and it is not in the visual perception that we find the way to express how things work to become a three-dimensional organism or object. It's not visual: it has to be intellectual, it has to be an idea. It is more like a formula to be thought. You can look at the paintings as diagrams and think in terms of molecules, or atoms, or a DNA chain, but at the same time they're not claiming to be scientific, of course. They're also ludic, they look childish and I think that is good also.

BUCHLOH: You said something today, which I thought was quite striking. When I was listing all the models of abstraction that we know in the twentieth century—there are quite a few and I don't want to repeat that now—you said: "No, it has nothing to do with any of those," and then you said, "It's much more like a tantric model, because Tantra constructs abstraction as an instrument." It was a totally striking statement because I never thought that any abstraction of the twentieth century from Mondrian to Ellsworth Kelly would define itself as an instrument. An instrument of permission, an instrument of perception, perhaps, an instrument of transforming, of structuring, and of defining experience? In what way would you define it from the tantric point of view of abstraction?

OROZCO: At some point I discovered Tantra and I was struck by the geometry and the body presence in this art. It's quite amazing, how the two together, the organic, the body, the sexual, is combined with the geometric and the mathematical. One possible way to see some of my work is related to this. And these paintings are also the idea of an instrument of knowledge, or an instrument of comprehension and enlightenment. Not religious, but an instrument of awareness—in the sense that when you look at it, you are aware of how it works. I think art can be an instrument of awareness in general. After you see a work of art, you are more aware of something about the world, you look at the world with more clarity in some aspects; I think that is the point of art in many ways.

Even though I was curious to explore the possibilities of abstraction, I don't quite think in terms of abstraction in art. I think in terms of fields connected through this structure, of making a geometric field such as, when you look at it, you become aware of something that is obviously very abstract. But it's also something that sounds or can be logical in relation with an organism, or in relation with how things grow or happen, in relation with abstract thinking itself, in relation with instruments, in relation with mechanicity, in relation with our body. Then there is gravity, those axes moving back and forward with no background, or a white background, and with that you have a kind of representation of a sculpture, but it's flat. Somehow it can represent the body too. But I don't think you can even call them abstract, because abstraction was negating all these representations. On the other hand, if they're instruments you can say they're technical, because I think they have to be a little bit technical to be instruments.

BUCHLOH: But they do look like diagrams.

OROZCO: But also they imply organicity. They imply a growing organism, they imply nature. But not the representation of nature from a window. A Mondrian painting is like a window, and I'm not into that. Because I'm a sculptor, I'm into gravity and I perceive the world in volumes, even though I use photography, drawing, or painting. I don't think in terms of window-like representation.

Spirograph: The Circular Ruins of Drawing (2004)

Briony Fer

> As soon as you tire of squares draw circles.
>
> —*John Ruskin*

> Circling, shattering: these are ways to disappear into space without ever reaching the limits of the sphere.
>
> —*Gabriel Orozco*

Drawings can be made or they can be found. They can be kept or they can be discarded. They are found in a photograph Orozco took of spirograph drawings on sheets of white paper laid out on a pavement in Delhi. The street context shows drawing at its most disposable, but retrieved by the photo and kept in the sort of limbo that seems to interest Orozco most—not entirely permanent but not entirely thrown away either. Spirographs for sale on a street. This isn't where we would expect to find drawing and yet here it is, as he might casually have come across it, at his feet, as he passed. These aren't his drawings, but drawing as happened upon. It invites us to think of drawing as a kind of transaction, connected to the way things circulate in the world, as well as something made in a fairly mechanical physical action. We probably all know how spirographs work, making intricate patterns by rotating a point in clear plastic circular stencils. The elaborately looped rings and wheels are made by rotating a smaller circle inside a larger one. There is something about the elements of a spirograph that resonates in Orozco's work. For a start, the rotating movement is always identical but, depending on the size of the inner stencil, the result is always different. Precisely the same turning movement of a stencil proliferates infinite difference—the lacing of lines tighter, the loops more extended, making endless circles that are more or less elaborate. The patterns were once futuristic, like fantastic planets or flowers in orbit, yet they now seem archaic. This kind of drawing has no art status yet can touch on something as infinite as a constellation of planets. This is drawing as cheap and ephemeral, pointless and playful. It is organized doodling that immediately invokes something both intensely handmade and intensely repetitive and mechanical. When Orozco produces drawings himself, these same elements seem to inform his sense of the graphic, and to impinge on everything he makes.

Historically, drawing has stood for both the greatest discipline (*disegno,* or design) and the greatest indiscipline (doodling). We might be inclined to think that modern art took up the second, improvisatory, experimental model, and abandoned the first. One might want to think that the spontaneous, the unplanned, and the automatic has taken precedence over the authority of drawing as a model of conceptual thought. *Disegno* was the term used in academic discourse to describe the conceptual articulation of compositional structure. The authority once associated with it may simply have migrated elsewhere, to other forms of orthodoxy. But drawing as a way of thinking and as a way of reflecting on what kind of thinking artists do is certainly not dead.[1] Drawing is nothing if not contingent. Over its history it has tended to attract a mixture of benign neglect and overinvestment. If drawing has been seen as less than painting or sculpture, then this view was always countered by the high claims made for it. Among other things, it stood for prolonged study and preparation—the long work demanded of art—and this was part of its allure. At the same time, its status as labor, the work necessary to make art, in terms of both practical endeavor and ethical value, was laced with anxieties about the *work* that art does in the world.

Nowhere was the process analyzed more closely than in artist and critic John Ruskin's 1857 manual *The Elements of Drawing.* On the surface, this volume teaches the discipline of drawing, element by element, in the face of the ever-present danger of failure, of a drawing becoming a "scrawling." But the intoxication of describing the intricacies of the process of observational drawing belies the mastering of the medium. The object of Ruskin's desire is the intense labor of the hand as it moves. He describes himself drawing in order to exemplify his method, with an almost narcissistic sensibility to the process. If Ruskin betrays the compulsion of drawing, then the exercises he describes betray his fascination with an almost bodily mechanics of drawing. Of course this is to read Ruskin against himself, to read his heightened sensibility against his own prohibitions. It is to imagine what the physical and mental labor of drawing means beneath what it says it means. But then drawing has always had that double edge—the capacity both to articulate the structure of representation and to disobey its rules—to tap into what the philosopher Gilles Deleuze has called in another context the "unconscious of representation."[2]

Ruskin's exercises involve the student holding up a sheet of white paper against the light or cutting a hole in another piece. They start with the most basic procedures and build up to the most complicated. The simplest thing to set before the eye, Ruskin says, is a sphere, and the most effective way to learn to draw a sphere is to work from "a child's toy, a white leather ball."[3] Rather than impart the rules of geometry, let alone convey a platonic ideal, Ruskin seems to advocate a pragmatic kind of improvisation, drawing on what is most easily found. "Go out into your garden or into the road," he hastens, "and pick up the first round or oval stone you can find."[4] He discusses setting up some of the exercises (placing a fossilized sea-urchin on a windowsill, for instance) in a way that suggests a slightly exotic and meticulously observed dream narrative or ritual; the look and feel of each element is lovingly described. It is as though the strictures of observational drawing license an almost excessive concentration of attention on the overlooked and fortuitous. Before they become pictures, in the sense of coherent compositions, things can be looked at in such a way as to make them strange. At moments when drawing seems most in thrall to the authority of composition and the symbolic, this precarious and disruptive desire, as in Ruskin's case, can also be most clearly felt. Drawing *without* thinking and drawing *as* thinking come to look, oddly enough, less like opposites.

One of the things they hold in common is the habitual character of drawing. Whether it is a study from nature or whether it is a spirograph, repetition generates drawing. Drawing leads to more drawing. It just goes on, to infinity. Drawing embodies a powerful sense of incompleteness. For Orozco, this seems something productive. He has always drawn. He always draws. He makes endlessly different kinds of drawing, from little sketches in his notebooks to computer drawings to automatic drawings to spit drawings. Aside from the fact that they are all made of paper they share little, on the surface at least. Although most artists draw, not all of them exhibit their drawings, or allocate to them the role that Orozco does. The fact that his drawings haven't been written about much almost proves the point that they provide a kind of background noise, something that just goes on. This doesn't do justice to the drawings themselves, but it is an important part of their dynamic.

Set starkly against this sense of endlessness is the way Orozco has used drawing to mark time. In his *Breathing Drawings* (2002), for example, which he has made since 1998, he sets himself an exercise—he closes his eyes and breathes. As he does so, he blindly draws a line on the page. The pressure exerted on the line of chalk varies with his breathing, and at the end of a breath he terminates the line. We could think of this process in relation to the model of automatic or "blind" drawing of Ellsworth Kelly who worked blindfolded, and Cy Twombly, who drew with the lights out.[5] But in a sense Orozco's exercise in drawing has less to do with the absence of sight than with the bodily rhythm of breathing and—most of all perhaps—with the *matter* of breath. It is more like the material trace of a breath he photographed on a piano in 1993 (fig. 34). In a small, simple gesture, these drawings both dramatize and trace the body's sensory circuits. In them, he does not draw blindly; he cuts off when a whole breath has been exhaled. It is a temporal marker. This is about as handmade and

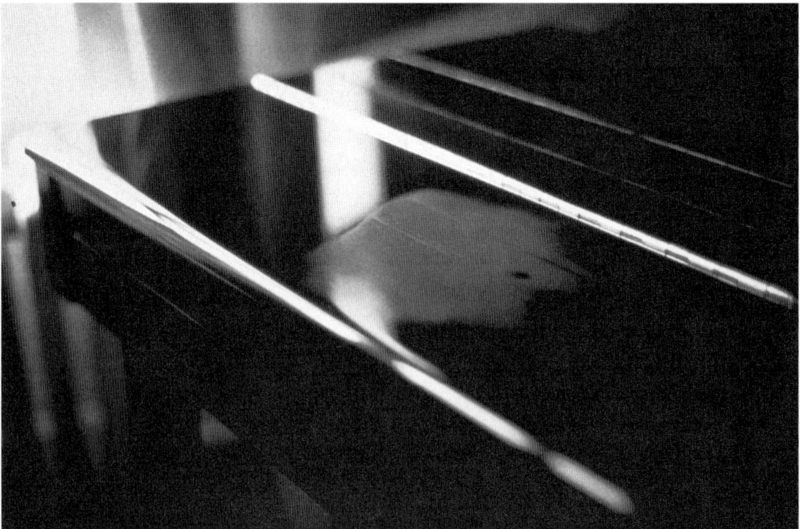

34 *Breath on Piano*, 1993.
Chromogenic color print.
16 x 20 inches.

as mechanical, as concentrated and as distracted, as a drawing can get. To make a work in the time frame of a few breaths is to make it in an instant. Yet to repeat the exercise will make a drawing that is completely different.

Drawing is like breathing. It, too, just goes on. Another meaning of the word spirograph is "an instrument for marking breathing movements." Orozco has spoken of the importance of Piero Manzoni, and this is reminiscent of the work that the Italian artist made out of breath, like his *Corpo d'Aria* series (1959–60). To do this Manzoni blew up a number of balloons, claiming to be breathing his soul into each one and making it eternal. As they shriveled he mounted them as relics on bits of board. Manzoni wanted to touch infinity. He also wanted to deflate it by the literal fact of its materiality. Manzoni's absurdist metaphysics, all his talk of infinity, was pneumatic: it blew things out of all proportion. It is as if he set up situations where the viewer enters into a kind of transaction with a proposition that is often absurd, as this one is, and bleakly targeted against the inflations of a commodity culture.

In 1997, Orozco began to draw on the surface of a human skull, resulting in the seminal work *Black Kites*. Unlike the creation of his breathing drawings, this was a long and difficult process—it took him six months to mark out and cover the whole thing. In his notes, he wrote at the time, "Line over volume. Topography of the cranium. Entering the eyes. Losing itself." The laborious task triggered other thoughts too: "To kill time." "To waste time."[6] How time-consuming can drawing be? (Even Ruskin never took six months to make one.) It is as if drawing, as it measures time, also eats away at it. Drawing competes with the skull as a *memento mori*. But it also consumes time the way Manzoni had made a spectacle of consumption—engaging with it and resisting it at the same time. In itself, the thing is a contradiction: a two-dimensional grid superimposed on a three-dimensional object. One element is precise and geometric, the other uneven and organic. The two are not resolved so much as overlaid one upon the other: a lack of fit almost perfectly rendered. "Volume made graphic," he wrote in a notebook at the time. And as quickly as he wrote it, he added, "Object made image."[7] This is a two-way street, or rather, a busy intersection. It is an extension of the computer-generated drawings he has been making since the mid-1990s insofar as it extends the grid to cover this most awkward of terrains: a skullscape. It is a graphic way of thinking volume. But on the other hand, he thinks about what the graphic means in the most material, not to say sculptural, ways. In an interview with critic and art historian Benjamin H. D. Buchloh, he insisted, "It's lead. It's metal in dust form over the bone,"[8] as if lead had been poured through the pencil.

One might be tempted to ask, therefore, what *is* drawing for Orozco? But I don't think this is the question. Rather the question he seems to invite is what *isn't* drawing in the world? There is another moment in the same conversation with Buchloh when Orozco suggests that works of his we might readily class as sculpture, like *La DS* (1993)—or as photography, like *Until You Find Another Yellow Schwalbe* (1995)—could equally well be called drawing. *La DS* could be drawing in the sense that the car was cut into sections. "It's the line that crosses," he says, "a line that cuts, a line that shapes."[9] Drawing as cutting and cutting out crosses over into collage, just as it does into sculpture. But the procedure of cutting also, as Buchloh has argued, "splits and splices industrially produced structures" and so crosses over into "the entire spectrum of spectacularized modernity."[10] Buchloh focuses here on Orozco's radicalizing of sculptural procedures, but the same case could be made, I think, for his drawing. The work he made for the 2003 Venice Biennale called *Shade between Rings of Air*, for example, seems to reflect on the condition of sculpture by replicating in wood the concrete sculpture garden that Carlo Scarpa designed for the 1952 Italian Pavilion, now a forgotten ruin in the patio outside (figs. 35, 36). Orozco doubled and turned the structure 180 degrees, yet if a line that cuts is drawing, then this scalloping and rotating of space is also intensely graphic, not so unlike the way he uses a compass with a blade to splice his airline tickets.

Orozco links this expansive sense of the graphic back to the tradition of Mexican illustrator and printmaker Jose Posada and "the graphic as a political instrument"[11]—the kind of drawing that infiltrates minds and brains (and seeps into skulls). Graphic models cut across categories and extend into mass imagery. But Orozco has also made drawings using coffee stains and spat-out toothpaste (*Untitled*, 1992) (fig. 37). Bodies seep into drawing as much as drawing seeps into minds. Just as this does not have to do with the medium of drawing as such, neither is it to be described in terms of the kind of hybridity or mixing of media that is now pretty much ubiquitous in contemporary art. Rather, there is a different logic at work, one that can be traced back to Manzoni, which focuses attention on the interlocking series that criss-cross Orozco's work in whatever medium, whether it is an object or a photograph or a drawing.[12]

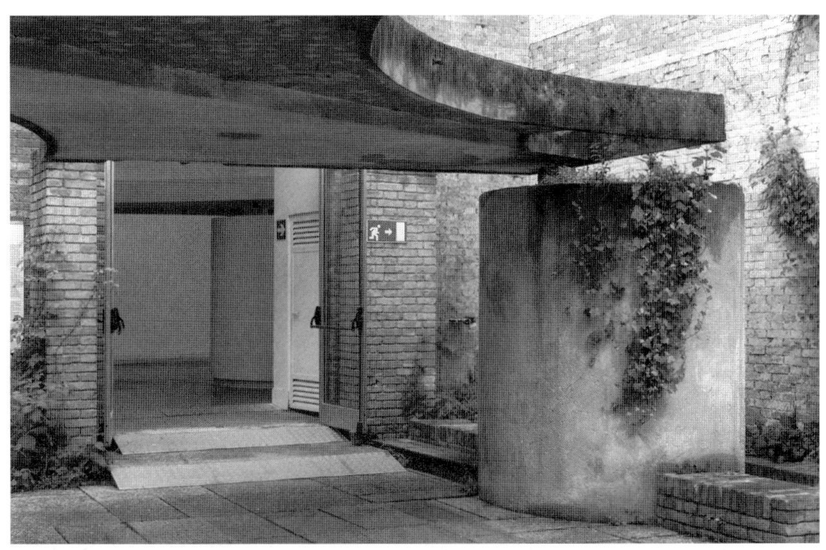

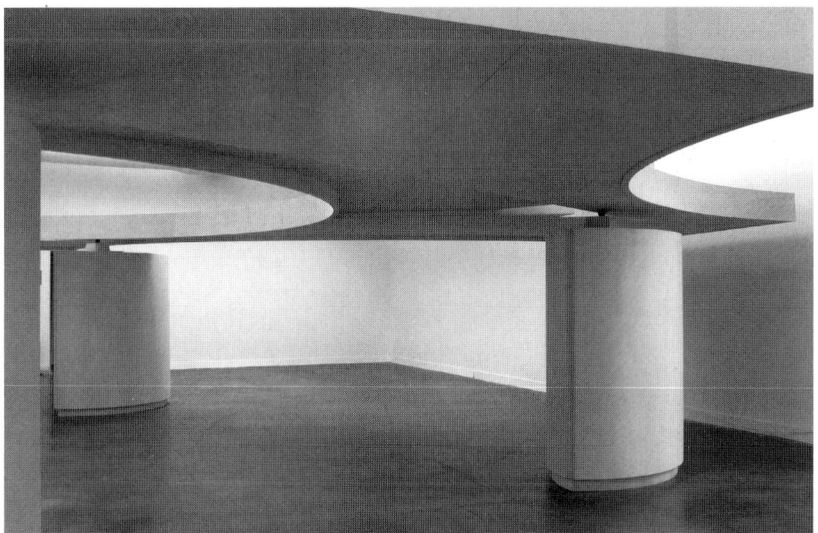

35, 36 *Shade between Rings of Air,* 2003.
Wood and metal.
45′ 11 3/16″ x 26′ 2 15/16″ x 9′ 2 1/4″.

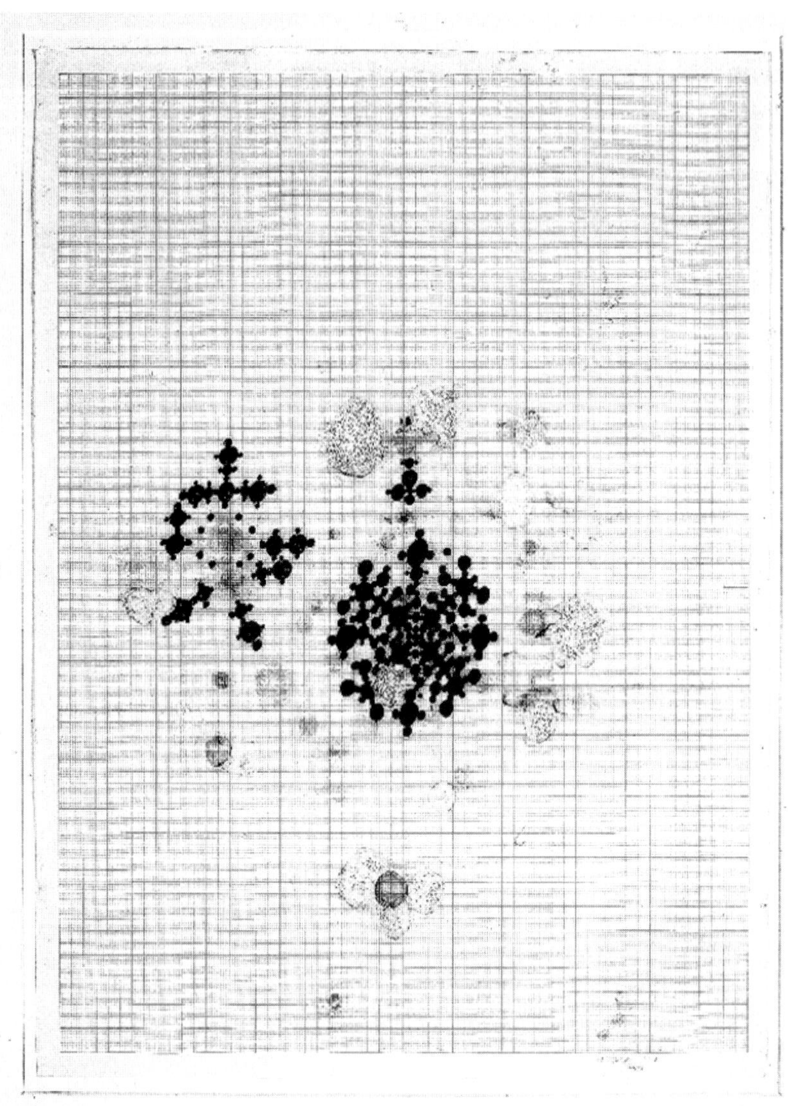

37 *Untitled* (*First Was the Spitting IV*), 1992.
Ink, graphite, and toothpaste spit on graph paper.
16 1/2 x 12 3/4 inches.

In some of the first drawings he did on graph paper, Orozco added small plasticine balls. He worked outward, expanding from the center. But there is an expansion, too, from the precise structure of the grid to the leaked stains left by the bits of plasticine. The elements of drawing in Orozco's work do not combine and compose but break up and disperse—and then reassemble in different combinations that are highly mobile. Since the mid-1990s, he has been producing computer-generated drawings, which he calls *Puddles* (1996–97) (fig. 38). These start off as templates of circles and grids generated by the click of a mouse. Then, at the center of each one, he adds more circles and half-circles, ellipses and eclipses, and it begins to unravel. Orozco creates a template and then colors bits of it in, from the center outward, by hand. In *Puddle 49* (1997), he has painted sections of the template in gouache, colored them in, and marked other squares out with little dots. In another drawing from 1996, he reverses the procedure and draws out little squares in pencil. Adding these elements destroys the coherence of the whole. Beginning at the center, he destroys the center.

Using geometric elements in this way invokes an earlier moment in the historical avant-garde, in particular the language of geometry as it was explored by the Russian constructivists. The monumental scale of the idea that art could transform life in the wake of revolution was encapsulated in what they preferred to call, not art, but "laboratory research." As Alexander Rodchenko put it, "Drawing as it was conceived in the past loses its value and is transformed into diagram or geometric projection."[13] Mechanical and technical drawing was the favored means to demonstrate the scientific validity of the practice. Although the endeavor was to avoid at all cost the arbitrary and the accidental, in practice, of course, the production of the work itself was makeshift, small-scale, and ephemeral. Rodchenko's folding hanging constructions are a testament to the kind of vast utopian idea that can fold away small (and vice versa). A vocabulary once associated with imagining a better socialist future now becomes a token or leftover of that earlier graphic model.

On the other hand, Orozco's use of computer-generated patterns is resolutely not about the technological or scientific, but points instead to the decorative and useless. A computer pattern has no greater use-value than spit or a spirograph. The computer seems more like a way of quickly making an infinite number of different possible patterns based on circles and grids; in the end it is more improvisatory than not. Orozco has said that when he made the series called the *Atomists* (1996) he had

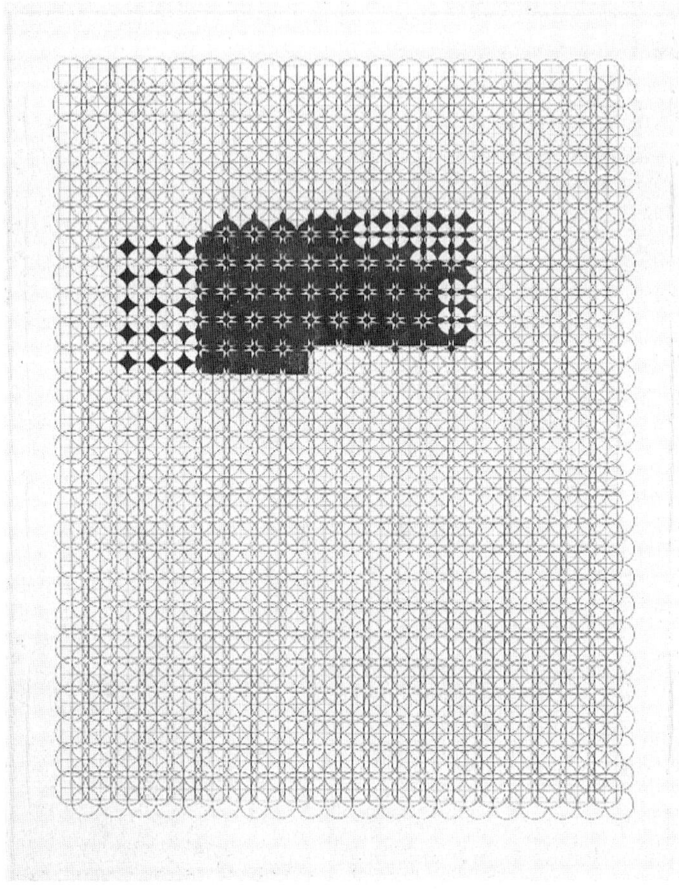

38 *Puddle 43*, 1997.
Gouache and graphite on inkjet print.
11 x 8 1/2 inches.

thought about the way Rodchenko combined graphics and photographs. In early Soviet film posters, Rodchenko shaped photographs into circles and other geometric patterns. Orozco reverses the process by superimposing circular geometric elements over photographs. It is as if he splits the term *photo-graph* into component parts. The split can be seen in a work like *Extension of Reflection* (1992), where rings of tire tracks pass through a puddle and intersect a manhole in a series of interlocking circles. He finds—or does he make?—the graphic in the photographic.

These are affinities across a great distance. A world shrinks and expands—could we say pneumatically? It is as if Orozco's use of repetition and repetitive patterns both draws widely disparate things close together and at the same time accentuates their differences. The computer-generated patterns he used in his small-scale drawings are enlarged in his series of *Blackboards* (1998), hung on the wall of the gallery, which in some instances spectators have been invited to draw on themselves. Even larger is the *Havre Caumartin* (1999) hung originally unframed, as a sort of double of the wall (fig. 39). These were produced by taking rubbings from the white circular mosaics in the Havre-Caumartin metro station, which Orozco was struck by when he went to Paris in the early 1980s. Blank walls might seem an unlikely thing to be struck by. They

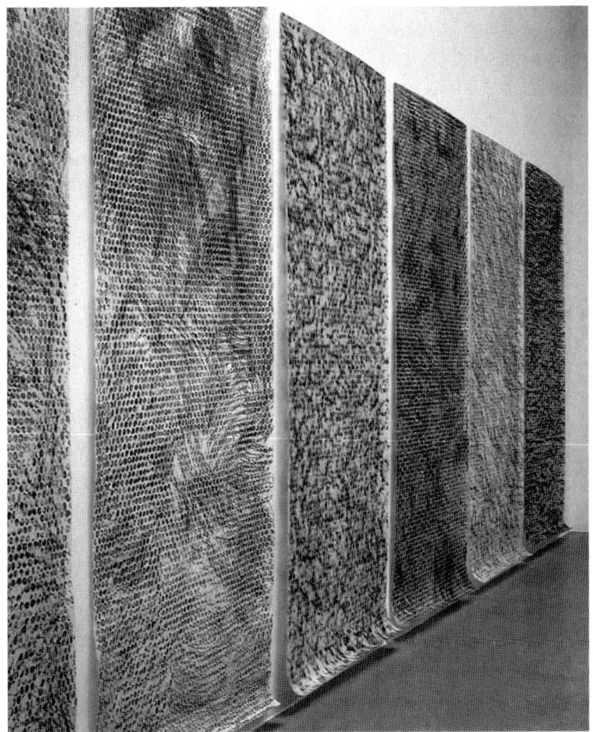

39 *Havre Caumartin,* 1999.
Installation view Galerie Chantal Crousel, Paris.
Graphite on Japanese paper, each 78 3/4 x 39 3/8 inches.
Image courtesy: Galerie Chantal Crousel, Paris.

are the kinds of surface you see without looking, yet they also stick in your mind as a leftover from a time when white circular mosaics signaled the new and the modern. Subway walls tend to be seen as dead spaces, but these frottages are intensely mobile and animated. Returning there some twenty years later, Orozco, with a number of assistants, made rubbings of surfaces that were, by then, far from new. What is striking about the series is how different each one turns out, depending on the pressure and the direction of the rubbed graphite. Orozco has commented on the bodily pressure required to make these large-scale drawings. There is a sense of intense physical labor here; the work is mechanical yet the results proliferate difference. Great swirls seem to break out in some, whereas in others the pattern is more regular.

In the foreword to his 1974 book *Species of Spaces*, French writer Georges Perec described how he was drawn to the ordinary spaces around us. Not the obviously spectacular though in reality "almost domesticated interplanetary, intersidereal or intergalactic spaces," but rather those closest to hand, like, he writes, the corridors of the Paris metro or a public park. To Perec the spaces we inhabit are broken into bits "and one of these bits is the metro corridor." A little further, he goes on: "At one time or another, almost everything passes through a sheet of paper, the page of a notebook, or of a diary, or some other chance support (a metro ticket, the margin of a newspaper, a cigarette paper, the back of an envelope, etc.) on which, at varying speeds and by different techniques depending on place, time or mood, one or another of the miscellaneous elements that comprise the everydayness of life come to be inscribed."[14] Rather than look toward the infinite, Perec wanted to capture that everydayness by describing the familiar spaces of an apartment or a street. The bits of experience that Perec selects—and the paper world that might offer that chance support he refers to—have a resonance, I think, for Orozco's work. But instead of opposing infinity to everydayness, Orozco positively invites that futuristic fantasy of planets and satellites, left over now as the residual forms of a utopian geometric vocabulary of intersecting circles. It is precisely the bringing together of an intergalactic space with a soap carton or a metro ticket that makes for Orozco's makeshift but spinning circuits.

The chance support of a wall, or a pavement, or a peso note, or an airline ticket. It is oddly apt that cultural critic Walter Benjamin chose the term *Anschaulichkeit* or "heightened graphicness" drawn from "the smallest and most precisely cut components" in his endeavor to "interpolate into the infinitesimally small."[15] These tokens or leftovers encapsulate everydayness. They link together like an endless series of coincidences. Orozco takes a ticket and superimposes upon it a series of intersecting circles. He may cut circles out, splicing a small thing into smaller segments. He may move its parts around, importing a globe from one ticket to another. Orozco has talked about how you can look at Kurt Schwitters's collages for a long time, "like complex space"—yet at the same time they are "just banal."[16] Some of the airline tickets have digital geometric grounds, while others are printed, superimposed by compass-drawn constellations or hand-colored in acrylic. One, *Red Air* (1997), uses the ticket's red carbon backing. He has cut out a circle, used it to rub through some of the ink in a residual trace that looks like a hovering aura, and then displaced it to the right (fig. 40). Turning around and turning over, parts are extracted and used to extend the collage beyond the edges of the ticket,

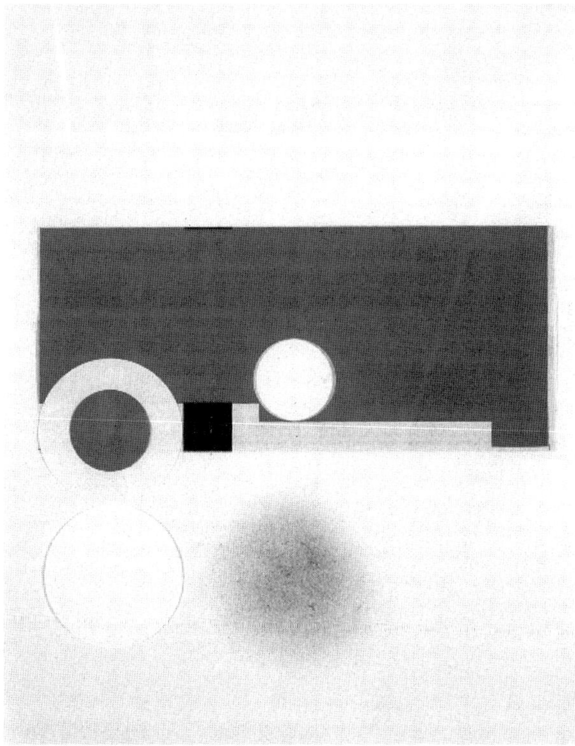

40 *Red Air*, 1997.
Cut-and-pasted red-carbon-coated airline ticket and red carbon on paper.
11 x 8 1/2 inches.

and to break it up into disparate elements. These collages seem to leap from one realm to another, covering a great distance in no time. Could this be space travel? It could be, on a very small scale—if you were able to keep it in your pocket.

It has often been remarked that Orozco is preoccupied with circles. But it is not only as a shape or form, but as a structure that circles interest him. There is a story by Jorges Luis Borges called "The Circular Ruins." In it the "obscure man" who is the protagonist comes from nowhere to the circular ruins of a burnt-out temple in the jungle. Few stories have such a vivid shape as this sequence of dreams. It is filled with circles but it also *is* a circle. It begins and ends at the same point. This story devours itself. It *is* a circular ruin, a perfect circle that disintegrates as it turns. The man is on a mission to dream another man and, as he dreams, the circular ruins give way to a circular amphitheater, only to reconfigure eventually as the beating heart he dreams, "the size of a closed fist." In the end he comes full circle to be consumed by fire at the very site where he began. And as he is engulfed in flames in a repetition of the original fire that destroyed the temple, "he understood that he too was a mere appearance, dreamt by another."[17] Circles do not simply provide the motifs in this story, they also describe its operation. To make a circle is also to break its circuit.

Orozco is not concerned with dreaming or dream narratives, but nonetheless he sets in train circuits that short-circuit. A formal vocabulary has been conventionally thought of as self-referential and hermetic. But Orozco's procedure is to use circles to *ruin* (there is no better word) rather than to endorse a formal system. Where formalism is a reductive logic, his logic of loops and circuits is expansive, encompassing ever more disparate elements in its orbit. The connections that are triggered proliferate outward. The spirographs being sold on a street with which I began were the subject of one of four photographs assembled in a work entitled *Discos Dados* (1997)—an arrangement that itself sets in train a rotation (fig. 41). In this constellation, spirograph patterns can move in the same orbit as a slightly blurred dandelion clock. The connections intersect with other work as if in a constellation, where the spaces between things become intensely animated. There is a drawing from 1995, for example, on a page of computer paper. It is full of circles but it can also be seen, if you like, as a circular ruin. There are coffee stains spread across it. There are patches of spat-out toothpaste. There are spirograph drawings, here partial and unfinished. These elements are all leftovers, just as the circles in his computer

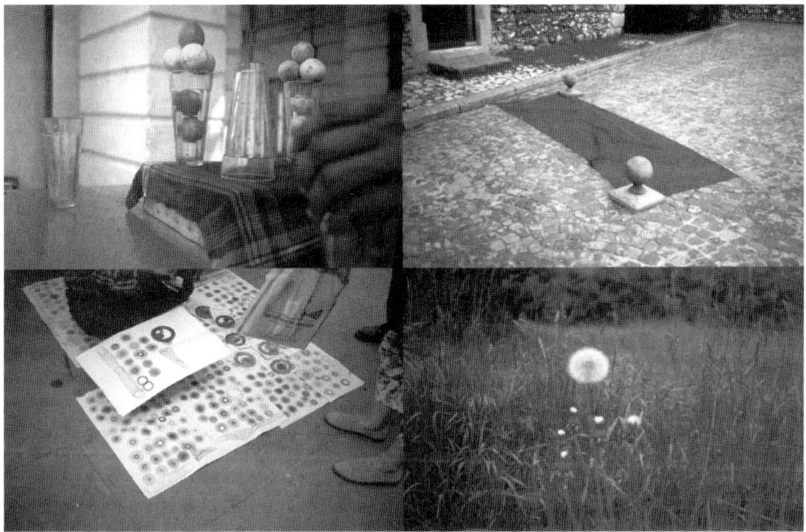

41 *Discos Dados,* 1997.
Inkjet print.
22 7/8 x 34 1/4 inches.
Image courtesy: Galerie Chantal Crousel, Paris.

drawings or *Puddles* are leftovers of a sort as well. And they cut across to others in the imagination, just as his incised circles cut through to other works he has made.

One of the striking things about Orozco's work is that it is impossible to think of his works singly—one immediately gives way to another. His method of displaying works on what he calls "working tables" creates the conditions for a field of action that is always multiple and always mobile, always in circulation. The tables, as much as a piece of paper, provide him with what he calls "platforms" on which to work. But they also provide a temporary, provisional ground that can be mobilized, not unlike Perec's chance supports. Orozco uses the temporariness of the exhibition to make this vivid, but it is there, already, in the work. It is as if the work that art does in the world, under present conditions, *has to be* contingent and incomplete. As a consequence, its radical possibility may precisely lie in its being something more like an exercise, something makeshift and improvisatory. Drawing is in no way the privileged site of such resistance, no more important than his sculpture or his photography. But Orozco's drawing nonetheless vividly demonstrates the twin action in his work, a ruination of center and an infinite dispersal of its elements. His endless series of divergences and recombinations are continually in movement in ways that dislocate the normal coordinates by which things are linked together in the world. As the French structuralist Claude Levi-Strauss put it, "If I may be allowed the expression, it is not the resemblances, but the differences, which resemble each other."[18] So it is that the smallest found object, like a spirograph, might intersect at an imaginary point with infinity—not because there is harmony in the universe, but on the contrary, because there is dislocation at the heart of our experience of the world we inhabit. The work of art is radically reconfigured in this process, its elements continually turning, its circular ruins creating momentum for generating the new.

Notes

1. See Deanna Petherbridge, for example, on the relationship between making and thinking in *The Primacy of Drawing: An Artist's View* (London: South Bank Center, 1991).

2. Gilles Deleuze, *Difference and Repetition* (London: Athlone Press, 1994), p. 14.

3. John Ruskin, *The Elements of Drawing* (London: George Allen, 1902), p. xvii. Quite inadvertently, of course, Ruskin's advice prefigures the chance effects of the found object as it was elaborated in surrealism. Margaret Iversen has recently discussed the genealogy of the found object with some reference to Orozco's work in "Readymade, Found Object, Photograph," *Art Journal* 62, no. 2 (summer 2004).

4. Ruskin, *The Elements of Drawing*, p. 43.

5. Yve-Alain Bois connects these two and discusses drawing "blind" in "Kelly's Trouvailles: Findings in France,'" in *Ellsworth Kelly: The Early Drawings, 1948–1955*, exh. cat. (Cambridge, Mass.: Harvard University Art Museums; Winterthur: Kunstmuseum Winterthur, 1999), pp. 23–24.

6. *Gabriel Orozco Photogravity*, exh. cat. (Philadelphia: Philadelphia Museum of Art, 1999), p. 148.

7. Ibid.

8. *Gabriel Orozco*: *Clinton Is Innocent*, exh. cat. (Paris: Musee d'art moderne de la Ville de Paris. 1998), p. 103.

9. Ibid.

10. Benjamin H. D. Buchloh, "Gabriel Orozco: The Sculpture of Everyday Life," in *Gabriel Orozco*, exh. cat. (Los Angeles: The Museum of Contemporary Art; Mexico City: Museo Internacional Rufino Tamayo, 2000), p. 91. In this volume, pp. 31–49.

11. *Clinton Is Innocent*, p. 103.

12. I describe this logic of series at work in Manzoni's *Achromes* of the late 1950s in my book *The Infinite Line* (New Haven and London: Yale University Press, 2004).

13. Alexander Rodchenko. "The Line," in *Rodchenko: The Complete Work*, ed. S. D. Khan Magomedov (London: Thames and Hudson, 1986), p. 294.

14. Georges Perec, "Species of Spaces," in *Species of Spaces and Other Pieces* (London: Penguin, 1997), p. 12.

15. Walter Benjamin, *The Arcades Project* (Cambridge, Mass.: Belknap Press of Harvard University Press, 1999), p. 931.

16. *Clinton Is Innocent*, p. 159.

17. Jorge Luis Borges, "The Circular Ruins," in *Labyrinths* (London: Penguin, 2000), p. 77. Molly Nesbit has discussed Borges in relation to Orozco in her fine essay "The Tempest," in *Gabriel Orozco*, ed. Alma Ruiz (Museum of Contemporary Art, Los Angeles, 2000). In this volume, pp. 59–83.

18. Claude Levi-Strauss, *Totemism* (Harmondsworth, Middlesex: Penguin, 1969), p. 77.

Cosmic Reification: Gabriel Orozco's Photographs (2004)

Benjamin H. D. Buchloh

We live on a sphere, we sculpt spheres and we make them sparkle.

—*Constantin Brancusi*

One day in the near future, the whole galaxy of objects will become readymades.

—*Marcel Duchamp*

When we try to identify the central features that conceptual artists introduced into the deployment of photography, three strategies emerge instantly as having been shared by all of the major photographic conceptualists (i.e., John Baldessari, Dan Graham, Douglas Huebler, Ed Ruscha).[1] The first feature was the systematic deskilling of photographic practices, a radicality that would soon enough come undone in the hands of the next generation of postconceptual artists (from Jeff Wall to Andreas Gursky), for whom the renewed emphasis on the carefully constructed and diligently produced photographic image would once again become central in the definition of artistic work. In manifest opposition to these tendencies, Gabriel Orozco resuscitates the conceptualists' original dismissal of photographic artistry and craft, and he continues their deskilling of the photograph: his images are distinguished neither by the high resolution generated by advanced digital camera and printing techniques, nor by extreme care and preparation in the preliminary phases of image selection and production. In fact Orozco's seemingly haphazard snapshot aesthetic conveys a sense of the universal equivalence and ultimate irrelevance of

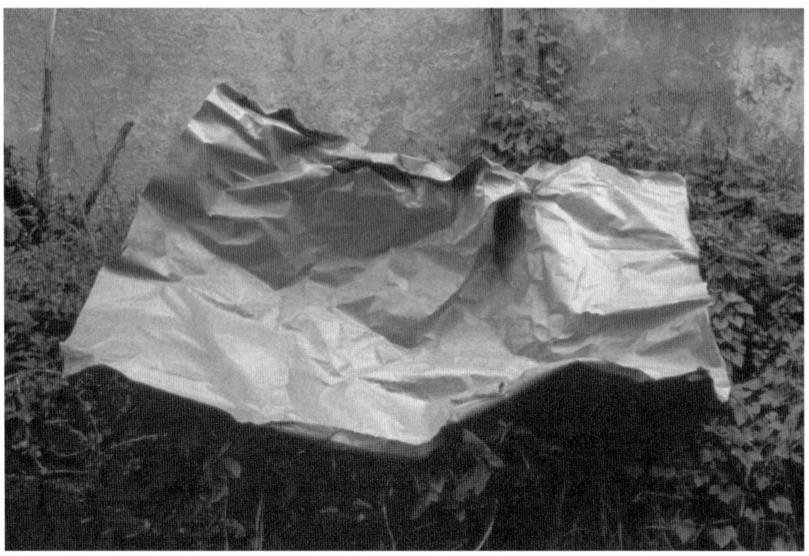

42 *Green Paper*, 1991.
Fuji crystal chromogenic archive C-print.
16 x 20 inches.

images (fig. 42). Least of all does he inflate his photographs to the size and scale of the very paintings that photographic conceptualism had, in fact, critically displaced.

The second feature of conceptualist photography had been its ostentatious denial of the viability of documentary and narrative traditions. Conceptualism acknowledged from the start the relative opacity, if not outright inaccessibility, of sociopolitical realities to photographic documentation. What is more, it even emphasized the insufficiency of the photograph to record the seemingly impenetrable complexities of a particular historical, ideological, or social formation. And the third manifest change in photographic practices, brought about by conceptualism's epistemological skepticism, is the development of new strategies that conceive and perform social interactions between a laboratory situation and theater (e.g., Vito Acconci, Dan Graham, Douglas Huebler), or that form collections of found semantic or architectural systems (e.g., Bernd and Hilla Becher, Ed Ruscha), or that initiate chance permutations or aleatory combinations of preestablished serial objects or modules (e.g., John Baldessari, Ruscha).

All of these strategies were clearly motivated by the insight that photography from now on could only give very limited and specific, and only relatively accurate, accounts of spatiotemporal and social processes. Furthermore, these strategies testified to the fact that photographs could at best enumerate and quantify objects, but not critically analyze their status and function in the variety of historical contexts that were photographically represented.

Conceptualist photography thus originated in a critique of some of photography's most traditional claims, namely to facilitate social transparency or to report on social subjects and relations, and to account accurately for quantifiable objects. In their stead, conceptualism now substituted lists and samples, staged systems and microsocial interactions, whose ephemeral, transient, and often random qualities only underlined the actually existing principles of a collectively governing anomic sociality, in which social relations, both those of production and those of communication, could no longer be properly detected or documented.

If the conceptual photograph succeeded in defining the authentic parameters of a highly mediated and alienated sociality and subjectivity, it had to confront a third, and equally complex, task: that of recording and representing a perpetually expanding, and increasingly unmanageable overproduction of objects. It does not appear accidental at all, then, that random accumulation and willful yet systematic quantifications would become the crucial strategies of conceptual art (both in its textual and its photographic operations). Two reasons come to mind in reconsidering the necessity of these enumerative and regulating formats. From now on, the list, the schema, and the permutation would appear as the solely adequate models of recording contemporary object relations.

First of all, if it had indeed become impossible to deploy photographs in order to situate a subject in its social context or spatiotemporal continuum, it would seem even more unthinkable to use photography to recognize a subject's relation to objects under the conditions of an advanced universe of reification. It is precisely in its attempt to give the most credible possible account of the subject's bodily situation in space and time, in its incessant recognition that only in a continuous fragmentation of that experience and in its quantificatory particularity, that conceptualist photography had also challenged traditional forms of sculptural production. In fact, it is on those grounds that it could claim to articulate the most credible parameters of sculpture available in the present. This necessitated, of course, a real insight into photography's capacities to collect and represent information on the subject's modalities of spatial and temporal experience within a medium that—all the more as a result of its manifest deskilling—was bonded to the everyday.

Second, one particular historically formed aesthetic had already corresponded to these advanced forms of totalized reification. Since the early 1950s, the experimental composer John Cage had abolished all criteria of aesthetic selectivity and artistic decision-making processes. Eventually this aesthetic was bound to have an effect even on a photographer's relationship to the world of objects. But while Cage's theory of a universal equivalence of all objects and structures had initially promised a total dissolution of traditions and a decentering of hierarchical criteria, it has clearly proven itself to be also an aesthetics of universal passivity and affirmation (as most obviously became the case in the work of Andy Warhol). The Cagean legacy would make it impossible even to begin the formulation of potential strategies for a radical reconceptualization of object experience, let alone for changing the object itself.

This Cagean aesthetic of a universal equivalence of all textures, procedures, and materials has had a tremendous impact on Orozco's conception of sculpture and photography in general, and on their interdependence in particular. From the beginning of his work, the multiplicity and simultaneity of seemingly incompatible materials and processes of sculptural production attest to that impact. Found industrial readymades (such as the *Yogurt Caps*, 1994, in his first exhibition at Marian Goodman Gallery in New York), or his *Penske Work Project* (1998), an unfathomable accumulation of construction debris, or a large-scale installation of suspended sheaths of lint (*Lintels*, 2001), are only a few examples of a truly inclusive and discontinuous theory of decentering and unstructuring the traditional materials and processes of sculptural production (fig. 43).

The same can be said for Orozco's seemingly random iconography of photographic images. These range from his careful arrangements in public spaces (e.g., *Crazy Tourist*, 1991, and *At the Cotton Factory*, 1993) and on the shelves of supermarkets (*Cats and Watermelons*, 1992), to the accidental encounters with natural phenomena (e.g., evaporation in *House and Rain*, 1998, or *Wet Watch*, 1993), to the circularity of the reverberating impact of stones in puddles (e.g., *From Roof to Roof*, 1993) (fig. 44). Those fortuitous relations of objects and constellations of materials, locations, and inhabitants seem to correspond to Orozco's search for sites and incidents where his complex concept of the sculptural can articulate itself in the

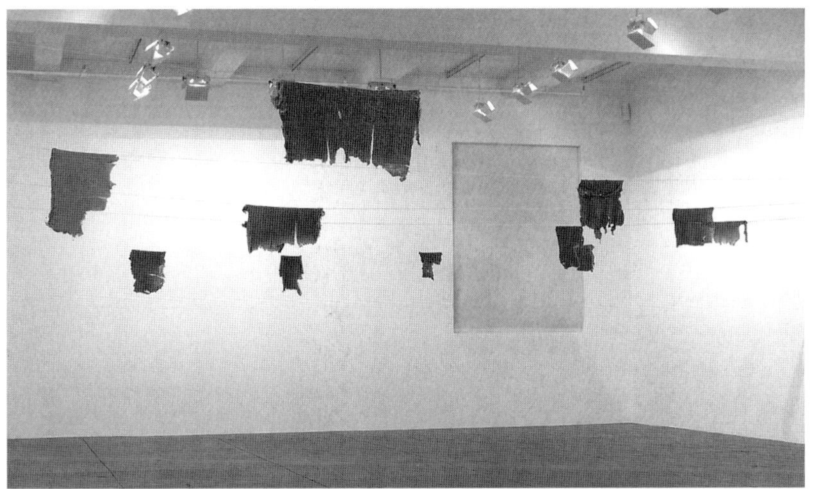

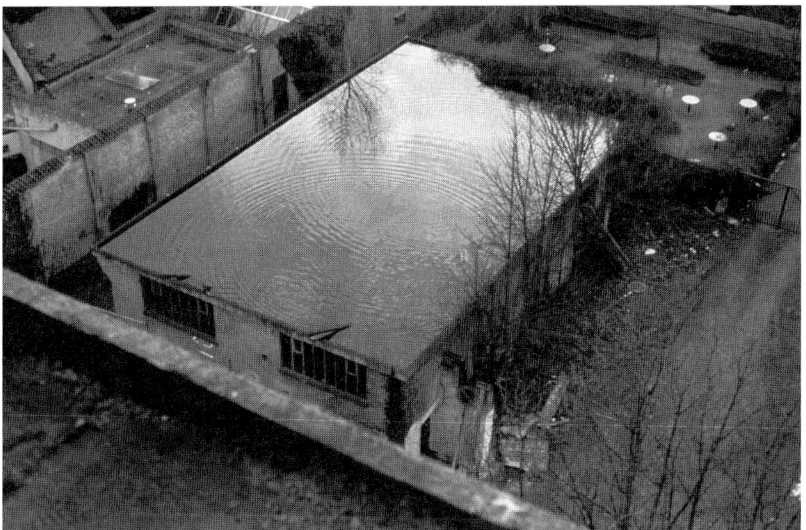

43 *Lintels*, 2001. Installation view,
Marian Goodman Gallery, New York.
Dryer lint. Dimensions variable.

44 *From Roof to Roof*, 1993.
Silver dye bleach print.
16 x 20 inches.

photographic record, almost as though sculpture was a naturally occurring phenomenon, and if not that, then certainly a project on the order of random play rather than planned production.

Obviously, Orozco's photographs (those taken by the artist as opposed to the found photographs of the *Atomists*, 1996, for example) simultaneously partake in this Cagean aesthetic and respond dialectically to the strategies of conceptual photography. The earliest example of Orozco's post-Cagean project of sculpture, and of the role that postconceptual photography can perform in this project, would be the image of a market in Brazil (*Crazy Tourist*). Here, at the end of the market day, the artist arranged a dozen or more found oranges on the empty display tables of the market's wooden stalls. A random constellation of found structures and the artistic intervention itself are defined as total equivalents. It becomes obvious that the wooden constructions or the roughly hewn and assembled stalls and tables are as "sculptural" as the artist's display of spherical objects (which, in their apparent state of untouched naturality, are used as stereometric and volumetric sculptural bodies).

A similar opposition is constructed in *At the Cotton Factory*, where Orozco has placed bundles of natural "raw" cotton fiber on the luggage racks of seemingly identical workers' bicycles parked in a perfect sequence at a textile factory (fig. 45). Beyond his obvious fascination with the sudden juxtaposition of the poverty of means (i.e., the naturally occurring fibrous material that had already played the role of nature in many of *arte povera*'s sculptural works, in particular those of Jannis Kounellis) with the mythical series of bicycle wheels, the photograph not only stages the work process itself and the misery of its compensation, it also reveals the cyclical conditions of exchange at the level of production: to leave the laborers at the end of the day with nothing but to continue to work the next day with the very same raw materials of production, so that the surplus value can be continuously extracted from their labor.

And in a recent photograph from a mosque in Timbuktu, Mali, *Total Perception* (2002), echoing the earlier constellations performed by the artist in *Crazy Tourist* or *At the Door of the Volcano* (1993), Orozco seems to have found his ideal of sculptural experience (fig. 46). Here it appears fully formed in a local mosque, without any intervention by the artist, as an encounter of chance, temporal flow, and the interaction of anonymous hands and materials in a natural environment. The random light projections (resulting from the perforation of deteriorated structures or the laceration of poor materials) appear almost as a historical travesty of

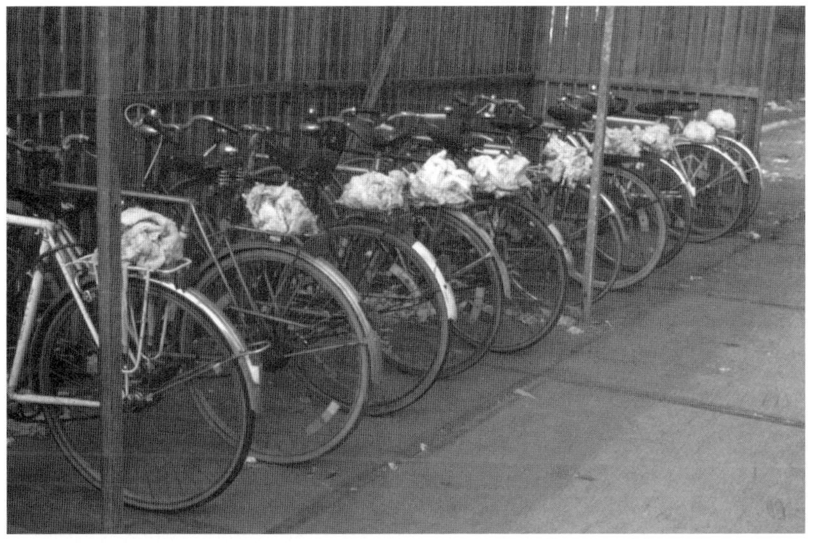

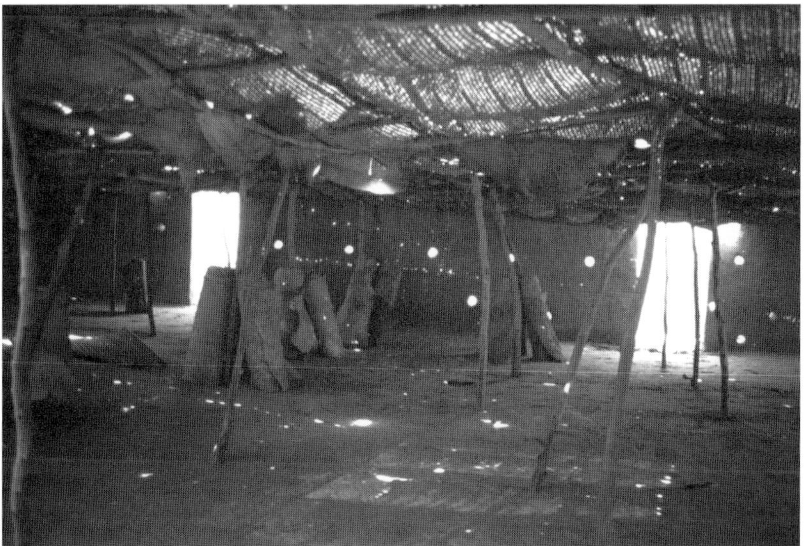

45 *At the Cotton Factory*, 1993.
Silver dye bleach print.
16 x 20 inches.

46 *Total Perception*, 2002.
Fuji crystal chromogenic archive C-print
mounted on Sintra board.
33 3/4 x 46 3/4 inches.

the techno-luminous projections of Laszló Moholy-Nagy's *Light Space Modulator* (1922–30). In their globular circularity these scattered projections of light fill this entire ritualistic space with the intensity of a desire for illumination and material transformation, a desire that is generally initiated in the circularity of shapes and spheres in Orozco's photographic and sculptural work. A burial ground, also in Timbuktu, seems to have offered Orozco the almost unrepeatable situation of a naturally occurring dialectic: if his images of the interior of the mosque offer the material evidence of a universally and collectively given access to the radiance of light and the emanation of energy, then the spherical clay containers serving as markers of the burial sites of the dead appear, if not as the literal *Urformen* of universal sculptural desire, then certainly as those of Orozco's conception of the sphere as sculpture. They offer concrete evidence of the body's maternal and material origins and destinations, and correspond to Orozco's profound sense that sculpture can articulate utopian aspirations as much as the conciliatory acceptance of the dystopian finality of the body.

When looking at images such as these for the first time, we might be led to believe that the artist is giving us images from zones of exemption, geopolitical spaces where the rules of universal reification have not yet taken hold, areas of refuge from the totalitarian control of production and consumption. But upon longer contemplation of the very same images, it becomes evident that they are not at all invoking the specificity of a regional culture (be it that of his native Mexico, or those countries where he has traveled such as India and Mali). Rather, while looking backward at these images of the pre-industrial past, Orozco seems to uncover their fate of being slated for an inexorable delivery to the very same principles of ecological devastation and the most ruthless forms of the exploitation of all available resources. After all, under the auspices of globalization, the hegemonic centers from within which he works and where he is situated as an artist are now incessantly expanding into those remaining parts of the world that have not yet been fully subjected to the universal principle of profit maximization. The continuously traveling artist, while not the perpetrator, is certainly the involuntary witness and messenger of that erosion.

Orozco's temporal tropes are those of a perpetual in-between, those of a temporal dialectic between the not yet and the nevermore. This is evident in the images of obsolescence that he collects as much as in the images of advanced forms of devastation, and neither obsolescence nor devastation bear any residual trace of a promise, let alone a transgressive utopian hope. In many instances, these constellations are directly derived from encounters with objects of design culture, either in a context of dislocation (e.g., *Dining Room in Tepoztlán*, 1995), or in a state of advanced dilapidation, as in the fixed row of *Waiting Chairs* (1998) (fig. 47).

These biomorphic Eames derivatives in the lobby of a museum in Calcutta at one time certainly held the promise of a better everyday life with which design deceived us into accelerated consumption. Now, in Orozco's photographs, these chairs are surmounted by greasy halos, the imprints of heads. And the pointless passing of time that the imprints have recorded stands in diametrical opposition to the pathos with which design once promised the new forms of everyday life. Or, in another example of the wreckages of design culture, we encounter a dramatically curvilinear wire frame (recorded several times, in water like a shipwreck and at other times as though abandoned and drifted onto a beach). This furniture concoction might have been at one time a fashionable Bat Chair; now it merely casts its linear shadows, extending and doubling as a skeleton of its once utopian insinuations. In a typical sculptural intervention, Orozco has affixed a spontaneously modeled sphere of wet sand onto the center of the

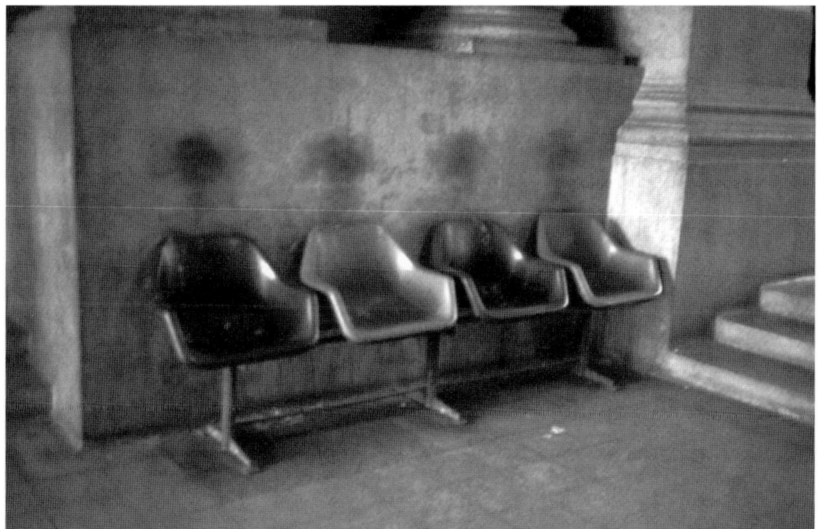

47 *Waiting Chairs*, 1998.
Silver dye bleach print.
16 x 20 inches.

ruins of a chair, anchoring it in its state of pointless dislodged drifting, and renewing the once-promising molecular circularity and energetic expansion that had initially inspired its design. Thus the transient sphere reminds us that a never-receding energetic process of flow and transformation continues even under the conditions of total dereliction and reification.

Both images also give us rather clear indications of the spectrum of forces and processes that Orozco considers to be valid, if not of the essential strategies and materials of his sculptural pursuits. These are first of all the traces of the flowing of time and the natural transformation of matter, preferably left by others rather than imposed by the artist. In that regard the shadowy grease marks are as crucially sculptural as is the artist's breath in his image *Breath on Piano* (1993), the condensation of water contained in the shell of *Wet Watch*, or the evaporating veils of water in his *House and Rain*.

Even, or we should say, in particular, his strangely atypical yet recurring images of animals (after all, there are never any images at all of human subjects in Orozco's own photographic work) articulate precisely the final condemnation of natural experience to the fallen world. Each and every one of them (*Sleeping Dog*, 1990; *Horse*, 1992; *Bat Dog*, 1993) confronts us with states of extreme ambiguity: between death and sleep, between resuscitating rest and definitive decay, between joy and rage (fig. 48). And hardly an image could proclaim the final loss of the natural more tragically, almost comically, than the lonely dog sitting in a pavilion staring out at a vast landscape or at the ocean in the manner of a Romantic landscape painting, where the subject had positioned itself at the frontiers of infinite nature to find its constitution, if not its liberation (*Dog in Tlalpan*, 1992).

Sculpture at this point in history inhabits the paradoxical space of having to refuse objecthood and simultaneously to reassert it. If the subject's bodily situatedness in the spatiotemporal continuum is one of the parameters within which sculpture is perpetually redefined, then its opposite would seem to be the subjection to the object, that is to say, the reigning conditions of object experience within which subjectivity is currently constituted. While these might not be the two most important conditions of sculptural reflection, it could certainly be argued that both parameters are integral to any theorization of sculpture in the present.

One particular group of images in Orozco's oeuvre inverts almost all of the principles governing his photographic production: the *Atomists* from 1996 (fig. 49). As with Orozco's own photographs, it is immediately evident that the artist has contemplated these found images primarily from

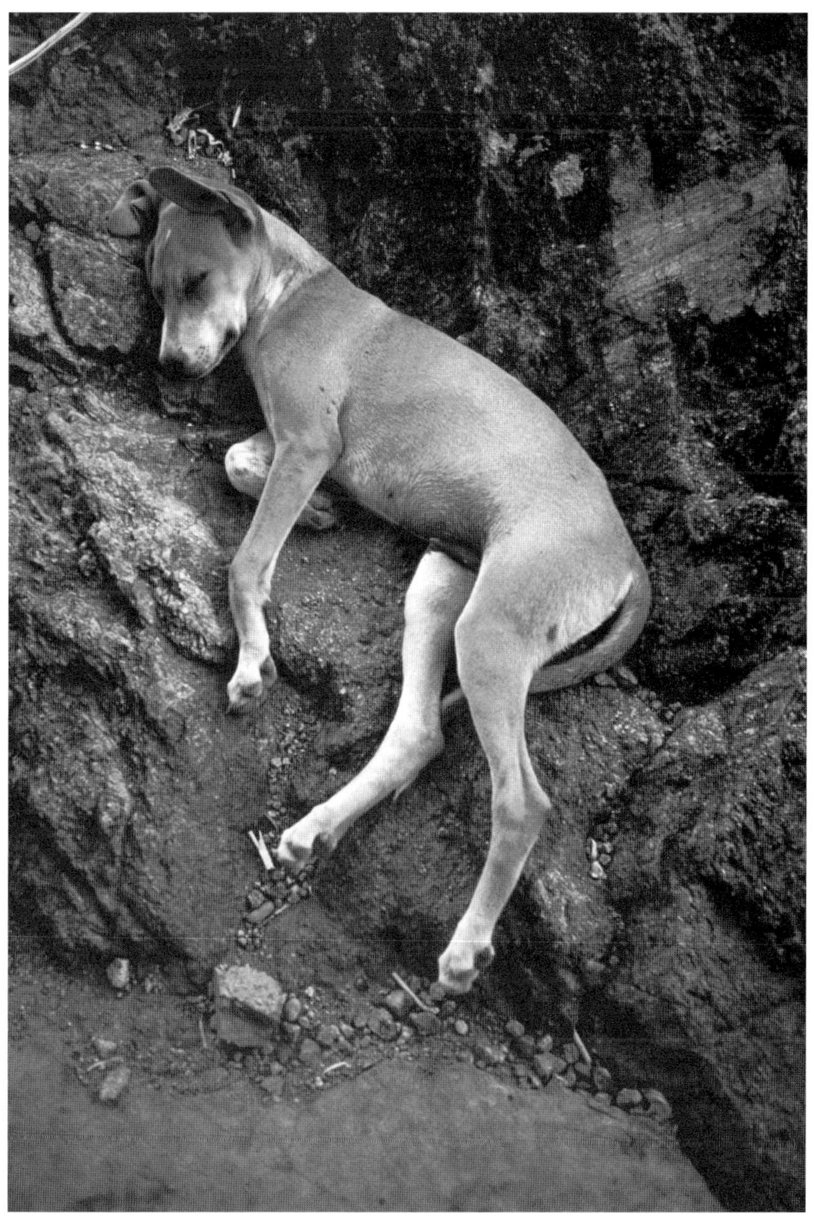

48 *Sleeping Dog*, 1990.
Silver dye bleach print.
20 x 16 inches.

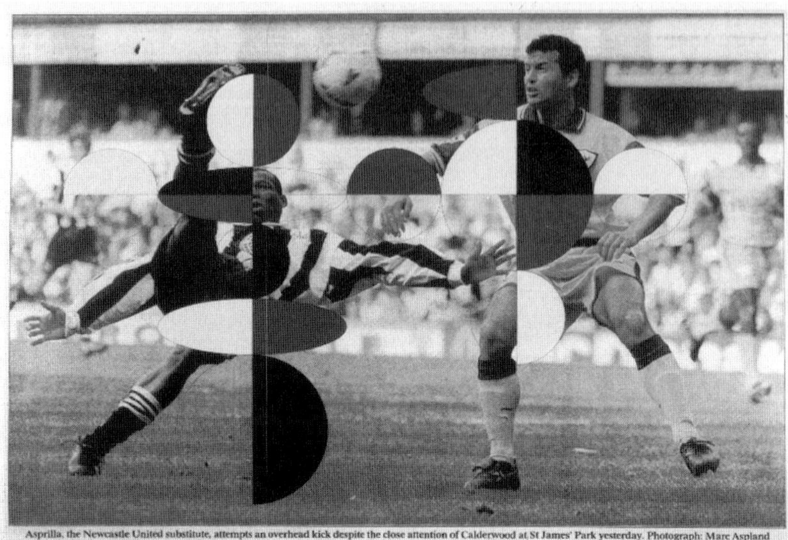

49 *Atomists: Asprilla*, 1996.
Inkjet print.
78 3/4 x 115 inches.

the perspective of the sculptor, yet from a position dialectically opposite to the one that defines his own image production. Apart from the fact that these are the only works by Orozco that deploy found photographs (drawn from daily newspaper images of spectacle sports), they are also the only images that deal programmatically with the representation of the human figure.[2] Moreover, all of these photographs have been recorded by professional sports photographers with the highest professional and technical competence. Once selected by Orozco, these images receive their painterly demarcations and are then enlarged with digital copying technology.

For each work in the *Atomists* series, Orozco chose images of mastered movement and arrested temporality. They represent moments of extreme bodily and psychological tension, industrial images of a ludic climax—moments, one could suggest, whose temporal intensity would decide, as the sociologist and film historian Siegfried Kracauer once famously stated, whether the photograph would trigger the athlete's transportation into the spheres of fame.

Painterly or photographic representations of the athlete in action constitute a peculiar and contradictory iconography in twentieth-century painting and photography, one that is clearly resuscitated in Orozco's *Atomists.* And though we should be careful not to compare two moments as different as those of 1912–13 (the year of Robert Delaunay's *The Cardiff Team*) and of 2004, a few historical remarks might be illuminating for the work in the present.

When the image of bodily performance enters the iconography of modernism, it originates more often than not in Etienne-Jules Marey's (and to a lesser degree in Eadweard Muybridge's) strictly scientific, chronophotographic images in which the performance of the body in a spatiotemporal continuum had not only become representable, but could also be analyzed and measured for the first time. Chronophotography was not only integral to the introduction of Taylorism, but also to the systematic improvement of the body's athletic performance powers.

Thus chronophotography contributed not only to the formation of modern athletic culture, but even more to the artistic celebration and cultural representation of that phenomenon. Increasingly, its social functions were to stabilize the industrial proletariat through physical exercise, but even more so through the production of mass cultural entertainment. Expanding further and further as the twentieth century progressed, the ideology of spectacle sports culminated in the mass cult's function to uphold collective anesthesia and incompetence in the subject's political self-constitution and self-determination in the processes of production.

Even though the cult of the athlete in the beginning of the twentieth century celebrated first of all the successful symbolic adaptation of the human body to the accelerated tasks of the daily performances of production, the artistic iconography of the gymnasts, athletes, and soccer players, in works from Delaunay to Kasimir Malevich, from Fernand Léger to El Lissitzky to Alexander Rodchenko, articulated a set of counteraspirations to the ruling ideological dimensions of sport. The avant-garde's cult of a successful fusion of the primitive inertia of the human body with the perfection of the productive machine in celebratory images of the robotic athlete was, of course, initially driven by its desires to disseminate the myth of a naturally given excellence and a universally accessible equality of the human subject, and therefore the images of athletes increased the evidence (along with those of the heroized worker) of an emerging historical reality of a classless society.

It became increasingly compelling, however, to recognize that the public spectacularization of the athletic body inevitably served to compensate for the systematic depoliticization of the subject in the mass public sphere. And that an increase in a celebratory approach to the athletic mass subject almost inevitably signaled either tendencies toward, or an already fully established condition of, totalitarianism.

Orozco's *Atomists* all partake in that complex iconographic tradition, and they are all the more remarkable for their modification of its contradictions. And if the human body appears in all of the *Atomists* in extreme forms of spatiotemporal animation, one might well consider them first of all as object lessons for the artist's sculptural projects. After all, it is here that we see some of the most advanced contemporary models synthesizing the subject's somatic, temporal, and spatial conditions of experience. Yet the subject in these images does not just appear as an example of exceptional bodily accomplishment and physical control, but also as a subject heroized in spectacle sports. In fact, one could argue that precisely because these images represent a spectacular synthesis of athletic discipline and gamesmanship under the conditions of an extremely industrialized leisure culture, they also confront Orozco with the precarious and problematic conditions of his own practices as an artist and sculptor in the present moment.

The industralization of ludic experience applies to artistic production at this point no less than it applies to spectacle sports, and as such it not only prohibits the redemption of the subject's desire for play as the primary motivation for a real unalienated human productivity, it fulfills the social function of a spectacular substitution for the eternally postponed promise of an abolition of alienated labor.

In almost all of the *Atomists* (except two out of fifteen) the object of the athletic pursuit is a ball, a spherical object, prominently visible in most of the photographs. The sphere or ball, as the ontological object of the desire to overcome spatiotemporal limitations while playing, establishes a manifest correlation between the circularity of Orozco's abstract design and the photographic representation of the spherical object. The incorporation of dynamism, speed, velocity, and physical movement has haunted twentieth-century art and sculpture since its beginning: after all, why would the very objects that promise radical transformation themselves remain static? Kinesthesia, the perception of temporality in spatiality, was the promise of futurism and of constructivism, the sculptural breakthrough of Naum Gabo's *Vibrating Column* (1921) as much as of Marcel Duchamp's *Bicycle Wheel* (1913). For Orozco, the kinetic performance of the athlete's body in his series the *Atomists* is just one of the examples of an unachievable sculptural synthesis, an ideal of velocity and bodily experience compressed into a manifest and concrete time-space continuum.

Beyond the selection process itself, Orozco's confrontation (and obvious fascination) with these hyperbolic images of performing athletes, with their bodily perfection and mastery of exceptional skills, seems to provoke an artistic response of almost elated modesty. Thus, in a careful and studious execution, Orozco constructs exact circular or elliptical segments with a compass and ruler, either as mere ink drawings or painted with tempera as monochrome shapes, and positions them within the photographic forcefields of spatiotemporal and specular arrest.

The circle is a strangely contested and precarious form in twentieth-century sculpture: for the most time absent, if not prohibited, it stages appearances nevertheless, furtive and marginal, again and again, only to disappear from the morphology and the doxa of what sculpture can tolerate and sustain in its formal vocabulary. Approximating the circle again and again, as if in a perpetual contestation, Constantin Brancusi in fact only adopted it in the design of elements of his bases or in the functional, almost utilitarian design of his *Table and Stools* (1937) as part of his larger project for Tîrgu Jiu. Painting, by contrast, has been more tolerant of the form, but even there pure circularity remained relatively rare: from Delaunay's *First Disk* (1913) to Rodchenko's compass drawings for his *Linear Constructions* (1920) and the group of extraordinary paintings entitled *Concentration of Color* (1920), culminating, of course, in his concentric and collapsible sculptures such as *Hanging Circular Construction* (1921).[3]

The hermetic and perfect form of the circle was apparently perceived for the longest time as a blockage to formal invention and artistic creativity. Its form is too parthenogenetic; there is an excess of self-enclosure that seems to exclude artistic interventions of any kind. The circle even exceeds the boundaries of the most radical efforts of playing the self-reflexive object against the authorial subject. The very fact that the perfect circle is a purely human construct proves that its vacuity or perfection can be neither improved nor enriched.

There is, of course, an additional, reasonable assumption to be made about modernism's slow adaptation of the circle. The geometric forms of the rectangle and the square (and the stereometrically corresponding forms) had articulated Cartesian rationality in the construction and representation of space, but as such they were, of course, also profoundly gendered. The circle as a radically alternate model of spatial organization dialectically abolishes perspectival directionality; it equates horizontality and verticality, and it dissolves what had been traditionally a clear hierarchical system of instructions for how to see and how to position oneself in space. By contrast, the almost autistic form of the circle is nonlinear and lends itself neither to the task of measuring and quantificatory delineation, nor to the task of temporal tracing.

In Orozco's *Atomists* only one circular unit is defined at a time, since each circular emblem is extracted from the photograph as a colored pixel that anchors the geometric construction and determines the chromatic definition of the abstract form (as though it were defining a digitally mediated version of divisionism). Thus Orozco conceives of a manifest opposition between the elementary image of abstraction, the molecular or the atomist conception of matter and energy, and confronts it with the representation of technology and the spectacularized and instrumentalized athletic body in many ways reminiscent of the extreme incompatibility already operative in Delaunay's *The Cardiff Team* or even in Lissitzky's photograph of a runner where the denotative figuration representing the athlete's body in spatiotemporal expansion is opposed to that of the molecular abstraction, based on a geometrically preconceived form of vertical striation and thus is derived from and directs the spectator into a totally different order of representation.

What Orozco actually constructs in these paradoxical networks of circular and elliptical forms that spread over the photograph's spectacular figuration is not at all a variation on the classical modernist grid in the manner of Piet Mondrian. It is a structure of spatial and cognitive mapping whose circularity, dynamic openness, and propulsion counteract pictorial concepts of Cartesian space with the dynamics of an atomistic image of energy and expansion. Simultaneously, it subverts the total arrest of the forces of self-realization and articulation that the technologically produced images of spectacle sports have produced.

Orozco's *Atomists* are similar in that respect to one of the greatest icons of postwar visual culture: Jasper Johns's target paintings. Here, the insistence on the ludic dimension of aesthetic production and reception had been equally fused with a radically altered conception of painterly and visual space. In a manifest declaration of opposition and of a simultaneous redemption of the betrayed aspirations of abstraction from Mondrian to Newman, Johns reinscribed the primary colors ostentatiously in a structure of circularity (rather than within the traditional rectangularity of the grid). More than that, he explicitly counteracted modernism's progressive insistence on primacy with a dimension of the subject's own access to the ludic experience, as though the ludic, then and ever since, were the only accessible modus for radical transcendence of reification.

Thus the return of geometric abstraction and of primary colors or monochrome color segments in Orozco's *Atomists* (preceded by a set of at first rather enigmatic lightboxes that Orozco had produced in the previous year, which had simply carried segmented circles in the primary colors alone) is not a mere resuscitation of long-lost modernist paradigms. Quite the opposite is the case: in its succinct simplicity, in the almost scholastic execution of the minute geometric forms, in its seemingly naive trust in the indestructible powers of pure abstract form and color, the *Atomists*' painterly elements provide us with a rather subversive constellation. They formulate the most elementary articulation of the self and of the subject with the universally available tools and languages of abstraction. Thus they construct a denial of the universal validity of the extreme forms of spectacularized figuration in media imagery that have become totalizing and incessant: our daily Riefenstahl.

Notes

1. Gabriel Orozco has asked me to clarify the somewhat enigmatic title of this essay. It is well known that artists in the twentieth century revert to the spiritualist references of their work, and of abstraction in particular, precisely at those moments when the artistic orientation, let alone implementation of concrete political, social, and ideological changes by cultural means, appear to be definitively foreclosed. These cosmogonic longings appear either in response to the massive return of ideological constructs that convince us that cultural practices *qua* culture never had the right nor the reason to make extra-aesthetic claims in the first place. They emerge from the condition that the cultural apparatus has been so systematically severed or voluntarily detached from all interactions with any dimension of social reality that the transference to the cosmic origins of avant-garde abstraction becomes once again the first and the last resort.

Under the current circumstances of an electronically implemented global system of control and consumption, it cannot surprise us that the aesthetic impulse toward the abolition of reification and defetishization would have to be deflected toward those spheres and realms (the cosmic ones in particular) where the laws of total reification seemingly do not yet apply. I thought my two epigraphs had indicated that this dialectic of total reification and cosmic longing had been articulated with artistic means before, in fact that it had a long history in the twentieth century.

Obviously, the conditions of avant-gardist culture of the 1920s are almost totally incomparable with our own in the present. But in order to support my seemingly speculative argument, I will add yet another statement, made in 1931 by Walter Benjamin in his essay "A Short History of Photography," where these contradictions are even more explicitly spelled out. Better yet, they are formulated in the context of the problems of the photographic practices that concern us here as well:

> What is creative in photography is its submission to fashion, and, not surprisingly, its motto is "The World is Beautiful." In that title, a tendency reveals itself that can position the montage of a soup can in cosmic space, but it cannot grasp any of the most elementary human contexts. Even with its most oneiric subjects, it still initiates more of the object's saleability than its cognitive insights into social reality. Since the true visage of this type of photography is advertisement, (de-)construction would of course be its rightful counterpart.

Or, if theories remain ultimately unconvincing to practitioners, allow me to point to a strikingly enigmatic image produced by Marcel Duchamp as a cover for the American journal *View* (vol. 5, no. 1) in 1945. Here it is not a soup can montaged into cosmic space, but a cobweb-covered bottle of Bordeaux that literally floats like a spaceship in the galaxy Duchamp would speak of later. Mysteriously, the bottle emits clouds of smoke and steam, like a rocket ship or a pipe. As we try to read the vintage of the Bordeaux label on the bottle, we discover soon enough that it does not only spell out the name Duchamp, but it is actually a copy of Duchamp's military identity card, clearly suggesting that the inevitable outcome of total reification is the need for war.

2. Of course, there are, as usual, exceptions to this overall principle governing Orozco's photographic production, the most notable being an image entitled *Maria* (1995), depicting the artist's wife from the back, standing on a beach, seemingly contemplating rocks. The others are two or three pictures (in more than 150 that have been defined as photographic works) in which children or figures appear from a considerable distance to be engaged in a variety of games (flying kites, playing ball, etc.).

3. It only appears at first sight that the circular and the spherical are less prominent in the modernist paraphrases of geometric and stereometric matrices than the square or their rectangular counterparts. What is significant, however, is the fact that in spite of their frequency, not to say ubiquity, the circular abstractions of modernist painting have always remained in a secondary or subservient position to the Cartesian rationality embodied in angular spatial constructions. There is, of course, a *Black Circle* painting by Malevich (1923), but it has remained relatively unknown, certainly by comparison to the prominence of the *Black Square* (1915). Equally one could say that Sophie Taeuber-Arp's extraordinary circular paintings of the mid-1930s have not received even the beginning of the historical and scholarly comprehension that they deserve, all the more so since it is in Taeuber-Arp's work that one could trace the logic of her formal and feminist critique of the hegemony of Cartesian rationality in pictorial and sculptural abstraction.

In the postwar period, the subversion of that hegemony is continued most brilliantly in the work of Jasper Johns and Kenneth Noland. These artists clearly positioned themselves against the seeming universality of rectangular abstraction (as embodied, for example, in the work of Ad Reinhardt or Barnett Newman). Yet this opposition would only culminate again with the work of Eva Hesse, for whom the circular morphology became a central strategy to literally reembody abstract form with psychosomatic dimensions. If any predecessor for Orozco's continuous insertion of circularity and the spherical into traditional modernist pictorial and sculptural orders could be suggested, it would be the work of Hesse.

Crazy about Saturn: Gabriel Orozco Interviewed by Briony Fer (2006)

BRIONY FER: Gabriel, I would like to ask you first to say something about the position or space you wanted to occupy as an artist at the beginning of the 1990s. How would you describe your position around at that time?

GABRIEL OROZCO: When I started to do my work in the early 1990s, my proposition was to deal with production and distribution and perception in a different way. I did not like mainstream '80s art, and I didn't believe in market movements and how they were producing and distributing work. I was skeptical of the '80s. I think it was a generational thing. I thought it was naive the way the media and popular culture were used. I wanted to use the infrastructure, the museums and galleries, in a different way and also to behave as an artist in a different way. I did not want to have a studio. I didn't want to have a big production machine. I wanted to deal with real life, with common things. Some of the results were surprising to people, from yogurt pots or a shoe box, to oranges at MoMA, to *The Yielding Stone*. Imagine them next to more spectacular art and then you can see the position I wanted to take.

FER: And how did this position relate to your own previous work? By this time you had already abandoned painting. Yet you studied as a painter, you started out as a painter. And you have in the last few years taken up painting again, which we shall talk about later. You made paintings up to the point you left to spend a year in Madrid in 1985, and you even made some on your return to Mexico.

OROZCO: I think I really stopped painting in Madrid. I did not like the kind of painting around in the '80s, the big formats, the German school of neo-expressionistic painting, which was very influential in Mexico. In a way, I was not so much against painting, but against that kind of noisy, sentimental painting. We also had a neo-Mexican tradition in painting that was kitsch and empty.

FER: Even though when you returned to Mexico you carried on making paintings for a while, as well as making actions and interventions out on the street?

OROZCO: I was taking fragments from Russian icons. I loved those paintings. I also like the objects, the thick wood, the abstract shapes, the gold. It is painting but with a readymade, conceptual approach. I didn't feel I was a painter. I was analyzing a painting, like a fragmented readymade and then presenting it. I did a show in Mexico of that work in 1989. Then I stopped completely. Then I started to move and travel, and use photography more and more.

FER: When, then, did you begin to use photography?

OROZCO: When I was in Madrid I didn't have a camera. The first time I used a camera I borrowed a camera from friends. It was here when there was the earthquake in Mexico in 1985. Many of my friends were going out taking photographs. I took some photos of the earthquake and the ruins, many details. But I didn't like photography that much then.

FER: So when did a camera come to seem like a useful tool to you?

OROZCO: When I lived in Brazil for four months in 1991. That was when I did *Crazy Tourist* with the oranges in the market. I was working outside on the street much more consciously and systematically then. I started to use photography at that time, about 1989, when the small automatic cameras came on to the market. Before that the cameras were too big. The portability of the camera was very important to me.

FER: You have spoken before about your exposure to *arte povera* when you were in Madrid, as well as to the more recent work of British sculptors like Tony Cragg. You could see these as sculptural alternatives to a minimalist aesthetic that has clearly never interested you. You have also spoken also about the importance of John Cage to you—a vitally important figure to you still, I think, especially his ideas of chance. But you have not spoken so much about what you were exposed to in Brazil.

OROZCO: I was following my girlfriend, that's why I went down to Brazil. But when I was there I was struck first by the physicality of the whole urban and natural landscape. My perception of my surroundings became much more sculptural than visual (even though I tend to be very visually orientated as a person). It was then that I got very interested in Brazilian art of the 1950s, like [Hélio] Oiticica and Lygia Clark. Before that I didn't know them. And I also got to know the work of contemporary Brazilian artists like Tunga and Cildo Meireles. I found I was in tune with other artists even though I was doing rather different things. I was not so close to Mexican artists then, even earlier conceptual artists. I was interested in sculpture, and in Mexico we don't have a very strong tradition in sculpture since colonial times. Of course, we have fantastic sculpture from the pre-Hispanic period, but less so after that.

FER: Did you see Lygia Clark's work in terms of sculpture, or action, or event?

OROZCO: I was interested in the sculptural aspect of the objects she made, even in the most action-oriented work. What I wanted to see was the final object and what intrigued me was their physicality.

FER: Can you say something about your relation to the material of sculpture? Perhaps you could begin by talking about *The Yielding Stone*, the work you made in New York in 1992.

OROZCO: I was working in plasticine on something else. Trying to make a shape out of plasticine, I always ended up with a dirty ball. I went to the roof of my apartment and rolled it to try to get the imprints. In New York, you have a black material on the roof [so] when you rolled it, it got really dirty. I had to accept the vulnerability of the material in terms of shape and dirtiness. Plasticine never hardens. It's always changing, always dirty, absorbing all the dust and the imprints. Then I did it bigger, and made it my own weight. That was the limit I placed on it, my own weight, my body rolling this other weight. I didn't want to make any kind of performance out of it, only some photographs.

FER: How would you describe the status of the photographs?

OROZCO: This is an important parenthesis. I distrust the documentation of the 1970s, where the documentation was what ended up in the museum. Amazing things that were happening outside the museum ended up as relics, after. I didn't like the way documentation came to look like the leftovers of a party. I try not to show documentation in that way. Not as an archive. I think the experience has to be a real one, interacting with a phenomenon, not a representation of one. It has to be something concrete and three-dimensional. When I cycle through puddles on my bicycle, I am alone. When I place my breath on a piano, I am alone. I do not have an audience. The photo is a witness of this intimacy. It is very important that I don't carry a lot of things with me, that I am empty handed. So I work in these actions with the materials that I find. I find the oranges on the floor. I find a puddle. This is an important difference for the status of the photograph in my work from that of conceptual artists in the 1970s. The status of the photograph hasn't got to do with scale or the size. The point is more about making something present, that inevitably, the only way to see something is through the photograph. The status of inevitability justifies it.

FER: Perhaps your work points to a contradiction that was always there in conceptual photography from the outset, but repressed. That is to say, you activate the space between the action and object and the photograph. In your work, it is hard to separate them out at a conceptual level, even though they exist in different media. For you, there seems to be no such thing as a single object. It's always already multiple. One event proliferates in time as well as different spatial contexts. Mobility triggers more mobility.

OROZCO: That's the key of my intentions. I always say that the work doesn't end in the museum but keeps going. The problem with the document as a kind of evidence is that it is an end. It is somebody else's leftovers, which creates a kind of intellectual passivity. When you have an object like *The Yielding Stone* it is still "breeding" and "living" that substance. It is something like an animal with an organic presence. My photography, of course, is a document, but it does not pretend to finish there; the event is still happening. You forget the photograph, but see the phenomena, the puddle or the breath. The photograph is like the shoe box. It is a recipient. That is an important idea for me. It is a recipient for the spectator. The status of the document is secondary, the phenomenon is primary.

FER: How does that idea affect the way you have shown your work?

OROZCO: I didn't want to show, for example, forty Schwalbe. The way I showed that work (1995) allowed you to walk along it, like putting a movie frame by frame in a room. It is always the same photo, but at the same time it is not the same. It is not the same street. You can see the differences. Some are inverted and printed so they all point from left to right. There is a straight line so the spectator has to move, in order to activate the photographs. Of course, that doesn't replicate my movements, which were more like a labyrinth and took place over a period of three months. With my yellow Schwalbe, I would find another yellow Schwalbe and park next to it. I also like to see the work as a vehicle, and not only a recipient. A car is a vehicle, an elevator is a vehicle, the yielding stone is a vehicle. Photography is a vehicle, a way of transporting an event from one place to another.

FER: In 1993, you had been involved in a show in Kortrijk in Belgium curated by Catherine de Zegher. Can you say something about your working process for that exhibition? Did you make the work there, or did you also use work that you had already made here in Mexico?

OROZCO: It was a mixture. That was my first solo show outside of Mexico. I took some works, some photographs from actions in New York, like the piece I made with watermelons in the supermarket from 1992 (*Cats and Watermelons*). And I also did something different, something new. Since then I have always done the same thing: I bring some works, I reconstruct some works. I like to displace old works and see them again in a new context. I tend to combine all these different systems.

FER: Do you see making exhibitions as part of how you make your work?

OROZCO: It is true that most of the time, in the 1990s, the place of the exhibition was important for me. It was important to consider the specificity and duration of the work. Again, you can compare it to the 1970s, when a work was just for that space: what was called site-specificity. It couldn't travel. Yes, I want to make a work for a specific place, but also for it to transcend that place and travel. Some travel better than others. The shoe box that I showed in the Aperto in 1993 has gone to many other places. And it maintains an awkwardness whenever it is shown. The yogurt caps from the Marian Goodman Gallery show in New York are more difficult to reactivate when they travel. The *Atomists*, which were originally shown in a gentleman's club in London, behave very differently out of the English context, making connections with a history of art rather than just British sport. It starts from a specific situation and then it starts to travel. It is important that the work gets out into the world and gets exposed to the erosion of different places. Specificity becomes a temporal development. That is true of all my work. It comes from a center, a cultural center. That doesn't mean a powerful cultural center. Every culture is a center and every culture is very local in many ways. And then it goes out into the world, and starts to travel.

FER: You lay great stress on this idea of beginning at a center in all your work. How does the idea of a center function in your work?

OROZCO: The beginning is the center. When we think of a beginning we often think of a straight line—you start from a point and you go somewhere. But if you think of a center it can go and grow in multiple directions. When I say I always start in the center or nucleus, with the minimal unity, it is of course metaphorical. What is the center in a shoe box? An empty space, surrounded by a cardboard empty skin, emptiness around an inside. And then in between the yogurt caps the center is the body of the spectator. I removed the center of *La DS*. The paintings start from the center and grow to cover the whole surface. When I first made the spitting drawings (which I made while I was in Kortrijk though I did not show them), I was working out from the center. I found that adding elements took something away, obliterated something. This was a way of approaching a piece of paper, which is also to destroy the center. It is the opposite of a vanishing point, which holds the center. It was a radically different way of thinking about the center.

FER: When did this preoccupation with circles, balls, and centers crystallize for you?

OROZCO: I have been fascinated since childhood with the idea of the planets. I was crazy about Saturn because you have the unity of the ball of the planet but also the rings moving around it. So I was fascinated by this idea of permanent movement *and* unity in a spherical body. Second, the tendency I have always had to cover over a surface—right from my earliest drawing and painting—was a way of generating a totality, a texture, a unity. It was as if you could put the left and right sides of the paper together and make a cylinder or something, as if the flat surface of paper could become a potential sphere. The third is very simplistic: I loved football and since I was a child I was playing every kind of ball game—volleyball, basketball, especially football. I loved the different kinds of ball, the bouncing, the permanent movement.

FER: Well, that brings us to the *Atomists.* This was the work you made for Artangel in 1996 in a London club. These have graphic elements superimposed over photographs of sportsmen. Are they closer to drawing? How were they made?

OROZCO: No, they are more like collage. The preparation of the work is based on newspaper photographs that I cut out. Then I imprinted a computer-generated drawing on top and colored it with wash by hand. So first it's a readymade, then a mechanical imprint, then it's hand-colored. I reproduced the image on a computer and made it bigger so the grain is enlarged and you can see the little dots as if they suddenly explode. Like an atom, the dot is the minimal unity of the photo. One dot divides into three colors, and the coloring of the graphic elements is taken from that. Then through those graphic elements, you cancel the movement in order to regenerate movement. Of course, there's a connection with some constructivist collages and sports posters too. It is important that the bodies are life-size.

FER: So that they correspond with the size of the spectator looking at the work? So that the circular motifs not only relate to the movement frozen in the photograph but also to the movement of the spectator in front of it?

OROZCO: Yes, the geometric elements have a strange presence. They exist between image and spectator, relating to both.

FER: I want to ask you about the work you have called the *Penske Project* that you did in 1998. It takes a rather different tack from the *Atomists* but it also says something about the way you like to recycle your work and the radical consequences of that recycling.

OROZCO: Well, I rented a truck from the Penske Company and drove around New York. At every trash can and every dumpster I stopped and collected material. And I did the sculpture, the piece, right there, on the spot. The timing of the making was important, not just the collecting. I was not just collecting garbage. The timing was important for me to be making a piece with this material in the street where I found it. Of course, I don't have a studio and it was a way of thinking about a mobile, portable studio. I was alone with sometimes one assistant and a bunch of tools and worked on the project for a month, making collages with objects. I made them on the spot but stored them in the truck, so the truck was for storage. It was a portable vehicle of the work. I didn't take photographs of the pieces. I just took polaroids to remember how they were done. I then showed them at the Marian Goodman Gallery. It was a weird show.

FER: Were the black and white game boxes also part of that same project?

OROZCO: They were not made in the street and they were not shown in that exhibition. But I took the boxes and thought I could make with them a kind of sculptural drawing. I did them a bit later.

FER: So they were the leftovers from that project.

OROZCO: They were the leftovers of the leftovers. They were boxes for educational films. I found them in the dumpster of a school. I made plasticine balls and inserted them into the holes that were for holding the film in place, pressing it and playing around with the plasticine balls. The stain of the black plasticine is important. So is the dirtiness and the traces of the action in the box.

FER: In what way are they games?

OROZCO: They are not an institutionalized game, but like a game you invent in a specific situation. When I was a kid, I invented games. Those are my favorite games, the ones you make up. You adapt the games you learn to a different field, like playing volleyball between two cars, or the games I made in these boxes. Also you can see *Black Kites* as a game to explore the grid. At one point I thought of calling my paintings game-boards. They are all games I invent with my own rules.

FER: You have often used natural materials. As early as 1991 you used terracotta to make *My Hands Are My Heart.* But you have also used leaves, bone, and organic materials of all sorts. Your titles often point to nature too. Why invoke nature in your work like this?

OROZCO: I have this tendency, which maybe I should avoid, but it is too late now. Many of my titles are nature-orientated: *Samurai Tree . . . Yielding Stone . . . Spine . . . Spume Tail.* I have always been interested in nature. Right from the start in my early drawings that I did while I was still at art school, fish disappear in mythical confusion in the texture of drawing. If you set nature against architecture, I am always on the side of nature trying to eat architecture, as it does in Mexican ruins. Think of the jungle eating a pyramid. I love abandoned houses, with plants growing through the ruins. I see the tree, or the structure of the tree as a perfect organism, and as an example of sculpture. So too the internal structure of a fruit is very important for my understanding of sculpture. It grows, and in the end you have a skin, growing out from the center. Therefore casting and molding don't interest me because they are just a skin around an empty inside, just a fake volume of something. In my ceramics there is a solid inside, or in the pots I am obviously thinking about a real emptiness, not just a fake emptiness.

FER: Nature is problematic for artists now because it comes with so much baggage. But for you it can obviously be separated from the sort of idealism in which it is usually couched. How?

OROZCO: My first take is to say that I don't know what nature is. I don't know what is natural and what is artificial. Those distinctions between the natural and the artificial, the geometric and the organic—these are the extremes that we navigate. You can say that the drawing on *Black Kites* is a kind of technical drawing. You can see it as clinical. You could say that there is something clinical in the way the moon tree inserted discs into each leaf (fig. 50). Something clinical inserted into the natural body. But nature can also be the moon tree or the DS. I use the car as if it were a fish or a natural body. It is a vehicle but is also the idea of the seed. A vehicle of transportation of movement for the seed. The DS is like a big seed. And so it is not clear what is artificial and what is natural, what is language and what are phenomena.

FER: What about the cultural symbols these things represent?

OROZCO: Cultural symbols are traps. Yes, a skull is Mexican. A DS, French. If you go to the Museum of Anthropology in Mexico, you can find lots of circles. The Aztec calendar is circular. There are many references to ball games in pre-Hispanic culture. But this is not the point. It is there, yes, but it is not the point. *La DS* was a reflection on three-dimensionality, for example, on speed, movement, gravity. When you get inside the car you feel movement. You feel speed. You get compressed by the resistance of the wind. Yes, it is a cultural symbol. *La DS* stood for a kind of design utopia, but that was secondary for me.

FER: What about the material, working on bone, or shell . . . is the material structural or symbolic?

OROZCO: I think they are pure materials. With the shells, it's graphite, which is lead on bone. It's very contrasted: shiny on matte. But the bone

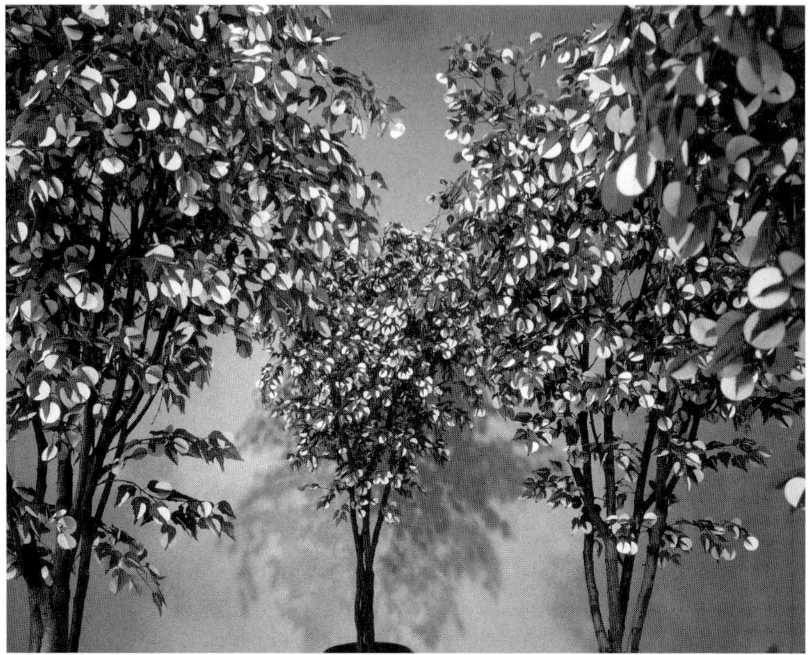

50 *Moon Tree*, 1996.
Wood, paper, and plastic.
100 x 66 x 66 inches.

absorbs the graphite. So does plaster. It has to do with a combination of materials that go well together. There is a tradition of decorating heads or shells in many cultures. I hope it's obvious that when I draw on a shell it is not a kind of decoration or tattoo on the surface, but has to do with the structure—with the topography of the object. Sometimes the lines follow accidents or the grain. I am drawing and looking at the same time, following the shape of the body. In *The Path of Thought* (1997), that's why I took the photograph, to see someone following the shape. I think I was drawing and comprehending the object through drawing. The drawing is a documentation of that.

FER: Materials like bone and shell have a particular resilience. They have particular connotations for thinking about time. Skulls have traditionally signified the fragility of human life. How do other natural materials you have used suggest temporality?

OROZCO: When I made the *Mixiotes* in 1999 (fig. 51), I made them for the *Market* show here in Mexico City. This was the opening exhibition of the gallery I was involved with—and it took place in a fruit market. They are made from cactus leaf with a rubber ball inside. They hang like fruit. They have the structure of a seed or fruit, like the mesh pieces too. *Mixiotes* means a food you prepare with the skin of a cactus around rabbit meat. I liked the word. And it was a very ephemeral material. I made it thinking it would not last more than a day, almost like a floral arrangement using very vulnerable materials. And then people took them home, and I kept some here in my place, and then I showed them in New York. There is something very physical in the making of small objects that I make with my hands with organic materials and shapes. But I also use very artificial materials in the same way—like the expanded styrofoam in the *Spumes*. In every material there is this possibility.

FER: These are hanging works. And you have always stressed the importance of gravity in your work.

OROZCO: The point of gravity is always important for me. In *The Yielding Stone* you can make a perfect ball, but as soon as you put it on the ground it makes a flat imprint, and through weight it starts to yield, pulling down the weight of the plasticine. I think I have a notion of sculpture in all my work—starting from the center, growing from the center. That center as a spine to the body, a center point of gravity, which connects the body with the Earth. A painter works with the idea of a vanishing point, with something flat and abstract, something in front of you. A sculptural mentality, on the other hand, is associated with the ground, from the floor upward. If you think in spherical terms, you have to mix the two, both a vanishing point and a gravity point. That creates movement too, orbital movement or centrifugal movement, a certain kind of turbulence, which is perhaps also why the sphere or the circle is for me the best way of showing both vanishing and gravity points. So in my paintings I am also thinking of the gravity point, the weight of a vertical axis, not only a vanishing point in the center.

FER: And hanging the pieces?

OROZCO: Hanging a piece always talks about gravity. In the *Spumes* (2002) (figs. 52, 53) I used liquid styrofoam. You cannot touch it with your hands. It is toxic. So I made what you could call recipients, latex sheets that acted as recipients, almost like hammocks, into which we poured the liquid

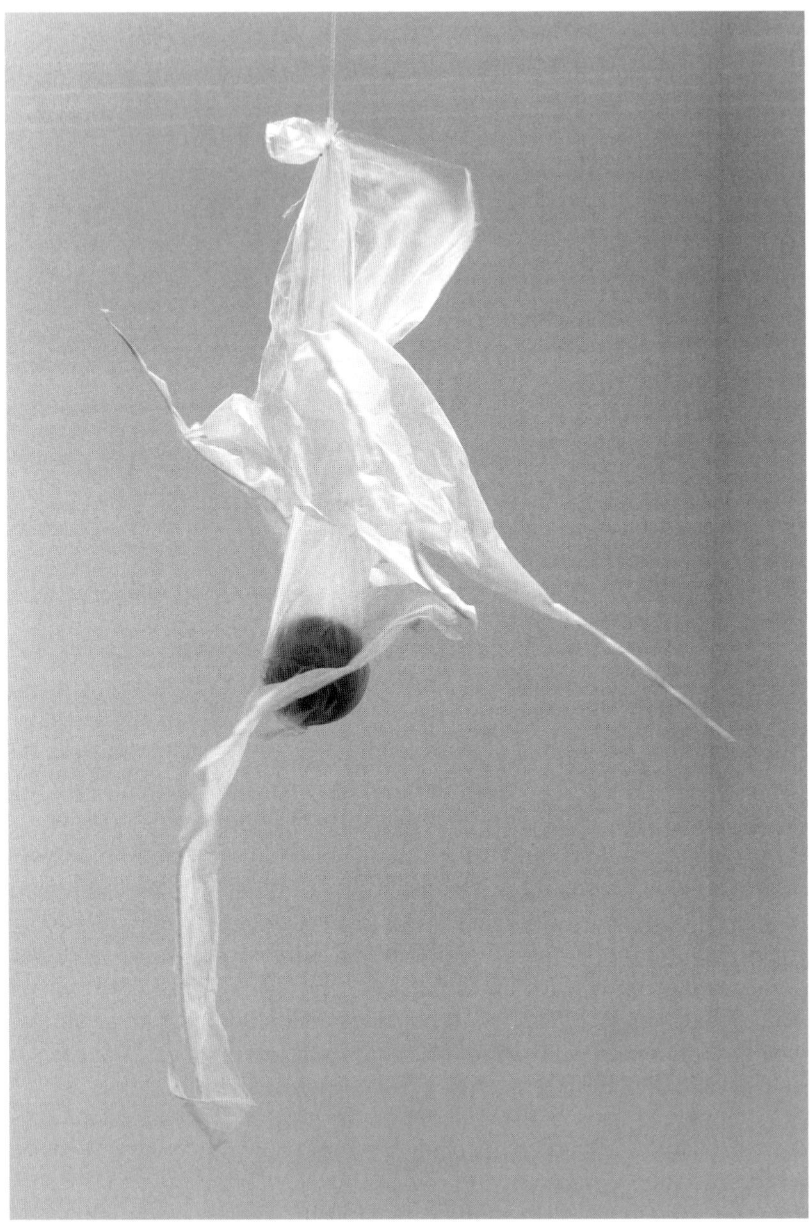

51 *Mixiotes*, 2001.
Maguey membrane, rubber balls,
plastic bags, and cotton string.
Dimensions variable.

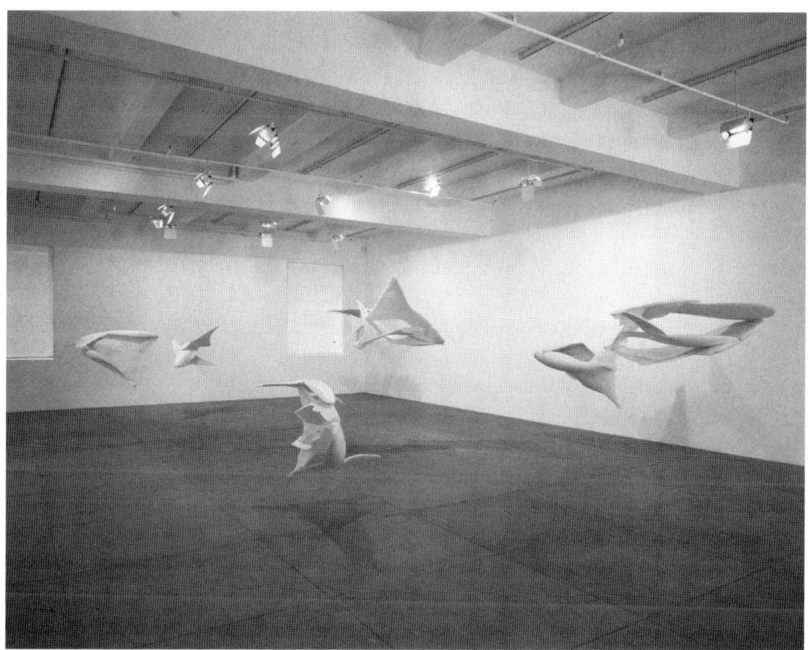

52 *Spumes*, 2003.
Installation view, Marian Goodman Gallery, New York.
Polyurethane foam. Dimensions variable.

styrofoam. As it was receiving the rolling liquid latex, I was also controlling it as it moved, like a river flowing. I was playing with the timing. Then I did it again. What happened to the liquid involved a kind of topography. It had a lot to do with time, like lava. You can see the trace of time.

FER: I am interested in the move from something as material as much of your work is, something as material as the kneaded lumps of terracotta that have been likened to amputated limbs or the *Cazuelas*—the move from that to these pieces, the large styrofoam hanging pieces and the small mesh pieces, which are hung from the ceiling and full of air. They could also be seen as yielding in some way, but now to air currents rather than to the pressure of solid ground. I am curious about the way you use air as material.

OROZCO: It is true that in *Mixiotes* and in the *Spumes*, the hanging styrofoam pieces that look like fishes or birds or bones or something, there is

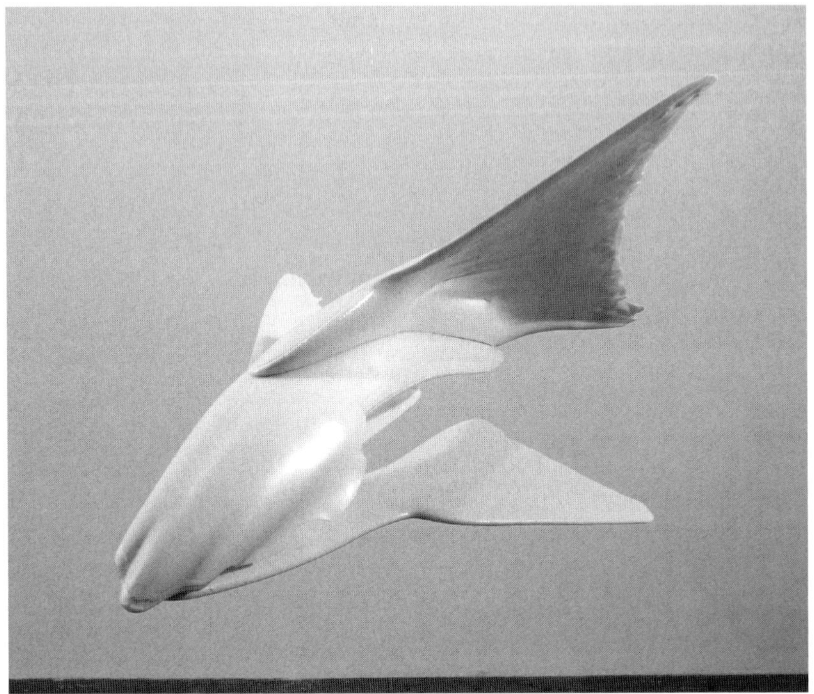

53 *Delta Tail,* 2003.
Polyurethane foam.
34 x 64 x 47 inches.

a lightness about them. They could be floating. It is true that the shape they have suggests wind going through them and shaping the form. It is true they could be eroded by the wind like some rocks. I like the idea of erosion. If you think of my terracottas, they are masses of clay somehow eroded by the pressure of my body. The red ones resemble body parts. The black clay pieces are more about trying to make a kind of geometric movement and less like body parts. In these, I throw the clay so it becomes very compacted, and then roll it around. More like *The Yielding Stone* in the way they are pressed against the ground into almost a diamond shape. Then there is also a work I made back in 1991 called *Recaptured Nature.* It was a rubber ball made from the inner tubes of the tire of a truck, which I cut open like a doughnut, then sealed and inflated. I was trying to recapture the utility of the material. It was a very similar procedure to the one I used in *La DS*, cutting it in half, down the middle, and then the reconfiguration of the body into a new shape. It is also a kind of topological exercise of transforming something, a body or a geometric structure, into a different shape yet which is essentially the same. In terms of mass and air, it is the same.

FER: There's the streamlining of *La DS* too, which you have talked about as almost like a fish in currents of water. I wondered about the idea of the kites, which seems like an airborne equivalent to *The Yielding Stone*. In your photograph of kites in a tree, and in particular in your video *Jaipur Kites*, a kite responds to the merest pressure of wind currents.

OROZCO: I never thought of that connection, but one of the reasons I love those kites in India is that they are square. It is a very basic kite. Contemporary kites are very fancy. This is a basic rhomboid—very basic and made of paper and wood pieces and a thread. To see the sky full of these little squares, all over the sky during the festival—fighting and playing all day long—was like a shoal of fishes, or like stars. You know when I did *The Yielding Stone* another title I was thinking of was a "wandering star," which was the original name given to the planets.

FER: Given how interested you have always been in mobile objects, and mobility and time, I wonder why you have not used video or film more?

OROZCO: One reason that is very important is that I am interested in the mobility of the spectator. That is, the mobility of the one who is activating the work in the museum space. I am not worried about my mobility, or the mobility of the planets. I know that. But what is interesting is how to express the movement and its reception by the spectator. The problem I have with video is that it is very static. You have to stand still. To use video and think you are really expressing movement and time is super-naive, I think. . . . It is not interesting. It's a very linear movement.

FER: You also made a series called *Kelly's Kites*. Do they connect?

OROZCO: That was a joke. The idea of the kite is poetic. It is an instrument, an invention that could be used in science or communication, but basically it is just a toy. I use that idea metaphorically all the time. I looked at some Ellsworth Kelly's paintings, but I could not believe in them. There seemed to be the intention of generating an illusion of flatness or a phenomenological presence that did not work for me. I could see shrinkage in the canvas, some real physical things happening to the pure color on the canvas. Then I received a catalog in the mail of a show he was having, and

I liked the reproductions better than the paintings. And I thought about remaking some three-dimensional movement in the reproduction of the flatness of the painting. So I began by cutting and pasting circular discs and then rotating them, generating shapes and configurations that were impossible in reality. It was a bizarre gesture on works that in reality I did not trust completely. The photographs had another physical status, and when I began to cut and paste, there was something interesting. Maybe the best way I found to express that was not to make a painting on the wall, but to make a kite.

FER: Is there a seed in that series of your own paintings?

OROZCO: Not really, because it is something about the image that I am interested in, in my paintings. I am trying to deal with the rotation of a body inside a flat plane. Not in the illusion of the body, but in the conceptual representation of an image. It is an abstraction, but not one which claims to be just a material phenomenon, but to be dealing with something else at the same time. Three-dimensionality, gravity, movement, light, symmetry, the organic, and so on—that is, all the same issues I am dealing with in sculpture and photography. So it is very different from abstract painting or minimalism. It is not about visuality.

FER: You stress a kind of internal contradiction in your paintings, that they both are and are not paintings. That's also something you could say exists in all your work. In your hanging mesh pieces, for example, it is the (heavier) mesh that looks light and seems to defy gravity and the (lighter) polyurethane foam that obeys the pull of gravity. Maybe that is a bit literal, but what is interesting is that at every level, such things stop behaving as contradictions in your work, I think, and act instead like very mobile and malleable reversals. But the ambivalence you have toward painting is crucial. After all, taking up painting again could seem a contradiction of your whole project up to that time. Can you explain how you came to make them? You showed the paintings for the first time at the Serpentine Gallery in 2002. How long had you been working on them?

OROZCO: For about a year before that. But the circles and the structure were always there somehow. A lot of my drawings had been with circles. I showed them maybe for the first time at the Kwangju Biennale in 1995. People did not know what to say about them. And I made a light box. I wanted to use it as a sign for publicity for nothing. I used the low-tech signage that you find all over Korea. I made several but I just showed one.

FER: What surprised me about your paintings was not the circular motifs or even the paint, but the canvas. It felt like a risk rather than a return to something. It did not feel like a return to painting. An established vocabulary for painting in some ways fails to fit your paintings.

OROZCO: People forget that I want to disappoint. I use that word deliberately. I want to disappoint the expectations of the one who waits to be amazed. When you make a decision someone is going to be disappointed because they think they know you. It is only then that the poetic can happen. It is not about entertaining the spectator, or working for the spectator. I knew they were going to be read as paintings, and I think they are not about painting. They are diagrams. The idea of a diagram has the pretension to explain how things work, how objects behave, and how plants grow. There is a kind of meeting point between the idea of the diagram and the fascination I have with icons. There is something very material about Russian icons. They are very flat, very geometric. Obviously icons played a role in abstraction, in Malevich, for example. But I am not religious. I am interested in their materialism. They are made of wood. In a conceptual way they behave as a geometric organism. It is also a game with certain rules, that I apply to these phenomena and see what happens, generated by chance phenomena.

FER: They invoke the first generation of abstract painting—the abstraction of the 1910s and '20s rather than the later, more expressive model of abstraction that gained ground with abstract expressionism in the middle of the century. Your references are often to the historical avant-garde.

OROZCO: I feel much more connected to the infantile, geometric approach to life you find in European art before the Second World War. I am interested in the way the art of the early avant-garde was based in childhood experience and had more connection with reality. Then art in the second part of the twentieth century, especially American art, got more into teenage experience. American culture is based on the teenager. It is decadent, self-indulgent. So much self-exploration with no connection to reality. Dada is for perverted kids, who shit and pee on the table. I feel much closer to that. In Mexico, the muralist movement was also infantile. I don't mean this pejoratively. It was infantile in that it was utopian, in its ideological energy, its approach to reality. Afterward, with Frida Kahlo, came teenagerhood. Surrealism was the perfect movement for teenagers.

FER: Maybe surrealism had to disavow the infantile in Dada. Another important strand for your work goes back to constructivism, especially Rodchenko's line and circle paintings, which were, of course, already, in a way, antipaintings, a way of painting that was not about the expressive idioms conventional to painting. Painting for him seemed to be a way of making an object.

OROZCO: Rodchenko is very important. The idea of construction is very important. It is not enough to cut a car in half. You have to build it up again. There is always a constructivism in my photography. It is not just to discard but to reconstruct, reconfigure, re-geometricize. I like Rodchenko paintings in photographs. When you look at them in reality, you feel he doesn't really like to paint.

FER: Color has been seen as the prime ground for expressive decisions, whereas you treat color not as a choice, but as a template, as what is predetermined.

OROZCO: What I hate about painting are all the small decisions, what goes with what. I like other kinds of decision. My research is more about space and bodies and action and movement, not about perception of color or about paintings. I made the decision to use four colors. The circle is divided into four parts, and so I needed four different colors. So I decided blue and red have the same weight, then white. Then gold, even more than yellow, because gold works as a noncolor and as a totality of light.

FER: Does that relate back to the icons?

OROZCO: Yes, in that it is physical. Like white, in Manzoni, is very physical. So it isn't decided by feeling, but it is technical, like dividing a chart. You need to see the four fields clearly. I vary the color according to the knight's move in chess—two and one. Two and one. Once I have put the colors at the center, then all the others follow.

FER: When you showed the series called *Samurai Tree* at Marian Goodman in the fall of 2005, you also included an animation of the color switches, which added another dimension to thinking about the paintings. All the color ways were animated, mobile, fast—as against the paintings that are slow to make, laborious to make even if they look quite mechanical. There seemed to be a point of friction there.

OROZCO: It happened like this: I was doing the paintings, and when I made the first drawing for the *Samurai Tree* series, I was very happy with it. I decided to work with the drawing, using the same rules of coloring. I called it *Invariant* because it is always the same. The location of color is different but the drawing is the same. I wanted to see the variations one by one. So I realized all the possible variations on the computer and made a kind of catalog. Then I could go to the catalog and choose the painting that I wanted to make. Helped by an assistant, we came up with 677 variations. Then we decided to see them one after the other, one second per image, and see how it looks. Finally I made a sequence, and we ended up with this animation. Somehow the animation came about from cataloging the variations of the drawings. You see the painting with all the possible variations, so it becomes a kind of mobile painting. For the objects themselves, I never wanted to use other techniques like screen-printing or computer-generated images. I like the technique of painting with acrylic. There is a connection with my own body. I work with one assistant, with great focus and concentration. At the beginning I didn't want to let anyone else produce the work. I wanted to do it myself. I am even going backward now, using egg tempera, a Russian icon technique, but I have some assistants to help me because I need to accelerate the process to see the results faster now.

FER: We come back to your own physical involvement with the work, to the resistance embodied in the handmade or the artisanal product. It is striking that you have drawn on craft techniques as well as computers—it is as if these technologies, whether archaic or digital, cease to be opposites and come to obey the same logic. I am thinking about the *Cazuelas (Beginnings)*—the project you made for Documenta in 2002.

OROZCO: Well, again, the idea of the recipient is important, as it is in all my work. I don't like making clay pots myself, but I worked with a potter in a workshop in France. When you make a bowl or a pot on a potter's wheel, you have the movement, you also have the idea of the wheel as a kind of vehicle. It is a brick clay not a pottery clay. As the potter was throwing, and I was indicating the shape I wanted, I was also making an arsenal of clay balls. And when the bowl was of the proper size then I was throwing the little balls at it, smashing them into it. It was like a game between baseball and basketball, trying to get the ball inside the bowl. The bowl was spinning, and the ball was a kind of meteorite. It was a whole exercise, a week of work. All the time, pitching and throwing, smashing the balls against the molds, and altogether they form a bowl. It was a reflection on pottery, erosion, movement, planetary space, etc.—it was all in there.

FER: You often seem to snatch back materials that circulate in a world of commodities—like various forms of packaging—and retrieve them for you own particular materialist project. I am thinking about the *Three Containers*—

OROZCO: I like the styrofoam containers—they are recipient molds—and I store things in them. Stuff becomes an informal archive of materials. I like that my own trash is a high-tech recipient. Over time this just happened. I did not intend to make a work, but I was testing materials over a period of about three years and suddenly it became a work. I like to use materials that are common and also not high-tech. I can use clay and egg tempera and styrofoam and wood and mesh. I use everything, not as a technology but because we use materials in everyday life. I use a computer but it is not about the computer. It is the materiality of the material. It is materialist, and it is a reflection on the material. There is never so much manipulation that you do not see what it is made of.

FER: This idea of bringing together a diverse collection of things over a period of time—not just in space but in time—seems also to be at the heart of your *Working Tables*. Perhaps you can speak about the temporality of the tables.

OROZCO: Well, the working table presentation came from having collections of objects stored in shoe boxes in my apartment, accumulating. Some of these objects I found interesting, but I didn't know what to do with them. Some of them were like tests that did not work. So after five or six years I thought why not show them all, on a table, successes and failures. I showed objects with drawings and diagrams which I did not consider finalized work either. I did not like the idea of a vitrine very much. I wanted them to look more like my table, covered with this and that, with trash, with instruments. I have always liked the idea of a mechanic's table in a garage, a rough, dirty accumulation of pieces. Every five years or so I pull out all the stuff I have accumulated. In the working tables, time is made actual. In many artworks today, you feel there is just one second there, one point, not time accumulated. Some of my best work has the pretension to have such an accumulation of time, so that you can spend quite a lot of time looking at the object. *Black Kites*, the skull with graphite, took six months to make, but I think you can maybe spend six months looking at it too. Then in the *Working Tables*, which are five years of work, process, tries, and tests, then you can spend fifteen minutes looking at them. Now is a moment of a high pressure of production on artists. There is a certain demand to work with this pressure, but the tables can only be made over time. They cannot be made in a week. You need all that accumulation of things left over. Production processes are coopted but these tables cannot be.

FER: Slow time.

OROZCO: Like Duchamp's *Large Glass* left to accumulate dust. Stopping time. It spoke about that quite consciously, a retarded work. In my case, I like the combination between this and the pressure of time. I like the pressure of time as well. I think you can also make a work in one second. The combination of scales is important in terms of size but also time. There's the work that only takes a moment and then there's the long-term project. There is the micro and the macro.

FER: I want to end by asking you about your attitude to architecture, and the relation of your work to architecture. For the 2003 Venice Biennale, you replicated a ruined sculpture court designed by Carlo Scarpa for the Italian Pavilion in 1952. The replica you made was like a ruin in reverse.

OROZCO: Scarpa made a small modernist pavilion to show modern sculpture in 1952, and then it was abandoned. It was a difficult space to show sculpture in, because Scarpa's pavilion is itself very sculptural. The room next to it is of very similar proportions. So I thought to make a replica next door and in wood. What interested me was the experience of walking between the two, between the ruin of the dusty, open-air pavilion and the wooden replica inside—one to one, almost like a model, which stood in a white room that was very pristine and clean. It was about the time between the platonic pavilion and the pavilion eroded by weather. It was a shiny new idea that was immediately eroded and accidented by reality. In the process of making the replica, there were many accidents that also occurred along the way. Then afterward, it traveled. It was shown in the Palacio de Cristal in Madrid, to see how it behaved differently, like sculpture. It was still a roof, but a roof behaving like a sculpture, making sculpture out of architecture.

FER: I want to come back to the point where we began. You spoke about wanting to occupy a position that was resistant to a spectacular culture, about wanting the work you did to interrupt in some way the circuits of production and consumption. In the light of that I want to ask you about two large-scale works that you are working on now. The first is the project for the Mexican National Library for which you plan to use the whole skeleton of a whale (fig. 54). Is this not a spectacular move? How does it relate to what you said at the beginning about a resistance to spectacle?

OROZCO: This is a big operation for me. Yes, it is spectacular, but it is so by accident, rather than to draw attention to it. I could have taken a team to film the search for the whale, but I didn't. I just wanted to go there myself. I still work pretty much the same way. I don't have assistants generally. I don't have a big studio. I take photos. The point is not about the literal scale of something. When I look for a skeleton I keep in mind my paintings and the idea of a spine. The paintings are like a spinal column or vertebrae in my work, not because it is painting but because of the geometry.

FER: Then there is the beach house you are working on, which picks up on the interest in architectural projects (fig. 55). You converted and reconfigured this house that we are sitting in here in Tlalpan. The beach house draws on a group of giant astronomical instruments near Delhi that you first encountered over eight years ago—and which has been in your mind ever since. A photograph of another part of the site called *Sundial*

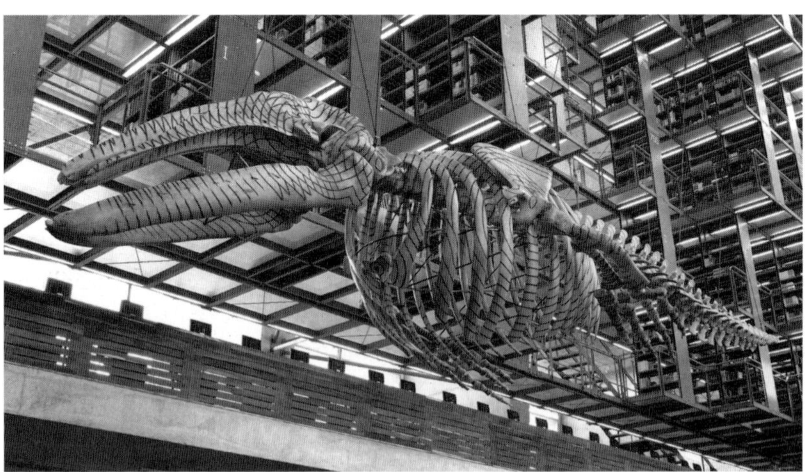

54 *Mobile Matrix*, 2006.
Graphite on gray whale skeleton.
100 x 460 1/5 x 80 3/4 inches.

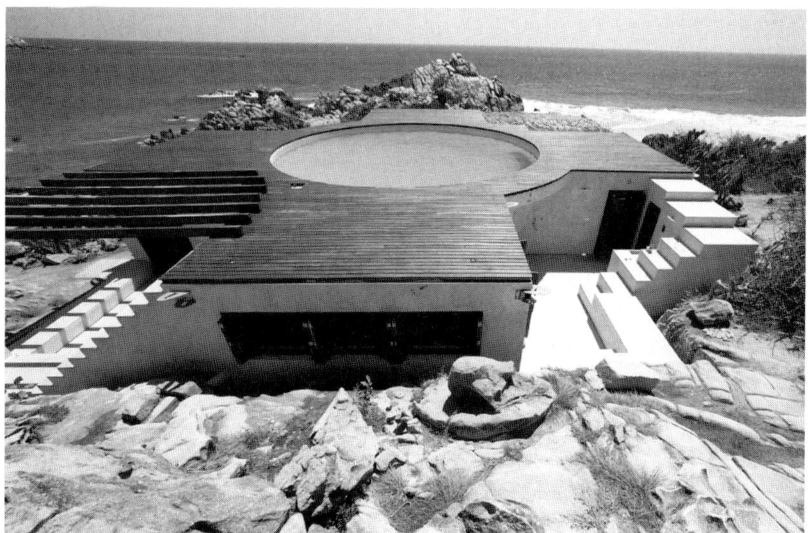

55 View of Observatory House on the Pacific Coast, Oaxaca, 2006.

Banana (1995) was included in your Smithsonian show of photographs in 2004. Rather like the Venice work, you are again transporting the shape of an entire building from one site to another. But on this occasion, you are moving one from one continent to another—an astronomical observatory in Delhi to the Mexican coast.

OROZCO: I think of making this house as a semiprivate thing. I am transporting the building somehow into a new context. I think other works might come out of this house. It is an experiment. It is an observatory, an instrument, a place of work. It will be my house, outside of the art world, inserted into everyday living, and outside the coopted world of the museum. This house is an experiment in everyday life for myself. It is important to keep it independent. I am not really interested in pavilions as such—that was the concern of a previous generation. It is not a way of speculating about architecture. I am not trying to be an architect. It is more like making sculpture with an architecture complex.

FER: These connections—not only the relationships between event, object, photograph that we started out talking about in relation to your work from the early '90s—but also now to architecture—are very mobile in your work. They spark off each other.

OROZCO: I call this a "deterritorialization" of style. I mean I do think in terms of a galaxy. A world of an artist generates planets and different constellations. I also think that the style or world of an artist can get into establishing a single, fixed territory, making a certain type of work, a certain style or brand. One artist, one idea. This style of working becomes a kind of fortress and I don't believe in that. I don't want to establish that kind of territory. The constellation of the world that the artist generates, that I want to generate, is in constant movement. The weight of each work is constantly questioned by the others.

FER: If the artist generates a world or a constellation, then how do you think of your own role in that? I mean in the sense of where you situate yourself. It seems to me that you actually avoid staging yourself, in a performative sense, in your work. Can you say something about that effacement?

OROZCO: I think it is better to empty that space of the actual body. Then that space can be reactivated, so everyone might occupy it for themselves. I want to open up that space as a recipient for the spectator to occupy. I want to erase my presence. It is very basic. When you impose yourself as the performative aspect of the work, that is not only expressing the narcissistic but also something tyrannical. It is a power mechanism, the artist imposing a legend on the anonymous public. That is what spectacle does, generate a persona, celebrity. In my photos I want to disappear. I don't want to impose my persona. Also I am very handsome and I don't want to make any enemies.

[*Laughter*]

Tlalpan, February 2006

The Tree and the Knight (2006)

Yve-Alain Bois

Edward Said was particularly fond of a quotation from a text by a twelfth-century monk, Hugo of Saint Victor. Said borrowed the quote from Eric Auerbach, himself a famous exile, just as I borrow it from Said: "The man who finds his homeland sweet is still a tender beginner; he to whom every soil is as his native one is already strong; but he is perfect to whom the entire world is as a foreign land."[1]

Let's advance a paradox at the outset: it is perhaps because he has reached the state of "perfection" to which the ancient author alluded that Gabriel Orozco, the quintessential globetrotter, the artist-immigrant, has been able to enter comfortably the land of painting—a domain resolutely foreign to him until very recently. And perhaps it is also why he can now come back to his native country without feeling the need to justify his departure, without fearing to be cast in the role of the returning Ulysses or that of the prodigal son. He had been apprehensive in the past—even before the hostile reaction of the Mexican art world, and particularly the art critics, to his first major exhibition in Mexico City in 2000. In 1998, for example, in a long and remarkable interview with Benjamin Buchloh, he refused to endorse either the position of "Mexican artist" or that of "international artist"—while he felt that the term "nomad" was too glamorous to describe his status.[2] "Returns" of any kind were then touchy topics for Orozco.

Yet, in the same interview, one reads his dismissal of the painter's practice (which he had abandoned while studying in Madrid in the mid-1980s—a sojourn that was crucial for the formation of his artistic identity, as he has stressed in numerous interviews): it was not so much with the medium of painting that Orozco had issues, but with the setting. To be a painter you have to have a studio, if not entirely distinct from your living space, at least from your kitchen and bedroom (fumes are toxic): you need to dedicate a space to your artistic practice, a place where your canvases can dry, where you can wash your brushes, where you can store your paint; you need to take root. Orozco long rebelled against both this sedentary obligation and the notion of an assigned allotment of space. For him, the working space had to be that of his daily life: "my apartment, just my apartment . . . the idea of the apartment is important; the idea of avoiding to have a studio or a factory, and just doing anything we can from here, from a common place; then going outside, having situations that produce this or that."[3] This explains, as well, Orozco's perpetual wandering from one medium to the next or, rather, between media, his ebullient versatility, which has dazzled all commentators.

Painting is a slo-mo activity that requires all kinds of paraphernalia; it is not something you do on the go. But if you are always "elsewhere," wherever you are, if "the entire world is as a foreign land," there is no longer any need to roam around, or much less so, no need to surf the whole panoply of nomadic media such as photography or readymades "*de voyage*" (to use Duchamp's apt phrase). There is no longer any prohibition, in any case, against establishing a studio. And who knows, perhaps this travel back in time, away from what I just called nomadic media to the sedentary activity of painting, is just the beginning. After all, except for frescoes, paintings have long been transportable objects; they too are nomadic in some ways (albeit only once they have been made). Their commerce began in classical Greece, where pictures called *xenia* (mainly still lifes) were brought as gifts to their host by visiting strangers (*xenion* comes from *xenos*, stranger or host). Will Orozco eventually engage in the old craft of fresco? And what about carving marble, casting bronze? He has expressly stated his disgust for such sculptural practices—as no longer credible, as pure kitsch—but even the land of kitsch can be inhabited by one who has attained the wisdom praised by our medieval monk. For his current series of paintings, Orozco is relearning the forgotten skills of icon painters: egg tempera on wood panel, gold-leaf gilding. Who would have ever thought such a revival possible, especially after the bad name given to "Byzantine parallels," not so long along, by a Clement Greenberg?[4]

I am not trying to be facetious here. In fact, for an artist such as Orozco, steeped in conceptual art and at ease with the most sophisticated new technologies, returning to the tradition of the so-called geometric abstraction in painting, which is what he has been toying with during the past three years or so, represents just as much an archaism as working with a clay potter at the wheel (which he has also been doing) or reading Cennino Cennini's manual *Il Libro dell'Arte*, in order to learn how many egg yolks (and what kind!) to use in a tempera concoction so that it does not ruin your colors or dry too fast. There is an obvious telescoping of time in that counterintuitive graft of a quattrocento practice onto that of a Mondrian, but this telescoping, in itself, signals that it is from the point of view of a stranger that Orozco looks at the whole development of Western painting, and that this exogenous, oblique point of view is perhaps the only one able to rekindle its flame.[5]

That Orozco's pictorial enterprise has little directly to do with the tradition I just mentioned comes out with particular clarity in a statement where he opposes his work to the "worst failures" of op art: "It's not visual, it has to be intellectual, it has to be an idea."[6] The conceptual nature of his involvement with painting is also at the core of his interest in Tantra, as well as that of his very first brush with Russian icons. As he declared that he had quit painting while in Madrid, Briony Fer reminded him of his first return to painting (and to Mexico) after his Spanish years. At this he retorted:

> I was taking fragments from Russian icons. I loved those paintings. I also like the objects, the thick wood, the abstract shapes, the gold. It is painting but with a readymade, conceptual approach. I didn't feel I was a painter. I was analyzing a painting, like a fragmented readymade and then presenting it. I did a show in Mexico of that work in 1989. Then I stopped completely. Then I started to move and travel, and use photography more and more.[7]

He no longer has to be so defensive; he can allow himself to feel as a painter—but his approach is no less conceptual than before.

Let us go back to his criticism of op art—for which he has often admitted a soft spot. It failed, he notes, because it was illusionistic—it wanted to generate, by visual means alone, the illusion of movement or three-dimensionality:

> They are very nice tries, they were fantastic and I like them very much, since childhood. But I don't think it's a visual problem to

> generate a three-dimensional proposition and it is not in the visual perception that we find the way to express how things work to become a three-dimensional organism or object. [We now switch to discussing his own paintings.] It's not visual: it has to be intellectual, it has to be an idea. It is more like a formula to be thought. You can look at the paintings as diagrams and think in terms of molecules, or atoms, or a DNA chain, but at the same time they're not claiming to be scientific, of course. They're also ludic, they look childish and I think that is good also.[8]

There is much to unpack in such a statement, all the more so since it is excerpted from a long conversation and refers in shorthand to things developed previously during a two-hour dialogue. The two main themes it encourages us to explore, and which indeed pervade all the declarations of Orozco about his work (in whatever medium), are *game* and *organism*. In the field of painting, the theme "game" translates into game-board (or board game), but more importantly, via the metaphor of chess, and in particular the move of the knight—which is, as Orozco reminds us, "the only piece of the game whose movement is conceived to represent three-dimensionality"[9]—it brings us to the artist's conception of his canvases as "platforms for action," as diagrammatic, conceptual representations of a movement, that of the "rotation of a body *inside* a flat plane."[10]

But let us start with the notion of organic growth, literally an obsession for Orozco (fig. 56). His model par excellence is the tree: "In a way, my dream is to one day make a world that is as fantastic and perfect as a tree. Trees are perfect things, the perfect machine, the perfect body, the perfect exotic things, trees are so strange and always surprising, very mysterious."[11] Differentiating his recent paintings from Jasper Johns's *Target* canvases, he states that the American artist

> was not starting from nothing, growing into an unknown kind of form, which I think is how organic creatures grow: they start from a center and there is no certainty about what kind of shape will be there at the end, and also how much they can keep growing. . . . I love the idea of how trees grow from a center. How they also grow underground and on the ground from a center and a horizon and they start to develop all the branches. A tree is a metaphor for me.[12]

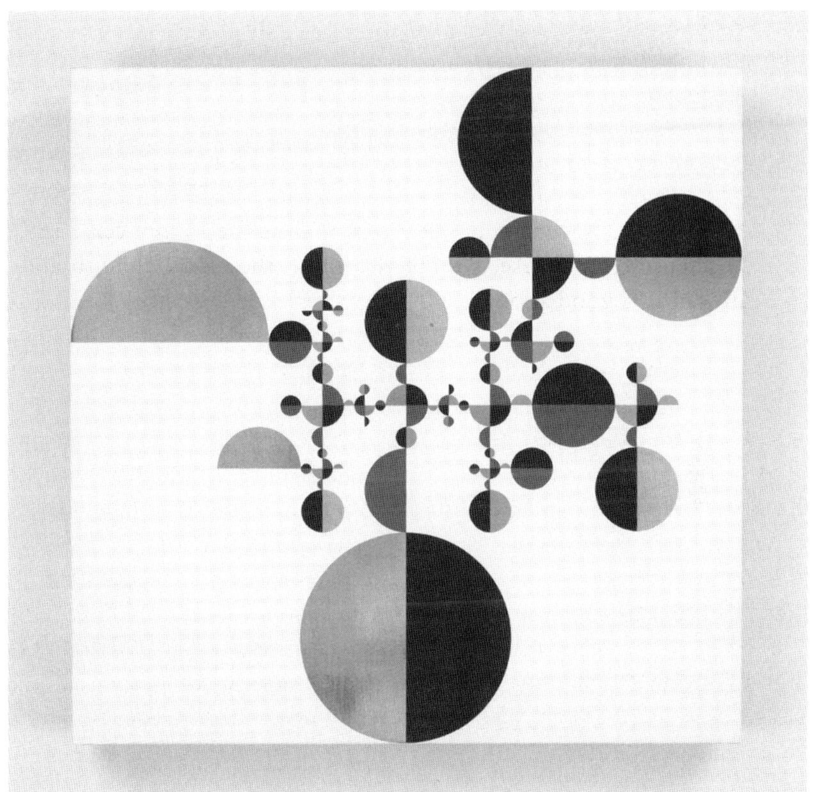

56 *Samurai Tree (Invariant 1S)*, 2005.
Tempera and gold leaf on wood.
21 5/8 x 21 5/8 inches.

The tree was, as well, a metaphor for many pioneers of abstract art—but only for very few of them was it a positive one for organic growth (Jean Arp being the most eloquent in this minority, to which belongs also Schwitters, an artist ranking high in Orozco's pantheon). Quite the contrary, and this is easily understandable in the context of these artists' necessary struggle against, or flight from, "the natural," the tree was for many of them the very emblem of mimetic representation (they had all been impressionists frolicking *en plein air* during their youth). An excellent testimony of this modernist chlorophobia is to be found in the answers to the questionnaire sent in 1933 by the journal of the association *Abstraction-Création: art non-figuratif* to the roster of its participants. Question two read: "What do you think of the influence of trees on your work?" Wladyslaw Strzeminski's answer was the most precise (this was to be expected—I have always held him as the most articulate theoretician among the abstract painters of his generation):

> Trees revealed to me what a work of art is not. The shape of a tree results from:
>
> a) symmetry (in the shape and in the distribution of leaves). This symmetry is the result of the cell division of a plant. A picture does not grow, its cells don't divide and thus there is no place in it for symmetry.
>
> b) the curving fluidity of the shape of the branches and trunk, resulting from the pressure of the wind, the direction of the sun (of light), the vaporization of sap in the plant. Such forces are nowhere to be found in a painting, therefore its form is different.[13]

(To the forces mentioned by Strzeminski, as we shall see, Orozco would add gravity.) But if during the first age of abstraction (from roughly 1915 to World War II), the tree was the symbol of mimesis, of "nature," the opposite insignia was the square as the emblem of the arbitrary, of "culture." Even after the tree no longer remained the mandatory opponent of the square in a paradigmatic pair, the latter retained its aura of pure artificiality, of belonging to the sphere of codification, of the semiological, of language—witness the answers to another questionnaire, this one sent to many artists and published by Lucy Lippard in *Art in America* in 1967 (there, the most articulate answer was given by a veteran of the first abstract wave, another of Orozco's heroes, Josef Albers, who justified his choice of the figure of the square by the fact that one does not see it in nature, except in some rare crystals).[14]

Of course, the artist who epitomizes best this struggle between the tree and the square during this first round of abstract art (or rather the victory of the square over the tree, even if squares are actually not that frequent in his oeuvre) is Piet Mondrian—and it is this painter above all, I think, whom Orozco addresses in his recent canvases. He himself alluded very explicitly to Mondrian's famous series of trees in the process of becoming grids. Here is how a statement partially quoted above unfolds: "A tree is a metaphor for me. But it doesn't mean you see the representation of a tree. That would be very Mondrianesque. Mondrian's vision of a tree is from the point of view of someone standing on the ground looking at a landscape. Vertical and horizontal lines make the structure and representation of the branches. But if you look at a tree from above, you see the center from where the branches start to spread in multiple directions."[15] Yet things are not as simple as that and Orozco might be in the end closer to Mondrian than he thinks—not to the Mondrian of the beginnings, of the trees series, nor to the painter of rarefied neo-plastic compositions, but to the author of *Victory Boogie Woogie*.

The path of Mondrian to abstraction via cubism is too well known, I certainly hope, to merit any development here. But I would like to insist on one point, which is that at first he envisioned the modular grid as a measure of suspending time, as a mapping of the autonomous space of the painting in which everything would be at rest, and that if he very swiftly abandoned this trope of the modular grid, which seemed so perfectly to answer his needs, it is because of a side effect that he had not foreseen, and which utterly undermined his quest for compositional stability: the optical flicker. This refusal of dynamism, of time (and thus of repetition and rhythm), was perfectly consistent with the war Mondrian waged against nature. The cycle of the seasons and the beat of our pulse were ciphers of the natural for Mondrian—and we should note how much Orozco proves him right: in the pulsatile flicker of the Mexican artist's animated film of the 672 color variations based on the "invariant diagram" of his *Samurai Tree* series (2005) (fig. 57), it is impossible not to sense an organic throb, be it blood or sex.[16] By the early 1930s, however, having reached a point of perfect classical stasis in his art, Mondrian began to change his view. The change was not abrupt, as it had been long prepared by his interest in jazz, but the click only happened in 1932, when he was able to translate his theoretical *aggiornamento* into his painting (with his use of what he called the "double line"). From then on we witness an amazing acceleration in what I have always thought to be a systematic enterprise of sabotage against his previous conception of painting as a necessarily static art.[17] Rhythm was admitted with a vengeance on Mondrian's canvases, now considered a key arsenal in his quest for a "dynamic equilibrium," the staccato accelerating throughout the 1930s. And at the end of his life, on the white walls of his New York studio, rectangles of primary colors floated unmoored, among them small mirrors disturbing the quiet austerity of this pristine space by their ever-changing reflections.

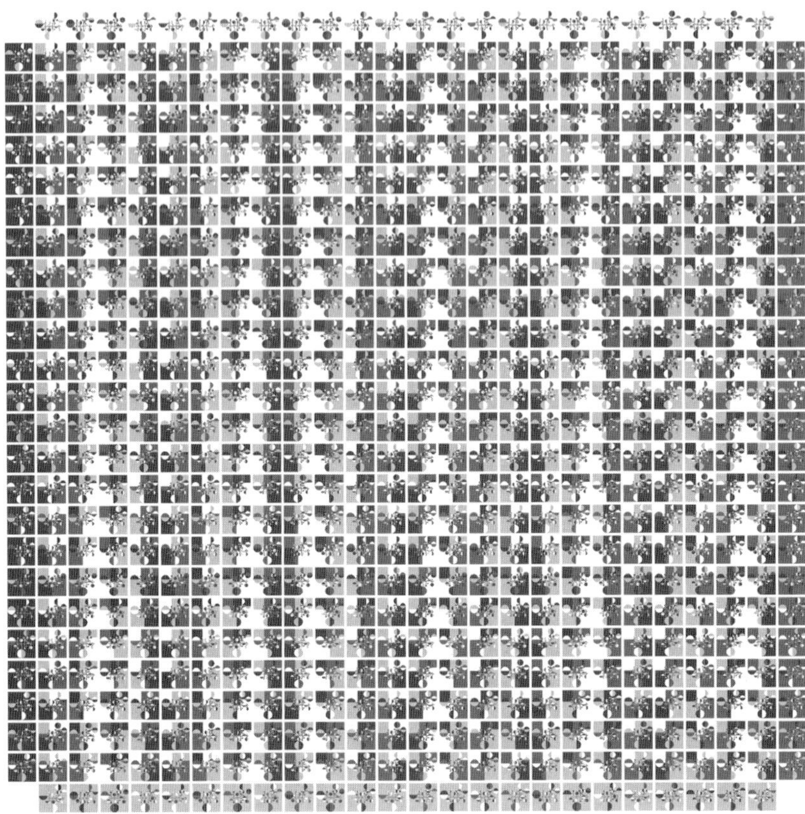

57 *Complete chart with 672 Invariants of Samurai Tree*, 2005.
Inkjet prints, series of 672.

But let us go back to the grid and its interpretation as a means of freezing time, which was common to all early pioneers of abstract art. (Strzeminski was particularly eloquent about that, though he saw this function as characterizing all tropes belonging to the generic category of deductive structures, the grid being only one of them.[18]) It might be this conception of the grid that prevented Mondrian and his peers from even thinking about chess as a model (even if his first three square modular compositions, all in a lozenge format, are based, like a chessboard, on a division of 8 × 8 squares).[19] Or, conversely, it might be that the conception of chess that was available at the time was inherently static. Witness, for example, Ferdinand de Saussure's celebrated use of the chess metaphor, in his *Course in General Linguistics*, in order to explain his concept of language as a synchronic system of signs, each of which is endowed with a specific oppositional identity that he called its "value." (Needless to say, the Swiss author's *Course*, posthumously published in 1916, just before Mondrian would be coping with the problem of the modular grid, remained a confidential opus known only to linguists until the late 1950s or early 1960s, with the advent of structuralism.)

Saussure's three points (synchrony, systematicity, value) are worth rehearsing, in part because a comparison of their applicability to Orozco's and to Mondrian's art will help in pinpointing the differences between the two. It seems to me that both Orozco and Mondrian would agree to the applicability of two of Saussure's concepts to their pictorial enterprise (language as a system; differential value of the sign). Here are Saussure's invocations of chess with regard to these concepts:

> *System*
> Language is a system that has its own rules. A comparison with chess will bring out the point. In chess, it is relatively easy to distinguish between what is external and what is internal [to the system]: the fact that the game passed from Persia to Europe is external; what is internal is everything concerning the rules. If I replace wooden pieces by pieces in ivory, this change has no effect on the system; but if I decrease or increase the number of pieces, this change has a profound effect on the "grammar" of the game.[20]
>
> *Value*
> Take a knight, for example. Is it by itself an element of the game? Certainly not, for in its pure materiality—outside its square and the other conditions of the game, it means nothing to the player; it becomes a real, concrete element only when endowed with value and wedded to it. Suppose that the piece happens to be destroyed or lost during the game. Can it be replaced by an equivalent piece? Certainly. Not only another knight but even a figure shorn of any resemblance to a knight can be declared identical provided the same value is attributed to it.[21]

The entire neo-plastic oeuvre of Mondrian functions as "Exhibit A" for Saussure's first point (about language—but also any semiological system—having its own internal rules), but this was verified with particular clarity in 1932 when the increase of Mondrian's pictorial vocabulary by just one element (the double line) completely transformed the "grammar" of his language (that is, utterly changed the rules of his game). As for Orozco, especially because the configuration of his canvases is based on something as specific, as exceptional, one could say, as the knight's move, it goes without saying that any alteration of that rule (were he to choose the rook's move or the bishop's as a guiding principle) would result in entirely different "compositions"—he simply would not be speaking the same pictorial tongue. Note that long before his return to painting, Orozco provided a perfect illustration for Saussure's metaphor in his *Horses Running Endlessly* of 1995 (fig. 58), consisting in a modified chess board (there were four times more squares than usual, and these were of four different colors, as opposed to the standard binary opposition). As for the pieces, not only were they also of four colors but each of the four pools of sixteen pieces (the standard number per team) comprised only knights.[22] Instead of a regulated tit-for-tat exchange necessarily coming to a close, only endless chaos (so says Orozco's title) could proceed from his "prepared" board (to use John Cage's word).

Saussure's notion of value, which is different from that of signification, is far too complex to be seriously examined here. To explain it in a nutshell, I shall quote his most famous example: the value of the French word *mouton* is not the same as that of the English word *sheep*, even though the two *can* have the same signification, "because in speaking of a piece of meat ready to be served on the table, English uses *mutton* and not *sheep*. The difference in value between *sheep* and *mouton* is due to the fact that *sheep* has beside it a second term while the French word does not."[23] Perhaps more telling—in that it seems almost a description of Mondrian asceticism, particularly in his barest canvases, for example his *Lozenge Composition with Two Black Lines* of 1931 (Stedelijk Museum, Amsterdam)—is the following remark: "If you augment language by one sign, you diminish in the same proportion the [value] of the others. Reciprocally, if only two signs had been chosen . . . all the [concrete] significations would have had to be divided between these two signs."[24]

On this point Mondrian and Orozco differ somewhat—the younger artist being more interested in the commutability, the exchangeability, of the sign (an abstract property deriving from its having a value, as is the case for currency) than in its identity. There is no better illustration of Saussure's hypothetical replacement of a lost knight during a game than Orozco's

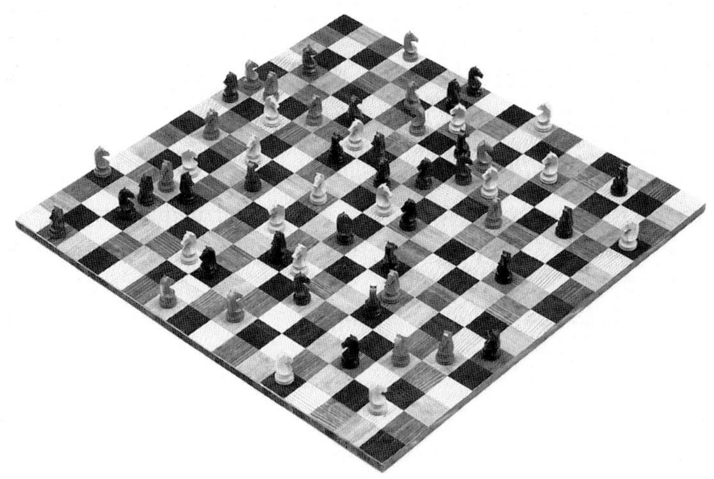

58 *Horses Running Endlessly*, 1995. Wood. 3 3/8 × 34 3/8 × 34 3/8 inches. Gift of Agnes Gund and Lewis B. Cullman in honor of Chess in the Schools. Location: The Museum of Modern Art, New York. Digital image © The Museum of Modern Art/ Licensed by SCALA/Art Resource, NY.

2005 animated film of the 677 color variations based on the "invariant diagram" of *Samurai Tree*: given that it is not the visual effect that matters to Orozco in his paintings, but rather the conceptual nature of the process of formation of the image, and given that in all the variations recorded in the film (of which only a few were actually realized in painting), the diagrammatic structure of the image itself remains unchanged; the value of a color plane is not altered, at least in theory, by its shifting from gold to blue or red or white.[25]

During most of his life Mondrian would probably have resisted the idea that such permutations were possible: even when he based several paintings on the same compositional scheme—and this is particularly striking for the classical 1929–32 series that immediately preceded his discovery of the double line—he could never change the color of a plane without modifying other elements of the composition (the size of this and other planes, the thickness of the lines, etc.). However, at the very end of his career, while working on *Victory Boogie Woogie*, Mondrian came close to the nonvisual, conceptual stance of the Mexican artist.

Here are two anecdotes. The first is well known: when Carl Holty asked him why he kept altering *Victory Boogie Woogie* (which he did to the very end) instead of making several paintings of the different solutions that had been superimposed on this canvas, Mondrian answered, "I don't want pictures. I just want to find things out."[26] The other story is more obscure but perhaps more revealing: as he was showing to James Johnson Sweeney a painting in progress in his studio (most probably *Victory Boogie Woogie*), Mondrian asked his interlocutor what he thought of a particular area of the canvas (covered with small rectangular planes of colored paper, according to the method used by the painter in New York). Sweeney answered that, honestly, he preferred the way it looked at his last visit, when there was an element of a different color in place of the red one he could now see. Mondrian was at first puzzled, until he realized that Sweeney was commenting on what he effectively had in front of his eyes as opposed to what he, Mondrian, had so clearly thought out in his head: he had only used red because he no longer had a paper of the other color to hand, he said, but "it was not red in [his] mind."[27]

Let us come at last to the third occurrence of Saussure's chess metaphor, concerning synchronicity. The passage is long, and even though it is stunning for its sheer theoretical brilliance, I have to resist quoting it in full. In it, Saussure wants to show that in order to approach a language from a structural point of view—as opposed, say, to a sociological one—it is only necessary to consider one of its "states." If we are considering its current state, a knowledge of its historical past is irrelevant. After an elaborate comparison of the nature of changes occurring in language with those occurring in a game of chess, Saussure concludes:

> In a game of chess any particular position has the unique characteristic of being freed from all antecedent positions; the route used in arriving there makes absolutely no difference; one who has followed the entire match has no advantage over the curious party who comes up at this critical moment to inspect the state of the game; to describe this arrangement, it is perfectly useless to recall what had just happened ten seconds previously.[28]

In other words, even though it has a narrative development (pieces are taken, the board gets less and less crowded, in most cases one of the players wins), a game of chess is for Saussure a succession of static moments—it is like a slide show, as opposed to a movie. Or rather, each move, even though it "has a repercussion on the whole system," is indifferent to the structure of the game itself: "In chess, each move is absolutely distinct from the preceding and the subsequent equilibrium. The change effected belongs to neither state: only states matter."[29] With this Mondrian would have concurred. But I gather that Orozco would not. In that respect, he is much more the heir of the only artist of Mondrian's generation to have seriously thought about the conceptual implications of the chess model, and this in direct opposition both to the whole dream of arresting time, and to the fiction of pictorial opticality: Marcel Duchamp, whose interest in chess, as Hubert Damisch noted, arose at the very moment when the static conception of the game was about to be upturned by the revolutionary tactics of the camp known as "the hypermoderns."[30] I would say that it is under the aegis of Duchamp (one of his prime ancestors) that today Orozco is revisiting Mondrian.

We should note, however, that Orozco's paintings perturb the model of the chess so dramatically that they radically transform the "grammar" of the game, and in doing so they also annul in the grid what had seduced Mondrian and many others—the fact that it is decentered, all over. This is a direct consequence of Orozco's organic model—and he has been very insistent in his fascination for growth, a growth he always envisions as originating from a center (the rhizomatic growth of mushrooms is not for him—a major difference with John Cage here!). But centeredness in Orozco's paintings—and thus symmetry (which, surprisingly, had the connotation of death, not organic life, at the time of Mondrian)—is also a function of the noncompositional impulse of which they partake. In that respect they belong to a long tradition—with several very distinct tropes (grid, all over, monochrome, index, fusion of field and image, etc.) that were all already explored during the first wave of abstract art. The prewar occurrence that is closest to Orozco's works—and specifically targeting Mondrian's neo-plasticism—would be Theo van Doesburg's notion of a programmed art, one in which all compositional decisions would be mathematically computed beforehand, generated by a set of simple rules that would be readily deciphered by the beholder in the final work. True, van Doesburg shunned symmetry no less than Mondrian—it is only after World War II that symmetry was revisited and, in a swing of the pendulum, became a positive factor as an emblem of non- or even antisubjectivity.

The "What I hate about painting are all the small decisions, what goes with that" of Orozco[31] directly echoes, like it or not, Frank Stella's attack on what he called the "relational aesthetic" of European postcubist abstraction (there, too, Mondrian's neo-plasticism, albeit not named, was the prime target).[32]

There is, however, a difference between Orozco's approach to the very idea of systematicity and that of his predecessors. As in their works, the rules he adopted for the distribution of color planes in his paintings are extremely simple (centrifugal expansion according to the knight's move), as are no doubt the rules controlling the size of the contiguous circles and their division into half or quarter, but mesmerized by the vibrating simultaneous contrasts produced by the juxtapositions of colors, we instantly lose track of these rules (I, for one, can never remember them and even less verify them, but that is undoubtedly due to my utter incompetence in math). We might wonder why the periphery of Orozco's canvases is less agitated than their central zone, but we do not connect this fact, while in front of these works, to the one structural limitation imposed on the otherwise very free knight—that the closer it comes to the limits of the chessboard, and especially its corners, the more restricted are its moves. Add to this the nonchalant license taken by Orozco, at any point of the process, to disobey the a priori rules he has set himself, and we find ourselves still at a further remove from the strict realm of programmed art as defined by van Doesburg (or, closer to us, Sol LeWitt, in his patient and exhaustive declension of geometric and arithmetic systems during the 1960s). Curiously, with what Orozco has aptly called his wish to "disappoint" in his paintings,[33] he rejoins Mondrian's deliberate attempt, culminating in *Victory Boogie Woogie*, to trump all our expectations and to destabilize our perception, and this despite the fulcrum provided by their originating center.

But let us go back to this center once more. First, let's note that for Orozco growth is also a form of destruction—he speaks about some of his artistic procedures as the "introduction of a virus," admires the trees that are eating architecture away, as the jungle does in Mexican ruins.[34] Even before his recent series of paintings he thought about the entropic potential of growth, for example when doing his "spitting drawings" while in Kortrijk in 1993: "I was working out from the center. I found that adding elements took something away, obliterated something. [Note how closely this matches Saussure's remarks about the value of a sign.] This was a way of approaching a piece of paper that is also to destroy the center. It is the opposite of a vanishing point that holds the center."[35]

The most important issue, however, is perhaps not the battle between organic growth and inorganic geometry, but Orozco's stance against the vanishing point, which he sees as the anchor of a painterly way of thinking, a pictorial code, remnant of the past, from which he is intent, if not to wholly cut loose his painting, at least to give it some slack. He hopes to do so, he says, by conceiving of his painting in sculptural terms:

> I think I have a notion of sculpture in all my work—starting from the center, growing from the center. That center is as a spine to the body, a center point of gravity, which connects the body with earth. A painter works with the idea of a vanishing point, with something flat and abstract, something in front of you. A sculptural mentality, on the other hand, is associated with the ground, from the floor upward. If you think in spherical terms, you have to mix the two, both a vanishing point and a gravity point. That creates movement too, orbital movement or centrifugal movement, a certain kind of turbulence, which is perhaps also why the sphere or the circle is for me the best way of showing both vanishing and gravity points. In my paintings I am also thinking of the gravity point, the weight of a vertical axis, not only a vanishing point in the center.[36]

This statement is a bit confusing at first because two themes are intertwined, that of rotation and that of the switch from the planar verticality of painting to the spatial, tabular horizontality of sculpture—but this conjunction is crucial, and it is precisely why Orozco has been so attracted by the knight's move as a conceptual model (its jump addresses gravity and space, its spin addresses rotation). This is also one more instance of a certain affinity between his canvases and the last works of Mondrian. It might be true that, as Orozco noted (in a quote made above), when Mondrian painted his series of trees gradually digitized into a grid, he was still operating, at a certain level, as a landscape painter contemplating a scene *in front of* him; it might also be true that while working on his neo-plastic compositions, from 1920 on, he was still occupying the frontal (in-front-of) position of the painter with regard to his pictorial field, despite his very strong anti-gestaltist drive and the fact that those works were painted horizontally, on a table. But gradually throughout the 1930s, and certainly in New York, he came to think of his canvases as objects inhabiting space—both as maps (that is, diagrammatical "platform for actions") and as endowed with a three-dimensional materiality. As such, they were escaping the purely visual realm and thus illusion—which is why an Alberto Giacometti, the great maker of gameboards in twentieth-century art, could praise Mondrian's art as "coming from the domain of painting and entering another domain."[37] It is to this last point that Orozco alludes when he mentions Mondrian (immediately after having invoked Duchamp) as "getting to a kind of inner space in the space of the painting. Inner space means the inner line, the space in the line."[38] There is a certain thickness in Mondrian's last works, a material (and no longer illusionistic) weave of planes, with an over and an under, that is very close in kind, at least conceptually, to the rotary collage effect achieved by Orozco in his centrifugal structures.

In his *Knight's Move*, published in 1923 (devoted to Malevich, Tatlin, Mayakovsky, and other totems of modernity), the Russian formalist critic Viktor Shklovsky characterizes the odd course of his eponymous figure as oblique. The knight can't go straight, he explains, because the direct route is blocked in front of it.[39] Perhaps this is why Orozco had recourse to this figure: offering him a detour by which he could bypass the formidable obstacles any artist finds in the road toward painting today, the sideway hop of the knight gave him the tool with which, without much concern with the burden of the recent past, he could rejoice at relearning very old skills.

Notes

1. Edward Said, *Reflections on Exile and Other Essays* (Cambridge, Mass.: Harvard University Press, 2000), p. 185.

2. Benjamin H. D. Buchloh, "Interview with Gabriel Orozco," in *Gabriel Orozco: Clinton Is Innocent*, exh. cat. (Paris: Musée d'art moderne de la Ville de Paris, 1998), pp. 85–87.

3. Ibid, pp. 55–59. The "factory" in the quotation is a direct allusion to Warhol, discussed just before in the interview.

4. Greenberg's "Byzantine Parallels," dated 1958, is the essay where the critic articulates most forcefully his conception of opticality (in *Art and Culture* [Boston: Beacon Press, 1961], pp. 167–170). It is this conception that led him, somewhat later, to interpret Pollock's use of metallic paint as an illusionistic, "optical" device, an interpretation emphatically denied, as Rosalind Krauss noted, by another lover of metallic paint (in the early 1960s), Frank Stella (see *The Optical Unconscious* [Cambridge, Mass.: MIT Press, 1993], p. 246). It should be noted in passing that the gradual disappearance of gold from Western painting corresponds to the shift from the medieval conception of the image-maker as artisan to the Renaissance

idea of the fine artist (see Christian Hecht, *Die Glorie: Begriff, Bildelement in der europäischen Sakralkunst vom Mittelalter bis zum des Barock* [Regensburg: Schnell and Steiner, 2003]. My thanks to Jeffrey Hamburger for this reference). This shift, and Orozco is well aware of this, is the direct result of a class struggle that, if "outdated," is still going on: "Many craftsmen are artists, but their social position means that they are considered craftsmen, and unfortunately what they earn corresponds to that status, so they earn less than an artist. Then there are many artists who call themselves artists but are actually craftsmen. . . . I see the division between art and craft as a political problem. We know that in earlier times, the arts were divided between arts and crafts, and when art was functional, like craft, it was seen as a trade, then when it ceased to be functional it became Fine Art in capital letters. This is a French model [actually, Italian] which continues to be applied and which is now rather outdated." "Gabriel Orozco in Conversation with Guillermo Santamarina, Mexico City, August 2004," in *Gabriel Orozco*, exh. cat. (Madrid: Museo Nacional Centro de Arte Reina Sofia, 2005), p. 140.

5. For an illuminating analysis of Orozco's "reskilling," see the conclusion of Benjamin Buchloh's essay in "Gabriel Orozco: Sculpture as Recollection," in *Gabriel Orozco*, exh. cat. (Mexico City: Museo del Palacio de Bellas Artes, 2006), pp. 154–207. The passage in question is pp. 176–207.

6. "Gabriel Orozco in Conversation with Benjamin H. D. Buchloh," transcript of a conversation organized by the Serpentine Gallery and held at Goethe Institute London, July 1, 2004. In this volume, pp. 105–120. See also his declaration to Briony Fer: "It is not about visuality." In "Crazy about Saturn," *Gabriel Orozco*, exh. cat. (Mexico City: Museo del Palacio de Bellas Artes, 2006), p. 109. In this volume, pp. 157–180.

7. "Crazy about Saturn," p. 51. In this volume, pp. 157–180.

8. "Gabriel Orozco in Conversation with Benjamin H. D. Buchloh." In this volume, p. 158.

9. Ibid.

10. "Crazy about Saturn," p. 109. In this volume, p. 172.

11. "Interview with Gabriel Orozco," by Buchloh, in *Clinton Is Innocent*, p. 69.

12. "Gabriel Orozco in Conversation with Benjamin H. D. Buchloh," in this volume, p. 117.

13. Wladyslaw Strzeminski, untitled statement in *Abstraction création art non-figuratif* 2 (1933), p. 40.

14. See Josef Albers's untitled statement in Lucy Lippard, "Homage to the Square," *Art in America* 55, no. 4 (July–August 1967), pp. 50–57.

15. "Gabriel Orozco in Conversation with Benjamin H. D. Buchloh," in this volume, p. 117.

16. The fact that a rhythmic pulse is almost inevitably perceived as organic might be an intrinsic property of abstract film: this phenomenon is already very clear in Hans Richter's *Rhythmus 21* of 1921 and Viking Eggeling's *Diagonal Symphony* of 1923.

17. This analysis is developed in much greater length in my essay "The Iconoclast," published in *Piet Mondrian*, the catalog of the touring 1994 Mondrian retrospective (Washington, D.C.: National Gallery of Art), pp. 313–372.

18. On Strzeminski and the deductive structure, see my essay "Strzeminski and Kobro: In Search of Motivation," in my *Painting as Model* (Cambridge, Mass.: MIT Press, 1990), pp. 123–155.

19. Those are numbers B 97, B 98, B 99, and B 100 in Joop Joosten's *Catalogue Raisonné* of Mondrian's work of 1911–44 (New York: Harry N. Abrams, 1998), pp. 268–272. The two "checkerboard compositions" (the nickname is not due to Mondrian), although rectangular, are based in a modular division of 16 × 16 units.

20. Ferdinand de Saussure, *Course in General Linguistics* (New York: McGraw-Hill, 1959), pp. 22–23. I have slightly modified the translation, due to Wade Baskin.

21. Ibid, p. 110.

22. On the least cropped photograph Orozco published of this pieces one can see sixty-three wooden knights, sixteen of each of three colors—white, yellow, brown—and fifteen of black (but two corners are cropped, and the sixteenth black knight might have been on one of them). See *Gabriel Orozco*, published by Museo Nacional Centro de Arte Reina Sofia, Madrid, Spain on the occasion of his exhibition there in 2005.

23. Saussure, *General Course*, p. 116.

24. This quote does not figure in the 1916 (and highly deficient) edition of the *Course*, but in the notes of a student who actually took the class. Quoted in René Amacker, "Sur la notion de valeur," in *Studi saussuriani per Robert Godel* (Bologna: Il Mulino, 1972), p. 14. For more on this point, see my "Kahnweiler's Lesson," in *Painting as Model*, particularly pp. 86–89.

25. Orozco calls each canvas in his *Samurai Tree* series an "invariant," in an obvious homage to Albers. He has expressed his admiration for Albers's work in *TATEetc.*, a journal published by the Tate: "What I admire about it is that he has one idea; he looks at one decision, and from that decision he can do a lot of things. You can follow that decision into all the possible variants. That makes the work a little bit mechanical in one way, but very experimental in another" (issue 6, published on the occasion of the exhibition "Albers and Moholy-Nagy: From the Bauhaus to the New World," in the spring of 2006).

26. Quoted in Carl Holty, "Mondrian in New York: A Memoir," *Arts* 31, no. 10 (September 1957), p. 31.

27. Interview with James Johnson Sweeney by Piet Hoenderdos in his film *Mondrian in New York*, 1980.

28. Saussure, *General Course*, p. 89.

29. Ibid.

30. See Hubert Damisch, "The Duchamp Defense," in *October* 10 (fall 1979), pp. 5–28. Concluding his discussion of this sea change in chess strategy, Damisch quotes a Znosko-Borovski, "whom Duchamp translated": "The statics of the positional game were succeeded by the dynamism of hyper-modern play" (p. 16).

31. "Crazy about Saturn," p. 118. In this volume, p. 174.

32. I am referring here to the famous interview of Frank Stella and Donald Judd by Bruce Glaser, reprinted in *Minimal Art* by Gregory Battcock (New York: Dutton, 1968), pp. 148–164.

33. "Crazy about Saturn," p. 109. In this volume, p. 183.

34. For the virus, see the interview with Buchloh in *Clinton Is Innocent*, p. 95; for the trees "eating" architecture, see "Crazy about Saturn," p. 80. In this volume, p. 164.

35. "Crazy about Saturn," p. 65. In this volume, p. 162.

36. Ibid., p. 92. In this volume, p. 167.

37. Quoted in Georges Charbonnier, "Entretien avec Giacometti," in *Le monologue du peintre* (Paris: Julliard, 1959), p. 170. For more on the "sculptural" aspect of Mondrian's paintings, see my "Piet Mondrian, *New York City*," in *Painting as Model*.

38. "Interview with Gabriel Orozco," by Buchloh, in *Clinton Is Innocent*, p. 119.

39. Viktor Shklovsky, *Knight's Move*, trans. Richard Sheldon (Normal, Ill.: Dalkey Archive Press, 2005).

Index